"Michael Parent has taken the general logos associated with Lean and Six Sigma and transformed it into a narrative fit for the individual, with robust examples, essential takeaways, and – above all – sensible connections that make a disparate canon more portable, referenceable, and actionable."

Dr. Ben Benson, MBB
Founder of Coax Business Solutions, Inc

"If you want to develop and pursue successful innovation strategy for your organization, this is a must-read book. Through the application of Lean principles, sustainable value is delivered to the customers; this is the avenue to success. I recommend this book because it is a compelling presentation for delivering the greatest possible value to customers in alignment with an organization's mission and strategy. This book carefully curates and references industry examples of successes and learnings; supporting the reader to benchmark, apply practices, and translate into higher success rates across industries and business activities."

David D. Larsen, PSP, PMP, LSSMBB
Performance Excellence Specialist, Lee Health

"This book should be required reading for any Lean practitioner who wants to expand their Lean toolkit to include growth and innovation. The roadmap from the traditional Lean cost-savings process to Lean innovation is spelled out clearly with a sprinkling of real-world examples to learn from. Lean isn't just for manufacturing anymore. I highly recommend it."

Randall Scheps
Business Unit President, Howmet Aerospace

The Lean Innovation Cycle

The Lean Innovation Cycle

A Multi-Disciplinary Framework for Designing Value with Lean and Human-Centered Design

Michael Parent

A PRODUCTIVITY PRESS BOOK

First published 2022
by Routledge
605 Third Avenue, New York, NY 10158

and by Routledge
2 Park Square, Milton Park, Abingdon, Oxon, OX14 4RN

Routledge is an imprint of the Taylor & Francis Group, an informa business

ISBN: 978-1-032-07286-9 (hbk)
ISBN: 978-1-032-07285-2 (pbk)
ISBN: 978-1-003-20634-7 (ebk)

DOI: 10.4324/9781003206347

Typeset in ITC Garamond
by SPi Technologies India Pvt Ltd (Straive)

To my wife, Anne, and my daughter, Eloise
Thank you.

Contents

Acknowledgments

I would like to start by thanking my family. Your unwavering support for me and my undertakings cannot be overstated. To my wife Anne, thank you for your constant adulation and support. Likewise, thank you to my mom and dad who have always been a bastion of support and provided sage advice and guidance. My mother, Cheryl, was one of the earliest copy-editors of this manuscript. And finally, to my daughter, Eloise. You served as a motivation for this book even before you were born.

Thank you to my editors Michael Sinocchi and Samantha Dalton. Thank you for believing in this manuscript and for believing in me as a first-time author. I am grateful for your dedication to this book, for your feedback, and revisions. Likewise, I would like to thank my publisher Taylor & Francis, Productivity Press and all the individuals who have participated in the publication, sales, and distribution of this title.

I would also like to express my heartfelt gratitude and thanks to my friend David Larsen. You have been a great colleague, friend, mentor, and coach. Whether I needed inspiration, criticism, or support you have provided exactly what I needed and when I needed it. I credit you as the chief catalyst behind this book and I'm exceptionally grateful for your friendship and support. I am esteemed by your endorsement of my book.

I would like to thank the entire Bridgestone Enterprise Quality Education Team, especially Debbie Detwiler, Walt Tletski, and Matt Wright. Your mentorship in Lean and Six Sigma has had a profound impact on my career. My genesis and development in Lean Six Sigma are wholly indebted to your sponsorship and counsel.

Thanks to Dr. Ben Benson. I value the support and mentorship that you've shown through my Lean Six Sigma Master Black belt. I owe a lot of what is in this book to the topics we covered throughout the LSSMBB. Your endorsement of this book is especially dear to me.

Thanks to Diane Fogel of the College of William & Mary, Raymond A. Mason School of Business. The MBA program was integral to first peaking my interest in design thinking and Human-Centered Design.

Thank you to Dr. Michael Luchs, founding director of the Ukrop Innovation & Design Studio at William & Mary. Your generosity with your time and sharing what you've learned about innovation, design thinking, and maker spaces has greatly refined my understanding of these topics. I hope this book reflects both your expertise in the field and also what a delight it was to speak with you.

Thanks to Janeen Shaffer who has mentored and coached me through numerous career transitions. Your counsel has greatly empowered me to take charge of my professional career, and your encouragement has served as a constant motivator.

I would like to thank the University of Michigan College of Engineering, the Industrial and Operations Engineering Department and specifically Wanda Dobberstein. Wanda, as my academic advisor, your dedication to helping me throughout my undergraduate academic journey has had a profound impact on my life and what I've been able to achieve. This book is a direct result of the care and commitment that you've shown me.

Finally, I would like to express my gratitude to Randall Scheps for providing an endorsement of this book. Thank you for taking the time to review some of the early manuscripts and providing candid and helpful feedback.

Author

Michael Parent is a management consultant and Managing Director of Michael Parent Consulting Services. Throughout his career, Michael has coached executives through strategic problem-solving, operational excellence, and execution and has led continuous improvement projects in a myriad of industries and disciplines, such as Manufacturing, Insurance, Product Development, and Human Resources. Michael has written several articles which have been published in peer-reviewed industry journals and websites. Likewise, Michael has participated as a guest and expert on podcasts such as "The Gemba Academy Podcast" and "The Lean Blog Podcast with Mark Graban." Michael holds a Bachelor's Degree in Industrial and Operations Engineering from the University of Michigan in Ann Arbor and an MBA from the College of William & Mary, Raymond A. Mason School of Business in Williamsburg VA. Michael is a certified Lean and Six Sigma Master Black Belt.

Introduction

Innovation, Customer Value, and Lean

For companies everywhere, innovation has long been the pre-eminent secret sauce to their successes. There is a growing consensus among CEOs and academics that in order for a company to stay relevant and maintain its position in the marketplace it cannot simply rely on what has worked in the past. Established competitive advantages must give rise to something new, something novel, something disruptive. For a company to survive it must innovate.

By just exactly what *is* innovation? Contemporary ideas about what innovation is are divergent. These colloquial talking points often excite the mind but hang on some oft-disputed assumptions. Circumventing the pervasive issue of defining what innovation is, business pundits speak to the effects of innovation within an organization. The dominant consensus of these discussions is that through innovation, a company can obtain a first-mover advantage. Though defined conservatively by Fernando Suarez as a firm's ability to be better off than its competitors as a result of being first to market in a new product category, business leaders usually take the first-mover advantage to mean something more [1]. Often, they take it a step further into ideas about substantial market penetration, brand loyalty and recognition, and anything else that makes it nearly impossible for competitors to usurp the first market incumbent.

Despite the consensus of what its effects are and despite the perennial inclusion on companies' 10-Ks and financial reports, the definition of "innovation" remains pervasive. One might think of innovation as leveraging a

DOI: 10.4324/9781003206347-1

new technology, another the technology itself. Some may think innovation is solely the output of product development, a new revolutionary product. Still, others might see innovation on an industry-wide scale like 5G networks. Some academics have caught on. Realizing there likely won't be any consensus on innovation's definition, they dryly note that people tend to use the term loosely to call to mind the concept of innovation to confirm whatever they aim to do [2]. Steve Jobs was a prolific product innovator and revolutionized the way the world interacts with each other. He shifted the paradigm of what we expect from consumer electronics. Jeff Bezos, on the other hand, used new, emerging technologies to revolutionize the way we shop, purchase, receive products, and consume entertainment. Should we consider one any less of an innovator than the other? The distinctions here are artificial lines in the sand.

In this book, what I attempt to do is draw another line in the sandbox. My purpose here is to bring an of-neglected part of innovation out of the shadows and into the light of public discourse. Similar to the distinction between Bezos and Jobs, the purpose of this line in the sand is not to put two theories in conflict with one another but is meant to describe key differences between approaches. My aim is not to pit Lean Innovation against the traditional conception of innovation. Instead, I aim to show that Lean Innovation is another avenue by which innovation can be pursued and which still relies on novelty, creativity, and curiosity. My aim is twofold. First, to develop and explain a new paradigm, one that provides the structure needed to execute Lean Innovation. And then demonstrate the effects of Lean Innovation both in congruence and contrast to traditional innovation efforts.

What is Innovation?

With so much to discuss, perhaps the best thing to do is begin. I want to start by supplying you with an operational definition of what innovation is. As you've already seen, the word "innovation" elicits different ideas for different people. I want to start by level-setting these ideas and begin to create a foundation that can be built upon.

Permit me then, to take some time to do a healthy literature review of common ideas and theories about innovation. As easy as it would be to simply put forth my own definition, it would be intellectually disingenuous to exclude the views of others. In this vein, two succinct definitions that summarize current views about innovation are presented. Their merits and flaws are discussed. Finally, in light of this current landscape, I present my own formulation of innovation.

First, an article published by *Forbes* magazine titled "What Exactly is Innovation?". In lieu of a single sentence definition, author Michelle Greenwood opts for four criteria that a business activity must meet to be considered "innovation." These four criteria are:

- Creating meaningful points of difference for products and services vs. current alternatives
- Fulfilling unmet consumer needs, by offering new ways to accomplish goals, or make lives or jobs easier, better, happier, more exciting, satisfying, or more productive
- Enabling brands to compete in incremental new markets or category segments
- Delighting/engaging/capturing imaginations of consumers to increase loyalty [3]

The first takeaway from this definition is what innovation is not. Innovation is not a product or service. Rather, innovation is a business activity. It's a means to some end. Innovation should not exist for the sake of innovation. It should further the needs of the business. But to this end, the criteria put forth are found wanting. Many of the criteria can be met by other business activities that do not add up to innovation. As an example, criteria #1: creating points of differentiation isn't innovation. A multitiered product strategy sufficiently fills Greenwood's differentiation requirements but hardly qualifies as anything more than product management 101. Likewise, differentiating products and services need not be innovation. Creating a men's razor with five blades instead of three certainly creates a differentiated product in the marketplace, but innovation it is not.

The criteria for innovation to enable brands to compete in new markets and categories is likewise problematic. Innovation need not open doors to new markets. Rather, innovation can also be used as a tool to strengthen your competitive position by means of creating barriers to entry or lowering the bargaining positions of suppliers [4]. Conversely, companies can enter new markets and categories without innovation. As a thought experiment, consider General Electric. GE can enter new markets whenever it wants. If tomorrow GE decided to enter the consumer grill market, it's doubtful that it would need to rely on anything besides its existing manufacturing capabilities and sales channels. Innovation can stay home.

Finally, the criteria listed in Greenwood's article have an undue focus on *consumer* needs. This approach to innovation is one of the glaring inadequacies found in innovation discussions today. The requirements put forth by *Forbes* follows colloquial trends equating innovation to technology and aesthetic, nothing more. More, these criteria omit just about any improvement in business-to-business interactions. Just-in-time delivery, online ordering, and the internet, by this logic, are only innovative insofar as they benefit *consumers*, not other businesses.

It wouldn't be fair to leave the discussion here. Michelle Greenwood does expound around her four requirements and provides context to her requirements with several examples. In particular, she mentioned that successful innovation in new products and services offer new characteristics, new features and attributes, and more opportunity for customer touchpoints. She points to Apple products as an example of innovation not just in terms of product design and functionality, but also in terms of aesthetic, material, and color, and points to the Genius Bar and retail stores as a way Apple innovated its service approach to be more inviting, easy, and fun [5].

Besides using the word "innovative" several times in its own definition, there are other problems with the examples given. Surely, these illustrations all meet her requirements, but they simply don't pass the eye test. Should we be content with saying that a new coat of paint is akin to innovation? No, we should not. Her examples do provide us with a lot to take away. Greenwood identifies innovation both in terms of performance characteristics (*Faster* checkout, *more* touchpoints) and in customer delights (Voice Recognition, tactile responsiveness). Later on in this book, we pay particular attention to these distinctions and introduce methods for how to identify and meet these distinct customer desires.

Conversely, the American Society for Quality (ASQ) takes a different approach to innovation. They define innovation as the ways in which an organization updates, changes, and improves its internal processes, manufacturing techniques, and management methods [6].

The ASQ goes on to specify that though this may be the definition of innovation, it does not guarantee its success. Therefore, the ASQ gives additional criteria that lead to success. These criteria are meeting customer needs, satisfying expense and return on investment requirements, improving employee satisfaction, and product quality [7]. The ASQ also goes on to differentiate types or modes of innovation, such as product innovation, process innovation, and business model innovation.

There is an inherent complexity and versatility to innovation and how it is applied, this is a point the ASQ gets right. The ASQ provides a much more complete and satisfying conception of what innovation is. The ASQ, like *Forbes*, also identifies innovation, not as a product or service, but as a business activity. But what is most striking about the ASQ's definition and conception of innovation is its internal focus. Rather than concerning itself with the product and how it interacts with or delights the customer, the ASQ looks inwardly at how the innovations are *created*, how organizations develop new capabilities, and the effect this has on the business. To the ASQ, innovation is not a product or even a phenomenon. The ASQ sees innovation as a competency.

So, in summary of the literature review, it's fair to say that the definition given in *Forbes* is far too incomplete and narrowly focuses on the product and consumer. And although the definition provided by the ASQ is sufficiently descriptive, its definition is too inwardly focused and doesn't give credit enough to the voice of the customer and user experience. However, it's far easier to tear down than to build up. Therefore, let me offer my own definition of Innovation.

> Innovation is the business activity of creating and delivering customer value in new, creative, and novel ways.

Some may find this definition a bit too simplistic. Taking the ASQ as a benchmark, it's not enough for businesses to be innovative, they must also ensure its success, its viability. Therefore, taking their thoughts into consideration, more is needed to gain a complete conception of what makes innovation successful. In order for an organization to innovate [successfully], it must meet four requirements:

1. Identify and understand some unmet want, need, or desire of its customer
2. Fulfill this need in a novel, creative, or new way
3. Gain acceptance from the business creating and delivering the innovation
4. Gain acceptance of this new approach by the targeted customer

Let's first start with understanding some unmet want, need, or customer's desire. This idea is not unique to my definition and is so implicit in discussions on innovation that it nearly goes without saying. The ASQ calls this updating, changing, and improving. *Forbes* calls this fulfilling unmet customer needs. Since this is a book about Lean Innovation, let me propose a bit of jargon. Innovation must *add value*.

Second, innovation must have a sense of novelty, newness, and creativity. To this end, the definition provided by the ASQ misses the mark. Innovation is about doing something differently. "The electric light did not come from continuously improving candles," as the saying goes. Innovation is often synonymous with technology for this very reason. It must do something different, be something different, or create something different.

Third, it must be accepted within the organization it is created. Nokia used to have the top market share in the US cell phone market, by 2013 they had a mere 3% and were eventually sold off to Microsoft for their handset business [8]. What happened? Nokia failed to adapt to innovations in cell phone technology culminating in the first iPhone. Likewise and famously, Eastman Kodak created the first digital camera in 1975 only to go bankrupt, disrupted by the very technology they created [9]. Kodak's failure to "innovate" was not merely technological. Even into the new millennium, Kodak created a line of ink printers and drastically adapted its product line. They invested heavily in technology, even digital technologies. And yet Eastman Kodak still clung to film instead of digital cameras. The lesson Kodak teaches us is that the technology alone is not enough to "accept" an innovation into the organization. Sometimes accepting innovation means throwing out the whole business model. Eastman Kodak's inability to accept both the technological and modular changes ultimately led to their bankruptcy [10]. These strategic blunders did not arise from an inability to create innovative products or add value to the customers. Instead, they arose from the unwillingness or inability of organizations to adapt to changing customer expectations and accept these transformations as the new normal.

Finally, and most importantly, innovation, as either a product, process, or business model, must be accepted by the target customer. Without customer acceptance, the innovation will not be successful. This may be another one of those points that goes without saying. Unfortunately, it's hard to find examples and write compelling stories of products that didn't work. But suffice it to say, when we think of bubble wrap, we don't think of it as a novel innovation in textured wallpaper. Play-Doh is known as a toy for children, not as wallpaper cleaner. In both these cases, the purpose that the product was originally conceived for was not accepted by its target customers. The paradox, of course, is that new customers saw different values from these products and used them for different purposes. This need not be the case. But it raises an interesting point: how the customer interacts with an innovation is part of the innovation itself.

So thus the definition of innovation. Innovation is a business activity. It is not merely the product or the customer experience. It is not strictly an internal or external business activity. Innovation incorporates internal capabilities to create value and novelty with external customer experiences and interactions. Innovation must deliver unmet needs, wants, or desires to its customers. In delivering value to these customers, it must do this in some new, novel, or creative way. Innovation has a sense of novelty, creativity, newness. Definitions or no definitions, this is the spirit, the essence of innovation.

Additionally, we say that in order for innovation to be successful it must jump the hurdles of acceptance. An innovation must be accepted within the organization it was developed, and it must be accepted by the customers it was created for. As the next chapters demonstrate, Lean Innovation is particularly astute at creating innovation mechanisms that gain wide acceptance in organizations as well as in the marketplace.

What is Lean?

So what is Lean? I've begun this Lean Innovation conversation by defining one of the words, so it's only fitting that I spend the rest of the chapter defining the other. Lean is often misconstrued as a set of problem-solving tools to help businesses improve their processes and operations. I'm here to tell you that it's not. Sometimes "Lean" is seen as just another buzzword like "innovation" or a management fad like matrix organizations, management by consensus, or autonomous work teams. This all may be true, but the trendiness and buzzwordiness of Lean ought not detract from why it merited its celebrity in the first place. At a fundamental level, Lean is two things: a set of management principles and a process for executing these principles.

First the principles. As originally stated in "The Toyota Way" by Jeffrey Liker, there are 14 Principles of Lean. I've altered them slightly for brevity and the purposes of our discussion on innovation.

The 14 Principles of Lean are:

1. Management decisions ought to be based on long-term philosophy over all else
2. A smooth, continuous operation will make problems easy to detect

3. Avoid waste by letting the customer *pull* the demand
4. Level the workload *Heijunka*
5. Build a *right the first time* quality culture
6. The foundation of your efforts come from standardization
7. Identify problems with visual controls
8. Use only reliable, thoroughly tested technology that serves people and process
9. Grow leaders who live the philosophy and teach others
10. Develop exceptional individuals who embody the company philosophy
11. Respect and help your suppliers
12. Go and see *gemba*
13. Make decisions slowly, implement quickly
14. Reflect to improve [11]

These principles outline a fundamental structure of beliefs. The structure, summarized in Figure I.1 as "The Four Ps": Philosophy, Process, People, and Problem-solving build a structural hierarchy where philosophy drives process. Process gives way to how organizations treat and respect people. And those people drive the activities of *kaizen*. Kaizen is the heart of Lean. *Kaizen* comes from two Japanese words, *Kai* meaning change and *Zen* meaning good. It is the philosophy of continuous improvement, a ceaseless

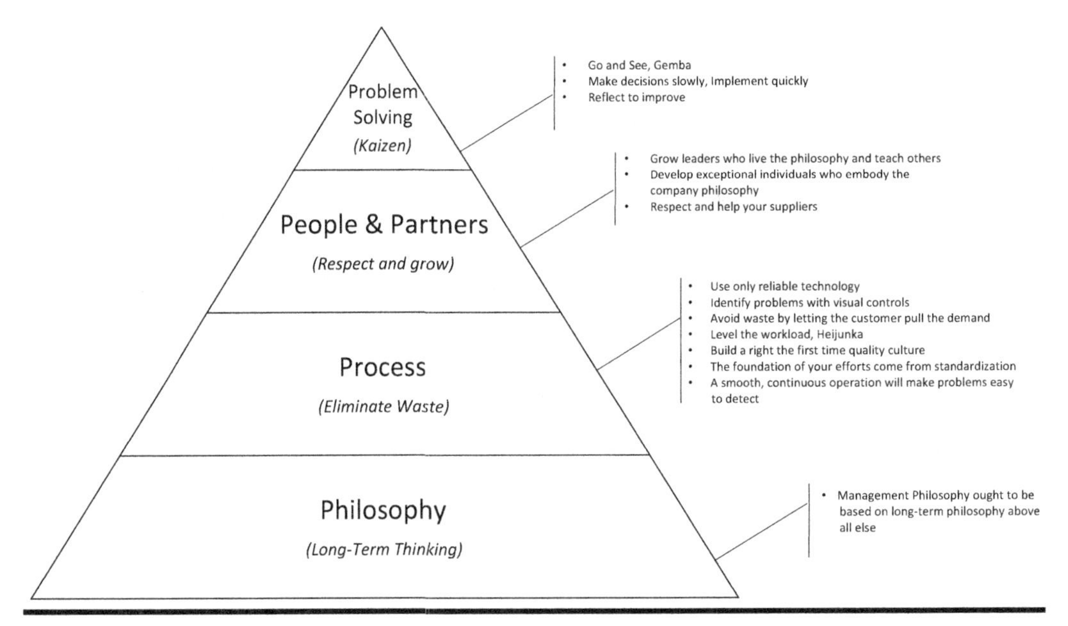

Figure I.1 The four Ps of Lean.

hunger to deliver more value to the customer than before [12]. For our purposes, it may be fine to think of this as problem-solving and innovation. All four Ps work together to deliver sustainable value to the customers, but the *Kaizen*, the act of doing, is what delivers the value. It is the summit of the Lean philosophy.

With the Lean philosophy introduced, next let's turn our attention to Lean as a process for applying the principles of the Lean ideology.

There are five steps in Lean as a process:

1. Define customer value
2. Define the value stream
3. Make it flow
4. Pull from the customer
5. Strive for excellence [13]

Defining customer value is number one with a bullet. In a Lean enterprise, everything else is subordinated under customer value. Whether you're engaging with Lean as a leader, team participant, or in some other capacity, everything must come back to customer value. In both Lean frameworks, the customer is pulling value from the business. The business is never pushing its products or ideas onto the customer. It never dictates to the customer what she should want or need or value. Instead, Lean facilitates an organization's ability to understand, define, and articulate what it is the customer actually values. Customer pull is one of the defining characteristics of Lean processes, enterprises, and as we'll see, innovation.

Process augments philosophy. Philosophy supports process. The Lean process identifies the need to define customer value and the Lean philosophy is the light on the hill. The philosophy, guiding in its wisdom, is proved impotent without the action-packed sequence demarcated by the process. The process is the roadmap and game plan for living the wisdom of the philosophy. The spirit of this strategy-process give and take is a concept the Japanese call the *Hoshin Kanri*, and in Lean, it applies to everything.

To English speakers, the *Hoshin Kanri* translates to "policy deployment." I can see the look of disappointment on your face. You picked up a book on innovation looking for something sexy, novel, and exciting. Instead, you're a few pages in and reading something on "policy deployment." Don't put the book down. Strap in. It will be worth it. The *Hoshin Kanri* is the means of cascading high-level objectives down throughout the entire organization across all functions. A guiding management philosophy of

Lean is to facilitate a give-and-take process of communicating up and down the organization. The *Hoshin Kanri* is the guiding force that enables novelty and independence to flourish throughout the company [14]. Why is policy deployment important to innovation? It empowers individuals in the organization to adapt quickly, identify areas of improvement, and take appropriate action. In an innovative capacity, it creates a culture that focuses decentralized creative efforts on the most important business objectives.

Lean: Not Just for Manufacturing Anymore

So far, all I've implied is that a management philosophy, widely successful in manufacturing, can also be used in guiding the innovation efforts of organizations. Can I really take such a leap? Is such a proclamation really supported? I just checked with my publisher, and she said I can. But if you won't take my word for it, consider some supporting evidence.

As we've just mentioned, Lean is a philosophy that guides management decisions and a process for delivering customer value. There is nothing about this that limits its scope to manufacturing and operations. It may have an archaic origin story, we all do, but there's nothing prohibiting the evolution of Lean from the primordial soup of manufacturing into a panoply of diverse applications, industries, and disciplines. In the past 20 years, industry observers have seen such an evolution. Lean philosophies have been applied in diverse applications and industries with resounding success. One such industry that has seen the positive impacts of Lean is the Healthcare Industry.

As the four Ps denoted, one of the core principles of Lean is to maximize customer value while minimizing waste; creating more customer value with fewer resources [15]. In healthcare, there is a lot of waste. Hospitals around the globe have begun to use the treasure trove of wisdom from Lean to remove this waste from their organizations. The results have already paid off. In one such example, the Policlinico San Martino – a university and community hospital in Genoa, Italy – has used Lean methods to transform their entire Oncology Department. Starting with the customer, the hospital team identified waiting times as key to their patient's satisfaction [read: customer value]. The less a patient has to wait, the more satisfied she will be. After a redesign of the office space and some additional retooling of their workflow, the hospital reduced the waiting time of patients by over

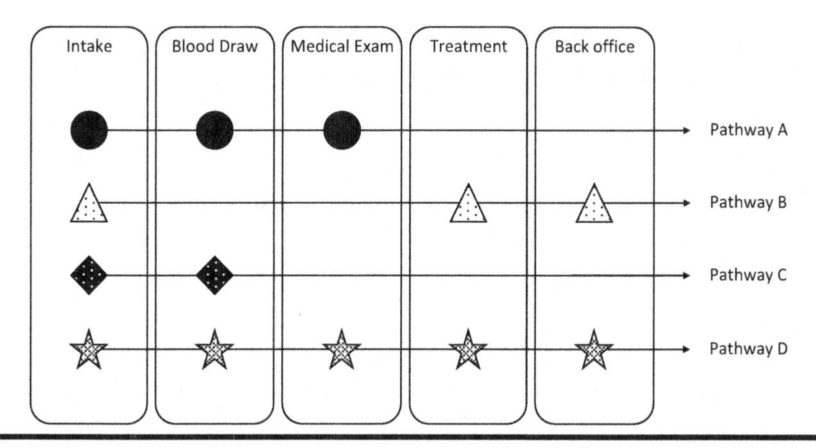

Figure I.2 Oncology workflows.

60%. By focusing on customer value, the hospital was able to identify four key archetypal pathways that dictated key metrics like occupancy rate and asset utilization. Informed by these insights, new procedures were enacted to manage equipment utilization and the physical redesign of the department, enabling the Italian hospital to prepare over half of all their Oncology procedures an entire day before the scheduled appointment! [16] (Figure I.2).

Lean isn't just about operations either. Disciplines outside the scope of traditional operations (supply chain, manufacturing, healthcare services) are increasingly adapting Lean principles to their applications. One such example in this Lean revolution is in the world of accounting. According to the Journal of Accountancy, CPAs are beginning to rethink how they organize their books. CPAs are getting rid of "product costs" and "departmental budgets" and supplementing these by organizing their books around customer "value streams." We'll talk a lot more about customer value streams later on. For now, just know that a value stream is the path a product or service takes to create and deliver value to a customer [17]. Likewise, standard costing is supplanted by detailed analysis of value delivery, not a predetermined book value. Many accountants have begun to note that as business demands of the 21st century begin to shift toward becoming more agile, flexible, and adaptable, the traditional accounting methods, developed to support mass production, don't quite fit the needs of today's enterprises [18]. As this example demonstrates, Lean supports a way of thinking about *how* a company delivers value to its customers and *what* it does to support this delivery. The customer focus of Lean has no borders and has made it the harbinger of change in the accounting industry.

Lean has applications in every industry and every discipline. When it comes to how Lean is being applied in non-manufacturing settings, these two examples aren't even the tip of the iceberg. The philosophy is lived, not simply applied. It espouses an unrelenting focus on customer value and is, for that reason, germane to the world of innovation.

Conclusion

Innovation is usually seen as an activity that creates disruptive, new, and widely different ideas that pull organizations in exciting new directions and propel change. This need not and ought not be the end of the innovation conversation. For all that it delivers, the traditional conception of innovation leaves behind significant blind spots that leave businesses unable to capitalize on unrealized opportunities, specifically unmet desires of the customer base it has already fought so hard to capture.

If this chapter addressed the "what" of Lean and innovation the next ought to answer the "how." How can Lean be adapted for innovation? How can teams create and deliver customer value in line with the process and philosophy of Lean? The stage has been set. The opportunity is knocking. Through the lens of unrelenting commitment to customer value, Lean Innovation provides a new and novel way of thinking about innovation.

References

[1] Suarez, F., Gianvito, L. (2005). "The Half Truth of First Mover Advantage". *Harvard Business Review.*

[2] Christensen, C., Raynor, M., McDonald, R. (2015). "What is Disruptive Innovation?" *Harvard Business Review.*

[3] Greenwood, Michelle. (2014). "What Exactly is Innovation?" *Forbes Magazine.* https://www.forbes.com/sites/michellegreenwald/2014/03/12/what-exactly-is-innovation/#345adfed5e5a

[4] Porter, Michael. (1979). "How Competitive Forces Shape Strategy". *Harvard Business Review.* https://hbr.org/1979/03/how-competitive-forces-shape-strategy

[5] Greenwood, Michelle. (2014). "What Exactly is Innovation?" *Forbes Magazine.* https://www.forbes.com/sites/michellegreenwald/2014/03/12/what-exactly-is-innovation/#345adfed5e5a

[6] American Society for Quality. (2020). "What is Innovation?" https://asq.org/quality-resources/innovation

[7] American Society for Quality. (2020). "What is Innovation?" https://asq.org/quality-resources/innovation
[8] Surowieki, James. (2013). "Where Nokia went Wrong". *The New Yorker*. https://www.newyorker.com/business/currency/where-nokia-went-wrong
[9] Shih, Willy. (2016). "The Real Lessons from Kodak's decline". *MIT Sloan Management Review*. https://sloanreview.mit.edu/article/the-real-lessons-from-kodaks-decline/
[10] Anthony, Scott. (2012). "Kodak and the Brutal Difficulty of Transformation". *Harvard Business Review*. https://hbr.org/2012/01/kodak-and-the-brutal-difficult
[11] Liker, J. (2004). *The Toyota Way: 14 Management Principles from the World's Greatest Manufacturer*. McGraw-Hill, New York, NY. pp. 37–41.
[12] Imai, M. (1997). *Gemba Kaizen: A commonsense approach to continuous improvement strategy*. McGraw-Hill, New York, NY. pp. 1–2.
[13] Womack, J., Jones, D. (1996). *Lean Thinking*. Taylor & Francis Group, New York, NY. pp. 16–26.
[14] Liker, J. (2004). *The Toyota Way: 14 Management Principles from the World's Greatest Manufacturer*. McGraw-Hill, New York, NY. pp. 217–220.
[15] Lean Enterprise Institute. (2020). "What is Lean". Lean Enterprise Institute. https://www.lean.org/WhatsLean/
[16] Guercini, J., Sobrero, A., Martelli, F. (2019). "Our New, Leaner Cancer Center". https://planet-lean.com/lean-healthcare-policlinico-genoa/
[17] Lean Enterprise Institute. (2020). "Value Stream". https://www.lean.org/lexicon/value-stream
[18] Journal of Accountancy. (2004). "The Lowdown on Lean Accounting". *Journal of Accountancy*. https://www.journalofaccountancy.com/issues/2004/jul/thelowdownonleanaccounting.html

Chapter 1

Lean Innovation and the Lean Innovation Cycle

The Introduction covered a lot. Both Innovation and Lean were introduced and defined. We created operational definitions for two of the most pervasive words in the business lexicon. The lexicon has been standardized. What a Lean thing to do! Now in this opening chapter, I introduce two definitions of my own: Lean Innovation and the Lean Innovation Cycle. As noted in the Introduction, the purpose of adding new definitions to the lexicon is to create a distinction between what lies ahead and traditional approaches to innovation. By creating this distinction, innovation can begin to be unpacked and understood at a deeper level.

Lean Innovation and the Lean Innovation Cycle

So what is Lean Innovation? Lean Innovation is the business activity of creating and delivering new value to customers in alignment with business strategy. It has a strategically different focus from that of traditional innovation. As the quick overview in the Introduction demonstrated, the focus of many organizations' innovation efforts is on developing technology and intellectual property. These, in turn, are to be used to create unique products, open up new markets, create stepwise growth, and the like. Just because the market is not new and the product not completely revolutionary does not mean innovation is absent. It is not always necessary for the target market, customer, and price point to change in order to create

DOI: 10.4324/9781003206347-2

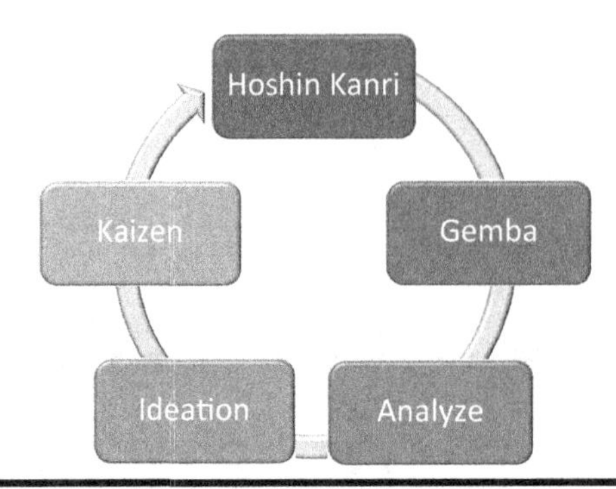

Figure 1.1 The Lean Innovation Cycle.

something novel or something that delights and excites customers. At a high level, Lean Innovation is focused on just one thing: delivering the greatest possible value to customers *in alignment with* an organization's mission and strategy. In this and subsequent chapters, I expound upon this idea. First, in this chapter, I introduce the mechanism for Lean Innovation called the Lean Innovation Cycle. After its introduction, I dedicate several chapters to dissecting each of the five steps in the model. In each deep dive, I explain the purpose and necessity of each step and the tools used therein. Then, in subsequent chapters, I provide ample examples and contrasts between the effects of traditional innovation and the Lean Innovation Cycle. Where traditional innovation struggles, Lean Innovation thrives.

Figure 1.1 summarizes the Lean Innovation Cycle as the mechanism to achieve Lean Innovation. There are five steps in the model and as the name supposes, these steps work in a cyclical fashion that perpetuates the continuous improvement of creating and delivering value to customers. The five steps of the Lean Innovation Cycle are (1) Hoshin Kanri, (2) Gemba, (3) Analyze, (4) Ideation, and (5) Kaizen.

What's the Difference?

What makes this model special? What makes this model a Lean model for innovation vs. any other? Take another look at the diagram. Did you see it? One of the most exciting things about this model, what makes this model unique and Lean, is that this model has customer pull.

First, the model identifies and explains how customers perceive value. In other innovation models the business pushes the innovations onto the customer. Usually, it starts in a traditional R&D department. A new technology or discovery creates a new business opportunity. The business either develops a product or a new way to deliver the product. The company then *pushes* this product into the marketplace, often with focus groups, in the hope that the product is adopted by its target customers. This is how many companies think of innovation today, and it underlies the distinction between traditional and Lean Innovation nicely. Additionally, these traditional organizations are usually departmentally and inwardly focused. Their structures dictate function. Only at the very end, once all the technical research and engineering has been completed, does the business begin to ask questions about anything related to a customer value stream. These efforts in innovation are not Lean.

The telecommunications industry is the best example of this sort of innovation. For over a century, the companies within this capital-intense industry have spent billions of dollars to invent technologies and create patents to stay one step ahead of their opponents. Bell Labs is a case in point, and their innovations cannot be underestimated. Radio astronomy, the transistor, even statistical process control (SPC) all got their start at Bell Labs [1]. To date, Bell Labs has been awarded nine Nobel Prizes, four Turing Awards, and a litany of others from 25 different organizations [2]. But suffice it to say that the Nokia Bell Labs Corporation no longer holds to the same strategic mission it had when it was created in the late 19th century.

Bell Labs is a happy story of traditional innovation efforts and by no means precipitates success. Bell Labs was so successful in creating innovations and technologies that it found its way by losing it. Not constrained by strategy, it was able to pursue innovation until the pursuit of innovation became its strategy! How many R&D or innovation organizations have pursued similar efforts, only to deliver technologies that have little use? The Lean Innovation Cycle is designed differently. It lets the values and desires of the customers dictate the positioning and development of business innovation, not the other way around. It keeps the business in the driver's seat while letting the customer take the wheel.

In a similar manner, the Lean Innovation Cycle is, in a sense, a value stream analysis with intense structure and exacting focus. In Lean, the principal goal is to create and deliver value to the customer. In Lean Innovation, the aim is to do the same with the added complexity of figuring out *what* the customer values and desires and *would* desire if it were offered to them. The model, then, is driven by interactions with the customer, analyzing these interactions, and then making changes that improve these interactions with, and add value to, the customer.

To illustrate the impact of the Lean Innovation Cycle in action, contrast the product development approach of The Wiremold Company before and after their Lean transformation. Their product development process was departmentally structured. The marketing department would focus on marketing and identify "opportunities" as either a defect in a competitor's product or an untapped market. They would pass this information to the engineers who, siloed from the rest of the organization, would design the new product. The result was products that lacked imagination and were often ignored by the customers they were designed to reach.

Following the Lean Innovation Cycle, The Wiremold Company determined their strategy, engaged with customers, analyzed their products in light of the new insights, and improved their products. For The Wiremold Company, the process challenged assumptions of performance characteristics like "cost per foot" and identified new applications and opportunities when considering previously disregarded characteristics like aesthetics and usability. The Wiremold Company didn't just apply the Lean tools. Removing waste would have just hurried poorly received designs to market faster. Wiremold first identified what was valuable to the customer and then pulled these insights into their operation. The results? 40% increase in sales, along with an increase in their gross margin [3].

Hoshin Kanri

The implication that the Lean Innovation Cycle proposes is that any innovation activity, any effort an organization makes to improve or innovate should first be dictated by the strategy of the organization. This is the fundamental principle of Lean. In the introduction, it was the bottom of the pyramid. *Hoshin Kanri* ought to dictate things like the target customer and industry. *Hoshin Kanri* ought to constrain innovation. That seems counter-intuitive, doesn't it? Innovation is all about creativity. Innovation teams should be challenging the status quo and breaking down barriers. Or should they? Creativity loves constraint. In a speech delivered to students at Stanford University, Marissa Mayer, Google's Vice President of Search Products and User Experience, shared that in her experiences, too much freedom creates an environment that is too unfocused [4].

Mayer is not alone in this sentiment. At the Cass Business School in London, Oguz Acar and his research team found that despite prevailing industry sentiments to remove structure, teams are able to create more and at a higher level when there is more structure [5]. Removing structure in lieu of creative space simply doesn't work. His research demonstrates that across different fields and applications and despite conventional wisdom, the key to unlocking creativity and innovation is not to remove all constraints. Rather, in order to innovate better, constraints such as time, funds, manpower, or other assets should restrict the innovation team [5].

Hoshin Kanri creates such constraints that increase performance. Rather than creating combative effects the strategic considerations of Hoshin Kanri determine the landscape of innovation moving forward. It removes the osmotic environment of possibility and supplants them with focused goals, which Acar and team would agree is helpful, not hurtful to creativity.

Hoshin Kanri should be a careful process of understanding an organization's own strengths and weaknesses as well as the external conditions it faces in the competitive environment. One of the principles of Lean is that if an organization gets Hoshin Kanri right, and it's communicated effectively, the whole organization, or in this case an innovation effort, is empowered to act autonomously and quickly. Guided by the strategic principles, innovation teams can make decentralized decisions to move in the desired direction and reflect the values of the organization.

Gemba

Importantly enough, Hoshin Kanri does not dictate the value a customer gets from a product or service. Believe it or not, the customer gets to decide what she considers valuable. Thus, we move into the next stage of the Lean Innovation Cycle, the gemba. Gemba is "The place work is done." When applied to manufacturing, this almost always means the production floor. For innovation it's different. The gemba is always in the hands of the customer. Another way to think of this step in the cycle is customer feedback and interaction. If you've ever taken an anthropology class, you may recognize this concept as "ethnography." Like traditional gemba walks, the purpose of this step in the process is simply to understand and observe [6]. Observe without judgment, observe without *a priori* beliefs, and observe without a desired outcome. Observe only for the sake of understanding. This is truly the most impactful and fruitful part of the Lean Innovation Cycle. Through these observations, we can see empirically how the customer interacts with a product. What does she enjoy about the product? Are her needs met by this product? What expectations does she have about the product? Questions and thoughts like these structure our observations. They allow the gemba to go beyond simple observation and exercise empathy for the customer. This "go and see" approach to customer experience will borrow heavily from Lean as well as a revolution in empathetic thinking known as Human-Centered Design.

In the past 20 years, there have been significant advances in the best practices for conducting a customer-focused gemba walk. Gone are the days of simple focus groups sitting around a table in a dimly-lit room discussing the newest product a company has already put to market. Gone are the days of cursory customer-satisfaction surveys. Instead, Human-Centered Design has reshaped the way people think about thinking. As its name implies, Human-Centered Design focuses on the individual and their experience using a product. It has been a watershed revolution that has shifted the methods of innovation to make way for something more value-added, more waste-resistant, more Lean.

Analyze

Once the gemba is completed, the model moves innovation activities into the analyze phase. This step of the model helps innovators make sense of the gemba. It helps us better understand who the customer is, how they interact and derive value from a product, and what changes to the product or its delivery will lead to the greatest value for the customer. The analyze phase is part of the process that is less swift and more thoughtful. If the purpose of Lean is to deliver value by eliminating waste, the analyze phase of the Lean Innovation Cycle ensures that the time spent on the gemba isn't wasted. The changes proposed will be impactful, will make a difference. The analyze stage of the process is made up of three different analyses: (1) Customer Journey and Value Stream Mapping, (2) Kano Analysis, and (3) Quality Function Deployment (QFD).

Ultimately, the goal of the analyze phase is to take the holistic experiences, interactions, and qualitative data that was collected in the analyze phase, and turn it into something more concrete and visual. The Customer Journey process mapping analysis is a logical jumping-off point. This phase of the analysis focuses on visualizing what you observed from the user experience. The analysis starts with creating a high-level process map, then quantifying the process, like time to complete each step and wait times. Finally, and most importantly, the customer experience of each step is considered and mapped. How does the consumer feel at each step? What are his or her frustrations, expectations, and wants?

Take, for example, the process of mopping the floor with a liquid cleaning product. The process starts with gathering supplies (the cleaning product, a bucket, a mop). Then the user turns on the water, waits for it to heat up, mixes the product and water in the bucket, moves the bucket back to the room with the dirty floor, and finally begins. Almost all of the prep work is non-value-added and there's hardly any interaction with the product! The user experience isn't just dictated by the interaction of the product itself but by the process as well. Identifying which parts of the process are non-value-added, take the most time, deliver the most frustrations, or don't use the product create fertile ground for future innovation.

The second analyze in the stage is the Kano Analysis. The Kano Model is a way to understand customer expectations and customer value [7]. The model is a bit technical, so I'll table introducing it until Chapter 4. For now, let's be content to say part of our analysis will allow us to differentiate aspects of a customer's wants and needs and desires. The Kano Model will further help us understand how a particular product or service meets this constellation of customer value.

Finally, the analyze stage concludes with something called QFD. QFD is one of those other-lesser-known Lean concepts. Developed in Japan in the 1960s, the purpose of QFD is to take the information from the gemba and Kano Analysis and relate it to something more tangible and alterable [7]. As an example, a gemba walk might reveal that customers want more fuel-efficient vehicles, safer vehicles, and quieter vehicles. Innovators then would have to consider certain trade-offs between these criteria. A lighter steel frame may make the frame more fuel efficient but at the cost of safety. Lots of soundproofing and safety features will increase the weight of the car and decrease fuel efficiency. The QFD analysis allows innovators to express the wants and desires of customers in terms of real *design parameters*. The design parameters then guide innovators through the ideation process, evoking trade-off considerations along the way.

Thus by the analyze step of the Lean Innovation Model, innovators have determined their strategic objectives, observed and interacted with customers, and thoughtfully considered these interactions. The three stages of analyzing start by looking backward at the Voice of the Customer and information collected in the gemba and end by transforming these raw data into more concise, better-understood ideas to be shaped and molded in the ideation phase. The analyze stage of the model is both holistic and technical. First, innovators seek to empathize with the customers and uncover what emotions the whole product experience evokes. At the same time, the Kano and QFD analysis allow innovators to pull back the layers and begin to better scope the design problem. For the innovator, the analysis phase answers two important questions: *What* does a customer consider important in a product? And most importantly, *Why* does the customer consider the product important?

Ideation

In continuous improvement frameworks, very little time is spent on discussing the methods for *actually* putting the improvement in place. It's assumed that a current state analysis or Lean value stream map is so conclusive, so compelling, that it takes little effort to synthesize new ideas on how to improve and move into the future state. Waste identification supports this paradigm. Simply remove the waste from the process to get Lean. This, as a generality, works for continuous improvement projects, but unfortunately, it falls short for the challenges of innovation.

One of the key outputs of the analyze phase is a better-understood, better-framed design problem. In the next step in the cycle, the ideation phase, innovators take this vetted, well-thought-out design problem and play with it. This phase in the process is what most people think about when they think about innovation. As we've said before, innovation is about novelty and creativity. The ideation phase involves two substeps, brainstorming and prototyping, both of which elicit the full potential of human creativity.

In the brainstorming substep, innovators synthesize ways to solve the problem. The most important aspect of this activity is not to generate good ideas but rather create an environment that breaks down barriers. In such an environment, people feel comfortable expressing even the most absurd ideas with no judgment. These absurd ideas often lead to the most creative innovations.

Harvard Business School has created an innovation incubator with this principle in mind. Its neighbor across town, The Sloan Business School at the Massachusetts Institute of Technology has done the same, calling it the "IdeaStorm" [8]. The cardinal rules for the MIT IdeaStorm are threefold and simple. (1) Have respect for others and for all ideas. (2) Don't beat down any idea. (3) Don't dominate the conversation.

On the other side of the United States, professionals at IDEO, one of the most prestigious design firms in the world, have noticed that how we ask questions make a difference in creating a safe, welcoming environment.

When asking a question about a particular product or design, they never start with "Can we..." or "What would it take..." instead, every sentence starts with three words, "How might we..." The goal of the "how might we" questions is to create questions in the brainstorming sessions that are provocative and meaningful while also inviting [9].

One of the biggest issues innovation teams have to overcome is "groupthink." Groupthink, also sometimes referred to as tunnel vision, is a phenomenon where members of a group begin to agree with each other simply for the sake of agreeing. Their drive toward conformity leads people to irrational decisions for fear of dissenting [10]. Nobody thinks critically about ideas because a consensus has been reached. This is the enemy of innovation. In the chapter devoted to the ideation stage, several techniques and approaches are offered to help combat the phenomenon of groupthink.

If the first substep in the ideation process is all about divergent thinking, then the second substep is all about convergent thinking. As fun as it is to think wildly about possibilities and come up with absurd ideas, at some point the project must be completed, a product must be delivered. Convergent thinking is the step in the process that helps reel in the divergent thinking activities and press forward with the most viable ideas. Prototyping is probably the important activity in the ideation phase, and it occurs once the divergent thinking phase draws to a close. Prototyping allows innovators to truly test the viability of an idea. It's a quick and inexpensive way to fail quickly, learn rapidly, and make adjustments that better satisfy the needs of the customer.

The ideation phase starts by taking an abstract idea of a well-thought-out design problem and transforming it into an idea for a workable viable product. This phase is truly where the magic of innovation blossoms. It's the space for human creativity to shine. And yet, it stands on the shoulders of deep analytical rigor. This is the paradox of ideation and innovation. Flourishing creativity works only as much as the thoughtfulness by which it was prepared. Divergent thinking elicits genius inasmuch as it can be reined in and converged upon. Thus the ideation stage is where innovators try new things, seek to fail often, and learn rapidly.

Kaizen

Finally, the *kaizen* phase of the model. The last step of the cycle is where the theory is put into practice. All the tools of Lean can be brought together to create and deliver value to the customer. As noted earlier in this chapter, the Lean Innovation Cycle is the mechanism of implementing Lean, with the added burden of identifying customer wants, needs, and desires. It should come as no surprise then that within the *kaizen* step of the cycle is its own PDCA cycle of continuous improvement. Just as in Lean for Continuous Improvement, in this stage of the Lean Innovation Cycle, kaizen isn't just about making changes. It compels innovation teams to think critically about proposed improvements, plan them out, make changes, and track how products perform.

In my research and own estimations, this is what is lacking in some of the other attempts to codify an innovation model. In Eric Ries's book, *The Lean Startup*, the issue becomes crystal clear. Ries proposes that a startup ought to create a very simplified minimally viable product (MVP) [11]. As illustrated in Figure 1.2, Reis recommends using a cycle of "Build, Measure, Learn" to pursue efforts to quickly learn and understand what customers want and expect, make changes, and release a new version into the market anticipating a higher value to the customer, and repeat the process [11].

As much as I admire the model and its approach, it possesses a blind spot that resembles naiveté. The Lean Startup model, as it's called, offers no structure to ensure that what was changed in one iteration made a discernable difference in the next. The worst thing an innovation team could do is create an "innovation" that amounts to nothing new as version 1.0. Therefore, each chapter rolls out a step-by-step guide for Lean Innovation Cycle. The kaizen phase will focus on internal validation to improvements as much as undertaking the improvements themselves.

The Lean Innovation Cycle is focused on delivering customer value. It isn't a hog-wild activity meant to run full speed ahead into the next iteration of a product. Instead, it is a methodical approach to understanding how your customer reacts to your business and thoughtfully design changes whose effects better align with the *Hoshin Kanri*, the goals and strategy of

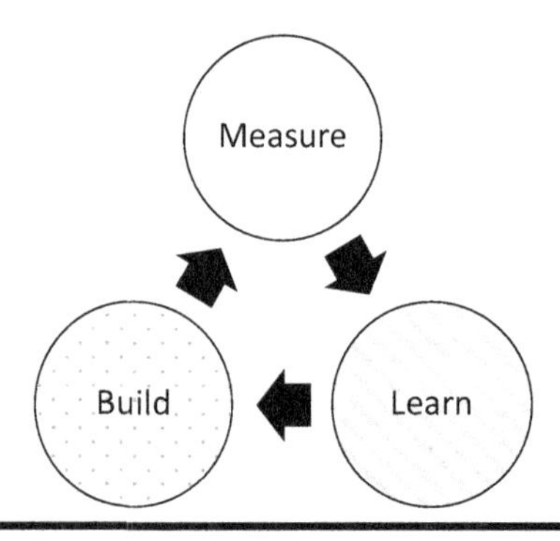

Figure 1.2 Lean Startup Cycle.

the business. Speed doesn't come from the model itself, it comes from the Kata of the Lean Innovation Cycle: practising the skills, the tools, and the approach will develop the organizational dexterity to move more swiftly and deliver customer value with exacting effectiveness.

Conclusion

Lean Innovation is all about delivering customer value within the established paradigm of an organization's strategy. Lean Innovation differs from other innovation activities in that it does not rely on high-stakes R&D expenditures or technological advances. Likewise, Lean Innovation has different aims than these endeavors. Rather than seeking stepwise growth or a new industry, customer, or marketplace, Lean Innovation is focused on delighting and increasing the satisfaction of current and adjacent customers. In so doing, Lean Innovation strengthens an organization's brand and the loyalty of its customers.

The Lean Innovation Cycle is the mechanism by which businesses create Lean Innovations. The five-step cycle takes the Lean framework for continuous improvement and adapts it to suit the needs of innovation. The adaptation of the Lean Innovation Cycle is Lean through and through. It is held together by the same Lean Principles that were introduced in the Introduction. It is a process with the chief aim and delivering customer value.

The cycle flows from one step to the next. Importantly, it always pulls value *from* the customer, never pushing *onto* the customer. Like the PDCA Shewhart Cycle, it starts with planning, the Hoshin Kanri, moves into the "do" of the gemba, "checks" and validates the information in the analysis phase, and then "acts" through ideation and kaizen. As with any adaptation of a paradigm, we'll develop new techniques and revisit some old tools that are tried and true. Throughout the cycle, the spirit of Lean is alive.

References

[1] National Institute of Standards. (2013). *NIST/SEMATECH e-Handbook of Statistical Methods.* http://www.itl.nist.gov/div898/handbook/ Chapter 6.1.1
[2] Bell Labs. (2019). *Global Recognition for groundbreaking Discovery.* Bell Labs Website. https://www.bell-labs.com/about/recognition/

[3] Mayer, M. (2006). *Creativity Loves Constraint.* Stanford Technology Ventures Program. https://ecorner.stanford.edu/videos/creativity-loves-constraint/
[4] Womack, J. P., Jones, D. T. (2003). *Lean Thinking.* Free Press. New York, NY.
[5] Acar, O., Tarakci, M., Kippenburg, D.V. (2018). "Creativity and Innovation Under Constraints: A Cross-Disciplinary Integrative Review". *Journal of Management* 45, 1, 96–121.
[6] Lean Enterprise Institute. (2020). *Gemba Walk.* Lean Enterprise Institute Website. https://www.lean.org/lexicon/gemba-walk
[7] ReVelle, J. (2004). *Quality Essentials: A References Guide from A to Z.* ASQ Quality Press.
[8] Landry, L. (2011). "Brainstorming and Ideastorming at MIT and Harvard: The New Springboard for Higher Ed Startups". *The Business Journals.* https://www.bizjournals.com/boston/inno/stories/news/2011/11/29/brainstorming-and-ideastorming-at-mit-and-harvard.html
[9] Program Fellows (2020). "'How Might We' Questions: Turn your perspective into actionable provocations." *Stanford Design School.* https://dschool.stanford.edu/resources/how-might-we-questions
[10] Janis, I. L. (1971). "Groupthink". *Psychology Today* 5, 43–46, 74–76.
[11] Ries, E. (2011). *The Lean Startup*, p. 75. Currency Publishing Co. New York.

Chapter 2

Hoshin Kanri

What is Hoshin Kanri?

With the first bit of housekeeping out of the way, we now turn to the first step in the Lean Innovation Cycle – Hoshin Kanri. Hoshin Kanri is a Japanese term that literally translates as "Direction" and "Management" [1]. Another way to think of it is that the *Hoshin* is the strategy a business pursues and the *Kanri* is the support of that strategy. At its heart, Hoshin Kanri is a structured and systematic way of providing direction to the rest of the organization. It is a management mechanism that ensures that everybody in the organization, regardless of their place in the enterprise hierarchy, is aligned to the same strategic goals. When Hoshin Kanri is properly implemented, it enables an organization to be more autonomous and flexible. These attributes are particularly helpful to innovation efforts whose effectiveness depends on a less rigorous structure and oversight.

One important principle that Hoshin Kanri reveals is that operational effectiveness is not valuable in its own right. It should not be seen as a means in and of itself. Famously, Michael Porter, one of the most influential business strategists of the 20th century, concluded something similar when he stated that operational effectiveness is not a strategy [2]. As Porter expounds, Operational Excellence is the ability to perform better, cheaper, faster, and with less defects. For Porter, Operational Excellence is incomplete because it does not dictate the strategic positioning of an organization – or how an organization distinguishes itself from competitors [3]. When we talk about operational effectiveness, or continuous improvement or a rose by any other name, we are specifically referring to the *Kanri*. Its purpose is to support the

DOI: 10.4324/9781003206347-3

Hoshin, the strategy of the organization. Both are important. Both are necessary. Neither are sufficient by themselves. An army without a battle plan is doomed so also is strategy without the means to execute.

This particular chapter focuses on operational nuances behind Hoshin: how goals should be determined and communicated throughout the organization and specific factors that are important to consider when selecting goals. The rest of the Lean Innovation Cycle will focus on the concrete steps of the Kanri, or how an innovation team can support the stated vision of the Hoshin through the subsequent steps of Gemba, Analyze, Ideation, and Kaizen. In particular, the Kanri is made impotent if the Hoshin does not answer three fundamental questions for the organization and the innovation team in particular. These questions are "Why does our organization exist?" "Who does our organization exist for" and "How do we know we've been effective in our mission?" Subsequently, once the Lean Innovation Cycle has been fully introduced, we will return to issues of strategy, competitive advantage, and sustainability from multiple, diverse perspectives.

High-Level Process of Hoshin Kanri

At a high level, the process of Hoshin Kanri is relatively straightforward. The first principle of Hoshin Kanri is that it takes a top-down approach. Lean and innovation are not grassroots movements. They require executive support. And if the purpose of Hoshin Kanri is to align the organization to common goals, it only makes sense that these goals start with leaders and decision-makers at the top. Executives make strategic decisions about what the company should be about. This includes items such as products, services, brand identity, and the target customers, but more importantly, the executive team provides a mission and a vision that aligns the organization to a common purpose. Usually, the executive team will also identify long-term goals that will help the organization realize their mission. Subsequently, after the C-suite has painted these broad strokes, these objectives are translated down to the next level of the organization, in what has sometimes been referred to as "waterfalling." At the next level, the strategic goals become more specific, pragmatic, and actionable. But importantly, as each goal becomes more granular, it is still tied to the original strategic goals. This waterfalling is in effect the deployment of the Hoshin Kanri. It ensures alignment within the entire organization because each person within the organization will be able to trace their particular goals to the organization's goals and mission.

Equally as important as selecting organizational goals is the periodic review and adjustment of these goals. The principles of Hoshin Kanri dictate that there should be a recurring review of the goals and how they are aligned to the internal and external forces facing the organization. A battle plan, no matter how masterfully crafted, will be doomed to fail if the circumstances that precipitated the plan have changed. A full-frontal assault will not work when the enemy has moved to the flank. As a recommendation, periodic review and re-evaluation of organizational goals should be done at least annually. It should incorporate all aspects of the business and generate actionable adjustments and changes.

Additionally, the re-evaluation, review, and adjustments should not just be conducted by organizational leadership and applied only to the strategic aspects of the plan. Likewise, the middle managers and agents of change that execute and support the organizational plan should evaluate their performance as well and make adjustments when needed. After-action reviews such as these are advantageous in assessing how well parts of the organization have performed to its goals. This can and should be done at all levels of the organization. Because these adjustments are not as affected by external forces, more frequent periodic reviews are encouraged. Support and operations teams that are responsible for executing strategy can learn more quickly through these after-action reviews and make adjustments in a timelier manner. At least once a quarter, after-action reviews should be conducted that assess areas of opportunity to improve and hold individuals accountable. Another way to hold individuals accountable is to frequently update the metrics. Like a telethon, the numbers are added almost instantaneously. This feedback is important for individuals responsible for the Kanri to feel and stay motivated. A frequent and timely updating of metrics will also demonstrate management's commitment to the vision.

Vision, Mission, and Breakthrough Objectives

The mission of an organization is the most important and fundamental guiding principle for formulating organizational strategy. Like a constitution or charter, its purpose is to clearly articulate why the organization exists, what it stands for, who its customers are, and how it aims to serve these customers. Examples of mission statements abound on the internet but they all have clearly articulated their purpose, customer, and service.

Similar to the mission statement is the vision statement. Rather than stating why an organization exists, the vision statement is more forward thinking. The vision statement clearly defines what an organization hopes to become in the future. The vision statement is an important guiding principle in strategy in that it gives direction in defining breakthrough objectives that will help the organization reach its desired future state.

In respect of Hoshin Kanri, the mission and vision statements have two purposes. First, they stand in their own right as the guiding light of the organization. They direct the organization where to go, who to serve, and what values to espouse. They act, in a sense, as the organizational constitution. Second, these statements must produce some concrete, high-level goals for the organization as well. These goals, what I call breakthrough objectives, should be long-term goals that are, at least in some regard, transformative in nature. The goals need to be challenging without being unreachable and progressive without being disruptive. Only three or four goals need to be selected, and while it's always better to be quantitative rather than qualitative in goal setting, the real purpose of these goals is to give the organization something to aspire to.

But be aware, sometimes goals can be far too aspirational as to be unreasonable. I once worked with a Japanese company who, in five years, wanted to be "Dan-Totsu" or the clear and absolute leader [4]. "The undisputed leader in what?" you might ask. "Everything," they would say. But this doesn't make any sense. Can a company really be number one in profitability, production volume, product performance, manufacturing cost, and revenue, in six different product categories around the world? At the time the firm was only best in one of those categories on just a few continents. It reminded me of a quip from one of my old college professors, "I am trying to make my family Hungarian. We are not currently Hungarian, but I am trying to move them toward it." It takes a whole lot more than aspirational thinking to make change happen. Goals that are too hopeful end up confusing and isolating the rest of the organization. Unsurprisingly, the Dan-Totsu pledge ended in dismal failure. Caught between competing priorities with no clear direction, the organization stymied in confusion and frustration. Dan-Totsu was never realized. Parts of the organization were sold off. There's a new CEO and leadership team now.

Taken together, the mission statement and the vision statement provide the foundation needed for any conversation on strategy. Without clearly articulating and understanding the reason for an organization's existence and the values it exposes, attempts to formulate a concise and effective strategy will be woefully ineffective. If a strategy is formulated, it will surely be rendered fruitless when the organization attempts to execute a strategy built without common purpose, values, principles, or ideals. As noted earlier, the Hoshin Kanri seeks to answer the question "Why does this organization exist?" The mission statement concisely answers this question and the vision statement provides added details about what the organization aspires to be in the future and how the organization's structure, service, delivery method, or customer may change.

Key Performance Indicators

The breakthrough objectives that come from the vision and mission statements beget another question of concern. "How do we know we've been effective?" The beauty of Hoshin Kanri is that it isn't just content with continuous improvement and it isn't content with just formulating strategy. In order for an organization to determine how well they've executed, it needs an **indicator**, some measurable way to determine how well the organization has **performed** on its **key** objectives. We call this a **Key Performance Indicator (KPI)**.

One of the biggest challenges of an organization is to determine what statistics, metrics, numbers should be tracked and counted as KPIs. Businesses in the 21st century have no shortage of statistics and data but not every piece of information truly translates to performance of key objectives. In selecting a KPI keep two principles in mind: alignment to objectives and agency. First a KPI must align to the mission of the organization, and as we'll see in the X-matrix, the specific breakthrough objectives that follow from the mission. Second, if a business unit or enterprise selects a KPI it ought to have the ability to influence the metric, what I call agency. Amount of revenue generated is a great KPI for a sales organization because it aligns with the objectives of the sales office and it's something a salesperson can influence – whether it's by selling more or selling better. Conversely, sometimes KPIs are poorly aligned to the objectives and agency of a business unit. I once worked with a talent acquisition team that wanted to keep track of the number of requisitions (job openings) they handled each month. But who cares? The recruiting group doesn't control the cadence of turnover, the growth of the organization, or any other factor that contributes to the number of requisitions on their plate. Rather, a more meaningful KPI like cost per hire, or time to hire, would have propelled them toward better operational performance and improvement. The cost per hire and time to hire metrics entail factors that the talent acquisition team can directly influence (agency) and can be tied directly to their role within the organization (alignment).

Similarly, I'm inundated by poorly chosen metrics in my own life in the form of LinkedIn notifications. Each week, I receive a notification telling me how many searches I appeared in last week. While it's an interesting piece of information, it's wholly misaligned with my goals as a user. People go on LinkedIn for a number of reasons be it to make new connections, interact more with like-minded professionals, drive traffic to a business website, or land a job. But nobody is going on LinkedIn to appear in searches. Nobody. The metric is wholly misaligned with the objectives of their users and provides little recourse to influence the result in the future.

Organizations face another challenge in selecting KPIs. Often, organizations become too narrowly focused on one part of their business. And this part is almost always finance. In order to remedy this issue, many organizations have adopted the Lean best practice of a balanced scorecard. The balanced scorecard is a high-level approach of selecting organizational KPIs that ensures that all of the stakeholders and key functions of the organization are represented [5]. It's a simple idea which has a profound impact. The balanced scorecard is also an effective approach because it limits the number of organizational KPIs selected. An organization cannot effectively manage a scorecard of 10 or 12 metrics. If everything is important, nothing is important, because nothing can be given priority. Instead, organizational decision-makers need to determine the critical few, most important parts about their organization, and determine which KPIs best reflect the desired performance. The scorecard compels the organizational decision-makers to identify the key stakeholders, a goal for each stakeholder group and a KPI that monitors that goal (Figure 2.1).

Leading and Lag Measures

In discussing the KPIs it's important to draw a distinction between leading and lagging measures. Lagging measures are easier to understand. They are backward-looking and decidedly demonstrate the past performance of a team or organization. These measures are also the most common measures reported, by nature of them being so much easier to obtain. Almost all financial measures are lag measures. Profitability, total revenue, and direct

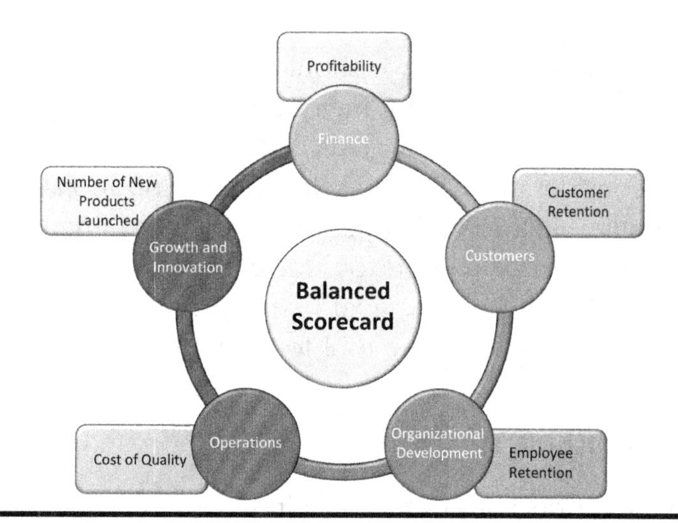

Figure 2.1 Example of a balanced scorecard.

labor costs are all lagging. Employee turnover is also a lag measure because the undesired event, attrition from the organization, has already occurred.

In contrast, leading measures are metrics that have a direct causal relationship to a stated goal. These measures are reported much less often, usually for the reasons that they're harder to obtain, track, and measure. Rather than compiling a summary statistic for each quarter for total revenue generated, a sales organization can predict the next quarter's performance by looking at number of cold calls and conversion rates. Wouldn't it be better if, instead of tracking employee turnover, you could predict if somebody was going to leave based on the length of their commute to work, job performance, and how many sick days they've taken recently? Generally speaking, by tracking and improving leading metrics, organizations are able to have a greater effect on their stated objectives and can generate these effects more rapidly. To return to the LinkedIn example, appearing in more searches might seem like a leading measure. Conceivably, the more searches you appear in, the more opportunities for networking are made available, and the more networking opportunities, the more likely you are to be interviewed and selected for a new opportunity. However, there's no evidence to support that this hypothesis holds in reality. And since a strong causal relationship can't be established, its effectiveness as a leading measure is spurious at best. Conversely, number of job applications submitted, or better yet, number of jobs interviewed for are much better leading measures that anticipate and predict number of future job offers.

With these two distinctions in mind, it's important for organizational leaders to select the KPIs that will have the greatest impact on the organization. As noted, leading measures generally have a greater and faster impact than lagging measures. And yet, we should be cautious about endorsing a balanced scorecard of *only* leading measures. Matters of organizational culture regarding how results and goals are reported and adhered to are also important considerations. When selecting organizational KPIs, it's far better to prudently select KPIs that fit within the prevailing culture of the organization. A KPI can be a good tool for guiding an organization in its transformation to become a more goal-oriented and data-informed organization. But it cannot be an all-in-one tool for compelling this transformation.

Tools for Hoshin Kanri

With the theoretical principles of the Hoshin Kanri defined, it's time to move the conversation to the actual deployment of strategy throughout the organization. There are all kinds of tools to help business leaders determine their competitive position and strategy, many of which are discussed later on in this book. Tools like competitive profile matrices, SWOT analysis, perceptual maps, and others provide frameworks for organizations to think analytically and critically about themselves and their competition. In each of these tools, the strategist is asked to consider how factors that are both internal and external to themselves impact their best course of action, their dominant strategy. But one tool that concerns us right now is the X-matrix. The X-matrix is essential for visualizing how the mission and values of an organization are transformed into breakthrough objectives, the KPIs, and small actionable goals.

The X-Matrix Tool

The X-matrix is a tool specifically designed for Hoshin Kanri. This tool takes the mission statement and values of an organization and diagrams a concise cascade of direct, actionable tactics, assignable to individuals within the organization. This approach is beneficial because it ensures everybody's goals and actions are aligned to the breakthrough objectives that come down from the high-level vision. Moreover, the X-matrix has the added benefit of demonstrating how all the organizational objectives are connected and support one another in the execution of a firm's mission, vision, and strategy. Finally, the X-matrix allows individuals' line of sight into the whole picture of the organization while still giving concise focus to what is particularly important to them. This organizational transparency further reduces the effects of "silos" and is more apt to create an environment suitable for multidisciplinary collaboration and teams (Figure 2.2).

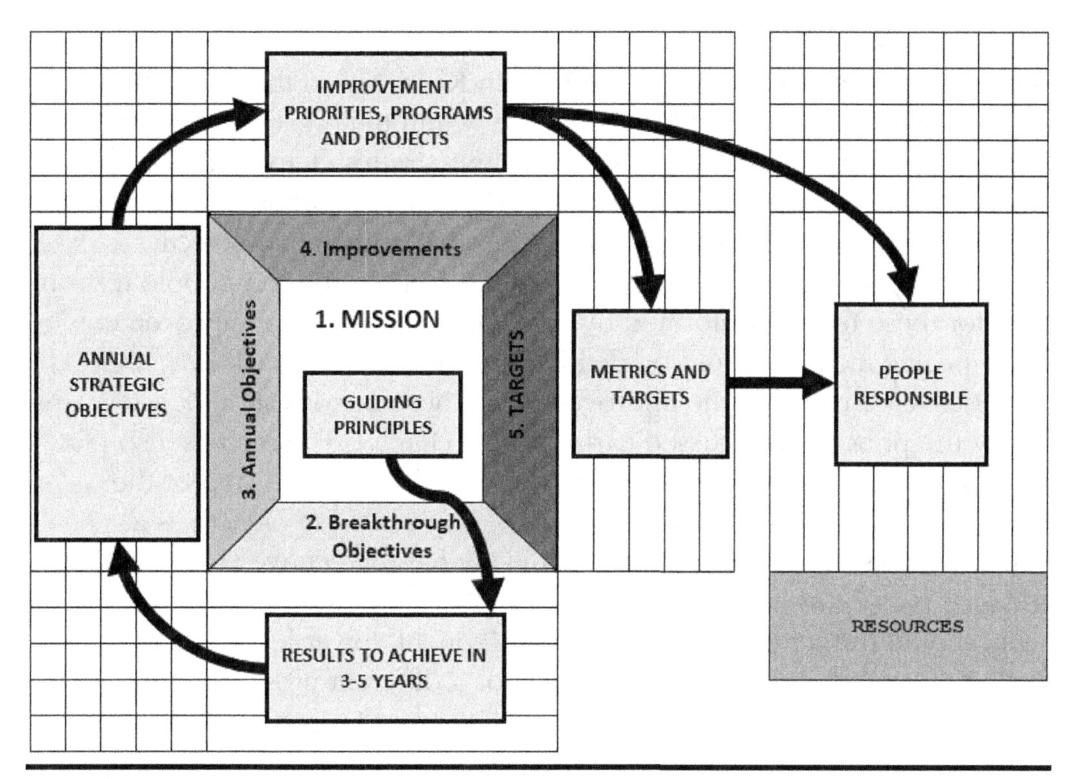

Figure 2.2 The X-matrix.

Suitably, the X-matrix starts with the mission and vision of an organization. These are the guiding principles that direct the organization's behavior and identity toward what the organization wants to accomplish and what it wants to become. Without a clear understanding of mission and vision, an organization runs the risk of losing focus and becoming distracted by other opportunities that are not part of its core mission. The next section of the Hoshin Kanri is the results. These are the long-term breakthrough objectives that the organization is trying to meet within the next three to five years. Guided by the vision and the mission, as well as the strategic tools discussed above, organizational leaders need to clearly articulate what needs to be accomplished to achieve or continue to achieve the mission of the organization and realize its future vision.

The next step in the X-matrix is the annual objectives. These further refine and articulate the long-term objectives into shorter-term and more manageable objectives and goals for the organization within the next year. Between the breakthrough objectives and annual objectives sections, the X-matrix provides a space for a dot matrix. This is a way to visualize how these two steps are related to and joined with one another. The dot matrix occurs in all subsequent steps of the X-matrix. After the annual objectives come what I like to call the *tactics* portion of the Hoshin Kanri. Given the breakthrough and annual objectives, what has to change within the organization? This step is labeled as “Improvements” on the X-diagram in this chapter. This step is one of the most consequential because it defines the actions that will be carried out in order to achieve the breakthrough and annual objectives.

The last two steps of the X-matrix are the metrics and the people responsible for these metrics. Informed by the direct action of the improvement step, specific metrics should be defined and recorded to track how well individuals are realizing the improvements. These metrics should also follow the principles discussed earlier in the chapter. The metrics also play an important role in accountability of individuals. The final step of the X-matrix is to cascade the matrix down and repeat these objectives at different levels. A C-suite X-matrix will likely have executive vice presidents and vice presidents in charge of some of their goals and initiatives. These goals should further guide and direct subsequent, lower-level X-matrices that articulate refined and specific goals for a different group of individuals at a different level within the organization. For any Lean practitioner, the X-matrix should also elicit ideas of the PDCA Shewhart Cycle: Plan-Do-Check-Act. Each step in the matrix facilitates a different step in the PDCA cycle, and at periodic points can be used to evaluate and improve the direction and plan based on the results (Figure 2.3).

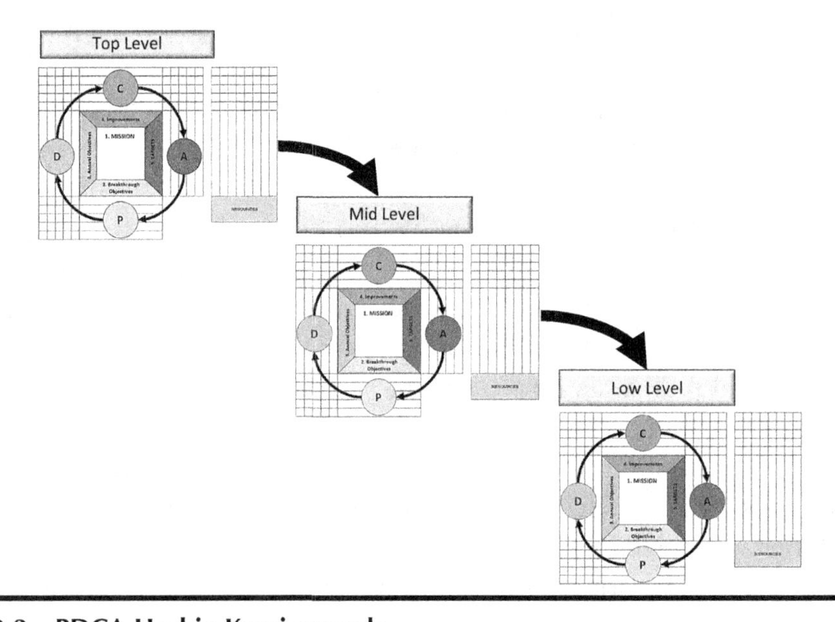

Figure 2.3 PDCA Hoshin Kanri cascade.

Market Segmentation

Traditionally, all of the key aspects of Hoshin Kanri have been covered. Operational tasks and execution should flow from the values contained in the mission and vision statements of the organization. The flow should be from the top down with periodic after-action reviews to adjust to improve the appropriateness of the strategy and operational objectives. But because we are dealing with innovation, the Hoshin Kanri cannot stand on its own as an internal mechanism for bridging the strategy-execution gap. Instead, any firm looking to innovate must also understand and appreciate the role that the customer or end-user has in executing strategy. In the previous section, it was noted that the mission statement should include, among other things, an idea of who the customer is that the organization is serving. It may seem like the mission statement, in addition to answering the question of "why does the organization exist?" also answers the question "What does the organization exist for?" However, in my estimation, more thought, reflection, and detail are needed to satisfactorily answer this question. The strengths of the Lean Innovation Cycle draw from its ability to extract insights from the customer. Without a comprehensive understanding of who the customer is, efforts to engage these customers and extract information from them will be stifled from the very start.

Market segmentation is a way for businesses to learn more about their customers and understand them at a deeper level. In particular, market segmentation is a type of analysis that looks to identify and categorize differences between all of the customers in aggregate. As an example, a book publisher will publish many types of books: textbooks, scientific journals, self-help, classic novels, and new releases. In each of these cases, the product is more or less the same – a printed book – and the customer is thereabouts the same as well – a purchaser of a printed book. But the example makes the distinction apparent. Clearly, there are key differences between these customers. The customers have different needs, desires, and interests. Customers realize different levels of value from different books, and it's not the case that a customer of one book, say a classic novel, will value another, say a textbook on organic chemistry. A college student is far more interested in textbooks than a saucy romance novel. It should also be clear, if it's not already, that ability to distinguish between classes of customers is powerful. A business *must* be able to discern differences in customers in order to remain competitive in delivering valuable products to the customers, positioning themselves appropriately in the marketplace, and exacting the highest profits it can for the value.

For these reasons, market segmentation is vitally important to starting on the path of Lean innovation for at least two reasons. First, Lean is about adding value to the customer. And rather than removing waste to add value, Lean innovation has the unique task of taking this value-driven ethos and designing something valuable from the beginning. Second, the Lean Innovation Cycle is customer-driven. It pulls insights from the customers, from the marketplace, and makes this the starting point for innovative design and thinking. Lean innovation does not push new ideas onto the market, it pulls the ideas from the customers. Market segmentation, along with the mission and vision statements, informs those within the organization responsible for innovation with the knowledge to be effective from the very beginning.

This isn't a marketing textbook, so it's not necessary to get into the weeds of how market segmentation is done or how classes of customers are determined. Rather, be conscious to know that there are different classes of customers that are separated in a number of different ways. For brevity's sake, I only introduce a few:

Demographics: Demographics are attributes about a person that are more or less outside of a person's direct influence and agency. Age, gender, race, ethnicity, education, employment, marital status are all demographics. These are all unchanging or slow to change.

Geographics: Geographic segmentation is a subset of one particular type of demographic, namely where a person lives. The specificity of geographic demographics will change depending on the scope of the business. A transnational company may look at differences between continents, cultures, and countries. Meanwhile, a US national country may look at differences between the Southwest, Northeast, and Midwest. Organizations, like state governments and electric and gas companies, will even narrow segmentation based on county, city, or zip code. In all, geographic segmentation seeks to use location to understand differences between stakeholders and customers.

Behavioral segmentation: Behavioral segmentation differs wildly from the previous two. Behavioral segmentation seeks to understand differences in stakeholders or customers based on what they do and how they behave. Your local supermarket is the best example of an organization seeking to understand customer behaviors. By scanning your shopper's card, you're providing the supermarket with information to understand how you spend including what you spend your money on, how much you spend, spending frequency, how often you buy repeat items, how often you buy new items, and much more. By understanding customer behavior and classifying customer behavior into different groups, businesses are empowered to advertise and price their products to maximum effectiveness [read: profitability].

Psychographics: The last type of classification I'll mention is psychographics. These take customer behavioral analysis even further. Psychographics seek to segment customers based on how they identify and perceive *themselves*. As an example, somebody who sees themselves as extra caring or concerned for the environment is likely to spend more money on products advertising green technology or is willing to pay more for products made from recycled and reused material. These product designs and product features are not informed by the behavior of the person. Instead, the self-identity of the customer is what drives the product's viability. As you can probably tell, psychometrics is harder to obtain than geography and demographics. Only recently have psychometrics been used in segmentation analysis. But it's also clear that the opportunity of finding a niche that resonates deeply with a person's identity has the potential to become very lucrative (Figure 2.4).

Market segmentation is a fundamental activity for any business but is also vitally important to the Lean Innovation Cycle. Along with the other aspects of the Hoshin Kanri, market segmentation acts like the Plan phase of the Shewhart Cycle or the Define phase of the DMAIC/DMADV process. Its purpose is to focus the attention of the business and innovation team on

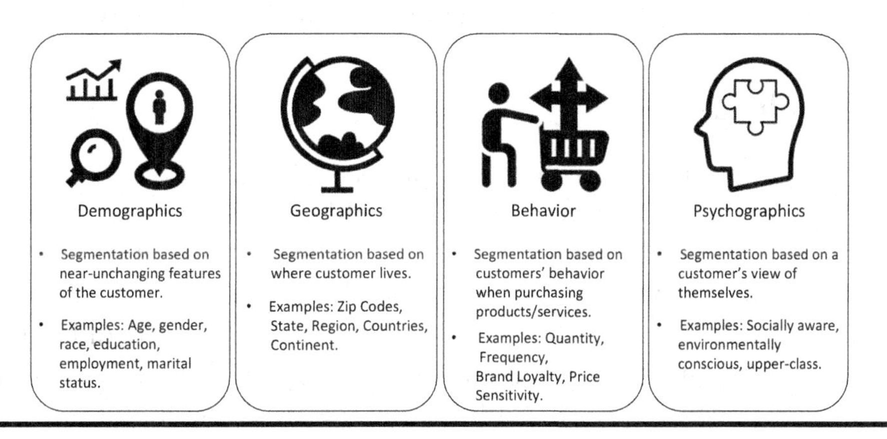

Figure 2.4 Types of market segmentation.

a particular group that shares a common idea and definition of value. These classifications become much more important later on because they dictate where innovative ideas come from which has a direct effect on the success of innovation.

The Innovation Team

Finally, one more addendum needs to be added to the discussion of Hoshin Kanri: How to structure and manage a team to execute innovation strategy? So far, we've looked at the higher-level considerations of strategy formulation in the Hoshin Kanri. Starting with the mission and vision statements we identified the values and purpose of an organization. Working our way through market segmentation, we realized a deeper understanding of the customers the organization will serve. And by thoughtfully and carefully selecting KPIs, we've ensured that the organization is able to evaluate how well it's performed to its stated goals. But these ideas can and should be applied just as well to each division, business line, or team within the organization, including the innovation team. That's the whole idea of Hoshin Kanri! Starting with the mission statement the innovation team should articulate its reason for existing and continue through the other ideas presented above with the added caveat that each of these steps should also align to the enterprise goals and subsequent hierarchical refinement. Additionally, the innovation team should consider who its customers are within the organization as well as the external consumer. With these things in mind, before going further into the next part of Hoshin Kanri, we ought to take a step back and give more consideration to the structure, function, and execution of the innovation team as its own entity.

Multidisciplinary Teams

In traditional continuous improvement projects, the green belt or black belt are not leading projects by themselves or conducting kaizens by their lonesome. The *modus operandi* of Lean and Six Sigma has always been to assemble a team of diverse team members. This assembly is often described as a cross-functional team. It should be a team that represents different roles, viewpoints, talents, and stakeholders. Traditionally in manufacturing, cross-functional teams consist of a few frontline workers, crew leaders, maintenance technicians, and engineers in addition to the project leader. A

Lean innovation team should follow similar principles. The team should be diverse in their talents and viewpoints, but this can be extended well beyond where the Lean framework leaves off. Lean innovation efforts can, and should, pull individuals from a variety of backgrounds. Backgrounds like sales, marketing, product development, and production and engineering can create synergy when they cooperate and collaborate together. Whereas Lean continuous improvement has often isolated to the world of production and operations, Lean innovation extends throughout all the divisions and disciplines within an organization.

The cross-functional, multidisciplinary team is essential for successful innovation. Cross-functional teams are unique in that they bring people from diverse perspectives into a single, cohesive group which is aligned to one unified goal. Innovation thrives within this multidisciplinary framework. By bringing together individuals from different functions, many different viewpoints, ideas, and perspectives are also discussed and thoughtfully considered. Diversity is particularly helpful in creative endeavors, like innovation, in that it mitigates tunnel vision of seeing a problem from the same perspective. These new perspectives naturally lead to the challenging of old assumptions and preconceived notions which can act as roadblocks for innovative thinking. But the most important part of the multidisciplinary team is that it creates a level playing field. Within a cross-functional framework, nobody is the hierarchical expert or leader. Every person brings their unique talents and perspective to a common direction. This too fosters creativity. It's an erroneous idea to suppose that because somebody has longer tenure or is higher up in an organizational hierarchy that they will have better, more meaningful insights into the desires and needs of the customer.

The multidisciplinary team is also one that can learn and grow at a much faster rate than other teams. Within a cross-functional team, there is increased momentum for change. Because the impact of organizational hierarchy is reduced, there is less "turf" to protect. People can make decisions that are aligned with the goals of the team. This allows team members to let down their guard, have more empathy for others, and grow in understanding of the organization as a whole and learn more specifics of different organizational functions. All of this serves to create a more creative and effective innovation team.

If you're looking for more concrete reasons to assemble a diverse team, consider the research of TRIZ founder Genrich Altshuller. In this book's Introduction, we also saw how different levels of innovation require multidisciplinary knowledge. Altshuller's research concluded that most innovations are simple, technical improvements to a product or process. This is, in a sense, where traditional continuous improvements make hay. These results shouldn't surprise us either because their advent is predicated on very little outside information. Technical experts can make improvements to the processes they know best. But Altshuller's research also showed that the higher levels of innovation, innovation that resolved physical contradictions and developed new technologies relied on knowledge from other disciplines and industries. Without diversifying the scope and source of the knowledge employed in innovation, innovation teams battle uphill in order to realize the more transformative and impactful types of innovations they desire. Thus multidisciplinary approaches, especially in assembling innovation teams, are a necessary condition for achieving highly transformative innovations.

The Lean Innovation Team and the Organization

While not explicitly part of the innovation team, it's important to get buy-in and support for innovation efforts from the top. Lean has never been a grassroots movement. Whether it manifests itself as competing priorities, lack of commitment, inability for action, or outright hostility toward the Lean framework, nothing dooms a Lean transformation quite like lack of executive support. Ideally, an innovation team will have its own place staked out in the company. Here, its chief responsibility is to generate innovative ideas and support business development. The leadership of the innovation team is likewise accountable, at least in part, for innovation. This structure is ideal because it creates an implicit commitment to innovation at the organizational level. But even in an environment where ideas like "agility" and "innovation" are given ample lip service, this structure is still a rarity in most organizations.

Therefore, in many organizations, innovation teams will need to act like internal consultants. They will need to create project proposals and produce project charters. They will need to have defined timeline and project deliverables. In this organizational structure, it's of the utmost importance to gain executive sponsorship for the innovation project – not just to remove roadblocks and free up resources – but also to gain a commitment to implementing the actionable items that come out of the project.

And finally, the innovation team must be led by a competent and dynamic leader. The innovation team leader should be a person with a panoply of tangible skills and intangible attributes. The leader should have a demonstrated proficiency in project management and facilitating collaborative sessions with teams. The leader should be able to coach their team to a higher level of performance as the team grows and matures, nurture the team when setbacks occur, and coach diverse personalities to higher individual performance as well. The leader should have executive presence and be highly persuasive and able to sell the ideas generated in course of an innovation project.

The leader should also be a "T-style leader." A T-style leader is a professional that has a deep mastery of a particular area of expertise, and a shallow understanding of *many* other functions and disciplines within an organization. This archetype is vitally important for successful innovation. As an example, take Leonardo Da Vinci. One of the most innovative people in world history. He was an engineer, a sculptor, a physicist, a geologist, a scientist of human anatomy, and an architect. Yet in all these endeavors he relied heavily on his absolute mastery of art. Without this mastery, he would have never been able to create some of the earliest drawings of the human anatomy, design his inventions, or conceptualize his sculptures and architecture. In a similar way innovators, and especially leaders of innovators must have some mastery of a particular function that anchors them and enables them to venture into other functions and empowers the multidisciplinary efforts that are necessary for successful innovation.

Managing an Innovation Team

Multidisciplinary teams come with their own unique set of challenges. For all of its merits, diversity has its drawbacks. We can't expect that after bringing a group of people with diverse backgrounds and viewpoints together that they will all get along seamlessly. In fact, the purpose of creating multidisciplinary teams is to create disagreement and challenge prevailing views and paradigms. A hands-off approach to leading this team will doom the innovation team before it even begins. And while there are many issues that can present themselves in managing an innovation team, the two most fundamental and important issues are that of trust and identity.

A team that cannot trust its leader will not be successful. In order to assemble a team that is effective as it is diverse, the team leader must first establish a firm foundation of trust. Trust for his or her leadership and trust between members of the team. As a leader, one of the most effective ways to create trust is to become more transparent. Make a conscious effort to unveil the man behind the curtain. By communicating how decisions are made, projects are prioritized, and performance is rewarded, leaders demystify if not eliminate many of the qualms and preoccupations many employees have. Like transparency, it's also important to be open and honest about your own performance. Candidly admit mistakes as they occur. If you or the team doesn't meet a goal or an expectation, explain why it's still important to achieve these goals and what the impacts of missing targets are. And likewise, don't hold on to failures – this is especially important for creative endeavors like innovation and will be discussed more in the ideation phase of the Lean Innovation Cycle.

Creating a team identity is also of paramount importance. Without a well-articulated and defined team identity, a diverse assemblage of people will not have a clear understanding of the role the team plays within the organization and their role within that team. The vision and mission statements should be the cornerstone for the team's identity. These statements clearly convey to the team, as well as any of its stakeholders, why the team exists and who it strives to be. As a suggestion, and painting with a broad brush, the team identity should be one that is collaborative yet methodical. The team should have a mission and vision to be collaborative, yes, but also highly efficient, effective and focused on achieving its results. With this tactical effectiveness in mind, another way to create and maintain cohesive team identity is visual management. And there's no better visual management tool than the *Obeya* or war room.

The Obeya

Obeya is also one of the later developments of the Toyota Production System and was introduced in the 1990s as part of the product development efforts for the Toyota Prius. In my experience its usage across industry reflects its late advent; many of the organizations I've worked with and benchmarked with still don't make effective use of an *Obeya*. In Japanese, *Obeya* literally means "large room." Within the Lean context, it has always meant something more. Physical space and visual management are always important in Lean. The gemba is the principal place to obtain information and progress toward goals that needs to be visualized. The *Obeya* is a natural extension of these principles and fits nicely into other principles of the Lean Innovation Cycle, which we'll return to in later chapters. The purpose of the *Obeya* room is to create a space for cross-functional leaders to come together and break down the departmental and divisional silos that separate them. It aligns the team to a common mission and purpose. *Obeya* is a tool like any other Lean tool. But instead of helping to identify and solve process problems, the purpose of the tool is to improve the cohesiveness and teamwork of a multidisciplinary team.

This is important to the cohesiveness and vibrancy of team identity. Cross-functional team members may sit in different parts of the building, in different departments and have duties or stronger networks in their functional areas. All of these factors are pushing them away from becoming a cohesive unit. Without the *Obeya*, the team exists only on paper. It's like a basketball team without a locker room. There's no place to prepare for the challenges that lie ahead, no place to game plan and talk about adjustments that need to be made.

Probably the best-known *Obeya* is not Japanese at all. NASA's mission control has been the coordinating mechanism behind the NASA space program for over half a century. At mission control, a diverse array of engineers, programmers, mathematicians, military veterans, and managers coordinate together for a common purpose – the current space mission. They make extraordinary achievements, because they're all very capable, yes, but also because of their environment and how it allows them to coordinate their diverse skillsets with each other.

With that high level of achievement in mind, it's worthwhile to ask, what exactly should an *Obeya* look like to help facilitate such successful performance? For starters, there should be no physical barriers. This allows for easier communication between team members. NASA's mission control of the 1950s and 1960s had something of a bullpen, long before open-office floor plans were in vogue. The *Obeya* should also be oriented towards the goals. With no walls or other physical barriers, it's easy for individuals in the war room to look in different directions and lose focus on the targets and goals. The *Obeya* ought to be oriented in one direction. This is the standard best practice across several industries and activities – newsrooms, mission control, orchestras, sports teams and even the Starship Enterprise. This best practice exists everywhere multidisciplinary teams coordinate together.

The most important aspect of the *Obeya* is the visual management. The purpose of the *Obeya* is to bring people together toward a common goal, and it's important for the team to be able to see and visualize this goal. The visualization becomes what the team orients itself to. It becomes the centerpiece of conversation, of investigation, and of action. This visual management need not be just KPIs and metrics. They can also be creative ideas, signals to other members, and diagrams for how things are connected. I once worked in a manufacturing plant that had tremendously high performing teams who used *Obeya* rooms. One wall had all the visualizations and metrics. Everybody was oriented to it, and there was nothing else to look at anywhere else. On that wall the goals were clearly stated, the KPIs regularly updated, the roles of each team member clearly identified. Each day, there was a brief 15-minute meeting where leaders brought either a red card or a green card. These cards communicated whether or not they needed outside help – not whether or not they met their daily goals. This allowed for quick nonverbal communication between the cross-functional group about who needed help and who could offer it. It facilitated a cohesive high performing team that could visualize how the team was doing, who needed support, and who could help.

The physical space of the *Obeya* matters. It adds support and structure to the cross-functional team and may be, amongst an ocean of competing signs, the only signal that team members get that they belong to a team with a unique mission, unique identity, and a unique role in supporting the Hoshin Kanri. Even within the scope of innovation, these principles should be adhered to. The *Obeya* should be the command center, the mission control for coordinating the team, building cohesiveness, identity, and teamwork and clearly communicating the shared objectives. Later on, in the more creative processes of the Lean Innovation Cycle, we return to the idea of the *Obeya* and see the changes that ought to be made to better facilitate a creative environment. But for now, be content with using the *Obeya* as a tool for coordination and mission.

Conclusion

Finally, I could not leave the discussion of the Hoshin Kanri without discussing its human aspect. One of the core principles of Lean is Respect for People. Without a clearly defined game of what is expected from individuals, how they'll be evaluated, and why they're asked to work on such and such a project, individuals feel unseen, disrespected, and confused about their impact and importance within the organization. The Hoshin Kanri X-matrix, for all of its technical and rigid bewilderment, has a deeply human focus that prioritizes transparent communication of vision, direction, and knowledge to each person in the organization.

The Hoshin Kanri may seem like a mixed bag of tricks. Mission statements, market segmentation, KPIs and managing an innovation team all seem to come from different directions. As all these tools and ideas buffet you from different directions, remember that the Hoshin Kanri creates the foundation for the Lean Innovation Cycle. In order to be effective at innovation, you have to be a good coach. And a good coach creates a winnable game for their team. You must understand why you're playing the game, that's the mission. You must know the score of the game, that's the KPIs. You must understand the strengths and weaknesses of your team and the other team and you must know schematically how your team will execute your playbook. The Hoshin Kanri accomplishes all of this before your team takes the field.

References

[1] "Hoshin Kanri: Connecting Strategic Planning to Project Execution". *Kanbanize.com*. https://kanbanize.com/lean-management/hoshin-kanri/what-is-hoshin-kanri

[2] Porter, M. (1996). "What is Strategy?" *Harvard Business Review*. https://hbr.org/1996/11/what-is-strategy

[3] Porter, M. (1996). "What is Strategy?" *Harvard Business Review*. https://hbr.org/1996/11/what-is-strategy

[4] Tire Review Staff. (2014). "Bridgestone Aims to Be 'Dan-Totsu'". *Tire Review*. https://www.tirereview.com/bridgestone-aims-dan-totsu/

[5] Kaplan, R., et al. (1992). "The Balanced Scorecard—Measures that Drive Performance". *Harvard Business Review*. https://hbr.org/1992/01/the-balanced-scorecard-measures-that-drive-performance-2

Chapter 3

The Gemba

I've recently developed a penchant for crime-based television shows. Whether it's a true crime documentary or a procedural courtroom drama, I've probably seen it. As I was watching a show the other day, it struck me how often we take for granted that perfect dramatic setting of a detective investigating a crime scene. The detective scrutinizes the scene, looking for clues about what happened and who did, or might have done, it. Though we never see it on screen, in reality a detective must get up from his desk, leave his office, get in his car, and drive several miles just to get to the scene of the crime. These are modern-day detectives, not characters set in Arthur Conan Doyle's Victorian England. These TV characters are an archetype of real law enforcement investigators that physically show up to crime scenes and solve real crimes. In the modern world, where forensic science dominates investigation and criminal court proceedings, why do these detectives bother to spend the time traveling to and from the crime scene? Surely the pictures, the DNA evidence, murder weapons, footprints, and anything else of the alleged perpetrator can be sent to the detective's desk, uploaded to the detective's computer, or at the very least moved to evidence locker. Surely, we have the capability for a homicide detective to get all the physical evidence without leaving the office. All of these pieces of evidence can be employed to sufficiently recreate a crime scene. In light of modern technology, it seems anachronistic and antiquated for a detective to actually visit the scene of a crime.

And yet, every police force on earth insists that a detective ought to go to the scene of the crime. It is a worldwide best practice. Law enforcement

DOI: 10.4324/9781003206347-4

knows that in order to really understand what transpired, the investigating detective must immerse himself into that environment. Even without further analysis, there is something intuitively correct in this. Imagine what a defense attorney would do with a detective testifying on the stand who never visited the crime scene. The defense attorney might ask how the detective was sure all the relevant physical evidence was collected and identified. How would the detective know if any relevant data was withheld from the analysis? The detective would lose credibility not just because he didn't do the leg work of traveling to the scene of the crime but precisely because without traveling to the scene the entire foundation and basis for his deductions fall apart. The same is true for problem-solvers, designers, and innovators. People in these positions need to do more than understand the "crime scene" – they need to immerse themselves within the scene and its surroundings. By fully immersing themselves, they are able to better understand the situation and solve the mystery. In turn, these environmental insights can point to areas of further inquiry and the unlocking of additional information that would otherwise be missed.

What has become a worldwide best practice in law enforcement can and should inform the way businesses think of their own operations, processes, and activities, and as is most relevant to the scope of this book, innovation. If the purpose of the detective is to solve a crime and identify who is responsible for the crime, then the innovator's purpose is to uncover the mystery of what the customer values and desires and how the customer behaves. The gemba holds the key to identifying these values and desires, and this chapter arms innovators with the tools and methods to unlock these insights.

Gemba in Traditional Lean

It should comfort the reader and all those familiar with Lean, that Lean as a problem-solving framework has a strong tradition when it comes to going to where the work is done, what the Japanese call the gemba. Taiichi Ohno was the founder of the Toyota Production System (TPS), which itself is the basis of Lean. Taiichi was scrupulous in ensuring managers first went to the gemba seeking to understand all they could about the problems of their operation. One of his most fabled efforts to get others to observe the gemba is the story of the Ohno Circle. As one version of the story puts it, he would draw a small, chalk circle, about 2 ft. in diameter on the production floor and have a manager remain in the circle for an entire hour [1]. Before Taiichi Ohno left the unwitting manager, he would give him one commission: "Identify waste." Then Taiichi Ohno would leave. It sounds like a sadistic punishment by western standards, maybe the "Oh No!" circle would be a better way to express it. However, there is subtle wisdom in Ohno's management techniques. I doubt any manager, after an hour, would say he couldn't find any waste. There's more to this story than just creative ways to get managers to see things your way. One such lesson, of course, is that nobody knows everything about a process. By the time Taiichi Ohno returned to the chalk circle, the marooned observer knew more about the process than anybody else in the building and owed all of his knowledge to simple and concentrated observation of the gemba.

The fact that foundation of Lean is built from the gemba is a foundational principle of Lean that merits repeating and emphasis. Only the gemba has the information to challenge our intuition and misconceptions. Further, the gemba is the only place where "good ideas" demonstrate their usefulness. This devotion to the gemba saturates the Lean philosophy that was introduced in the Introduction and inspires many of the other tenets of practising Lean. One such tenet within the Lean management philosophy is acknowledging the line workers (or for innovation purposes, end users) as the process (or product) experts.

By characterizing experts in terms of time spent on the gemba, managers shift the focus away from management philosophies, good ideas, and solutions that work on paper and move toward demonstrable solutions to empirical problems. The process expert is not understood as the engineer with the most advanced degrees or the manager with the biggest office and a prestigious job title. This is foundational to the Lean approach of innovation. Lean Innovators must first understand the user before developing any product or service. It is only after the user is completely understood that innovators are ready to synthesize solutions.

In my own personal experiences, I have seen gemba pay huge dividends as it relates to problem-solving and identifying root causes of chronic issues. Once, when working on a project in a manufacturing facility, I was trying to identify the root cause of issues on an assembly machine. Every two or three cycles, the cycle time would increase by about 30%. My project team and I observed machine operators and noticed that several of the operators were deviating from the working standards.

However, it wasn't until we went onto the floor and talked to the operators that we learned that the reason operators were not adhering to the standard was because the machine would fault out every third cycle if they didn't trick the machine by changing their method and deviating from the work standard. The gemba walk identified this root cause and allowed us to find a process solution, rather than blaming the operator for not adhering to the standard. This experience exemplifies two important ideas about the gemba observations. First, the standards were written without a gemba walk. These standards are akin to any type of product or service in the marketplace. It was as if the standards were *designed* without actually seeing how they will be used. Second, *how* a gemba walk is performed matters. Different insights require different approaches to observation and data gathering. My team and I observed that the standards weren't being followed, but it wasn't until the machine operators were interviewed that the root cause was truly uncovered. I return to both of these ideas later on in this chapter.

What Are We Looking for in the Gemba?

There is a lot missing in the story of the Ohno Circle that concerns us, however. For instance, the story fails to mention why that particular location for the Ohno Circle was selected. Confident as we may be in the platitude "Waste is Everywhere," most readers will be hard-pressed to imagine a world-class company like Toyota being pell-mell in selecting where they spend their resources and managers' time. The question has already been asked and answered in the previous chapter. Hoshin Kanri sets strategic objectives for the organization and then deploy these objectives down through the organization into concrete, actionable goals. Thus, the output of the Hoshin Kanri stage of the Lean Innovation Cycle becomes the input for the gemba phase. Moreover, without the guiding light of the Hoshin Kanri, the subsequent activities in the Lean Innovation Cycle, including and especially the gemba stage, would have no assurance of alignment between organizational goals and innovation activities. The Hoshin Kanri does more than select the target audience for a new innovation: it instructs where innovators look for insights into what customers expect and value. The gemba is the place where end users reveal their experiences, motivations, and emotions and where innovators experience customer behavior firsthand.

From Simple Lean Gemba to Lean Innovation Gemba

When applying Lean to innovation, the themes of the gemba expand. The gemba is no longer just about observing the process, the actions of a machine operator, or the environment. Rather, the gemba becomes the entire experience of the end user. This end-user experience includes their emotions, frustrations, and delights as they interact with a product or service. Later on, in the analyze phase of the Lean Innovation Cycle, we'll see how different tools can help distill these experiences into meaningful insights, but for now, it's simply important to be mindful about how and why we are collecting the data.

Applying Lean to innovation and design requires new skills that process-improvement practitioners do not necessarily possess. One of the biggest and most frequently occurring gaps is a practitioner's ability or willingness to properly immerse themselves into the gemba. While Taiichi Ohno was monumental in getting problem-solvers and managers out onto the production floor, we see that many of those efforts never went further than distant observation. Prescriptively, the managers in the Ohno Circle were expressly forbidden to leave a 1 ft. radius, thereby limiting their immersion into the process and the experience of the machine operator.

Unfortunately, the Lean toolbox is not well endowed or adept with tools and approaches for a better immersive experience into gemba. Certainly, there are check sheets, standard work, and all sorts of waste-walk templates to direct, focus, and guide gemba activities, but in all of these, the focus stays surface level. Gemba waste walks often remain superficial and are driven primarily, if not entirely, by observation alone. If Lean is going to be the breakout star in the innovation space, it needs to adapt and meet the unique challenges that come with innovation, design, and the considerations for the end-user experience.

The good news is, we don't need to reinvent the wheel or create these tools from scratch. One of the strongest undercurrents of Lean has been the philosophical principle of *yokoten*. *Yokoten* means knowledge sharing. Whether we're sharing knowledge between facilities, work teams, or individuals, when we think of knowledge sharing, we think of some sort of best practice or *method* for doing something. And this remains true when benchmarking the Lean framework with other problem-solving frameworks, like Human-Centered Design. Human-Centered Design is a strong problem-solving framework that focused on developing and employing methods for better understanding end users and designing solutions for these end-users' needs.

One of the principal foundations of Human-Centered Design is its insistence on learning from the user. Only by listening to the problems expressed by the user can a designer create a high-leverage solution. If it doesn't sound familiar it should. One of the core principles of Human-Centered Design is the same gemba principle preached by Taiichi Ohno. As a side note, Human-Centered Design, sometimes called Design Thinking, has in recent years become as much of a movement as it is a framework; Design for Six Sigma (DFFS) classes often incorporate ideas and approaches that were developed in design incubators like the D-school at Stanford, IDEO, and MIT Design Lab [2].

The purpose here is not to give a full treatment of Human-Centered Design. Rather, it is to quickly introduce the framework, take the relevant methods, and apply it to our conversation on Lean. As mentioned before, the purpose of the Human-Centered Design framework is to provide designers a human-centered roadmap for creating a solution to a unique challenge faced by a specific and particular end user [3]. This approach presupposes what we take for granted in Lean; the end user is more familiar with the limitations and opportunities of a product or service far more than any designer or problem solver could ever be. As Figure 3.1 demonstrates, the framework has 3 phases – Inspiration, Ideation, and Implementation [4]. In the inspiration phase, designers seek to understand the end users and opportunities for improvement. During the ideation stage, the design team converges on a design idea and quickly learns about design feasibility from low-resolution prototyping. Finally, in the implementation phase, designers put their ideas into practice. As you can probably tell already, there are numerous parallels to Lean and Six Sigma. What's important now is simply to focus on the methods contained in the inspiration phase. Since this phase in the Human-Centered Design framework focuses on gaining insights from human interactions, it's important to dissect the methods contained therein.

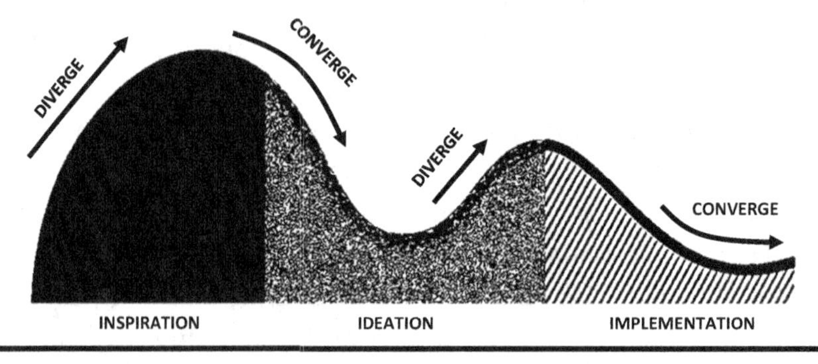

Figure 3.1 The Human-Centered Design framework.

Immersion Tools from Human-Centered Design

As noted, the benefit gained from incorporating the multidisciplinary concepts of Human-Centered Design into our Lean approach to innovation is that this approach provides a more thorough set of tools to understand the end user. Whereas Lean focuses on the observation of the gemba, Human-Centered Design insists on going further. Human-Centered Design calls this immersion. Its focus is to understand the experience and emotions of the end user, not to just observe it. In a word, the inspiration phase is about Empathy. Without empathy, the designer can only propose arbitrary solutions to the problem as he sees it. Dr. Prabhjot Singh, Director of Systems Design at the Earth Institute, summarizes the idea. He quips that he spends more time thinking about the design of the bridge and not enough time thinking about the needs and experience of the people who cross it [5]. In order to create better products and services, innovators and designers must think more about the user than the product. Without anchoring solutions to the people affected by the problem, it's very unlikely that the innovator will design a meaningful solution at all. The immersive tools outlined below are meant to generate empathy by creating immersive interactions with the end user and customer. By creating immersive experiences with the end user, the innovator can more readily understand the needs of the customer. The innovator can see and feel what the customer feels, including hopes, aspirations, fears, and self-identity. The deeper this understanding, the better the solution.

Who to Observe?

Observing a customer or end user of a product is a bit different than a simple gemba. In a traditional Lean manufacturing facility, the gemba is the factory floor. Generally speaking, more thought isn't given to *who* to talk to or *where* the gemba observations take place. This is not the case for Lean Innovation. Lean innovators must expand their paradigm to consider other aspects of the gemba. Returning for a moment to the Hoshin Kanri phase, recall that the customer is a specific demographic or subsection of a population that is being targeted for strategic reasons. This targeted approach did a good job of identifying demographic features about the user but the principles of Human-Centered Design require much more. Within the target group, there exist subcategories which each yield specific and refined

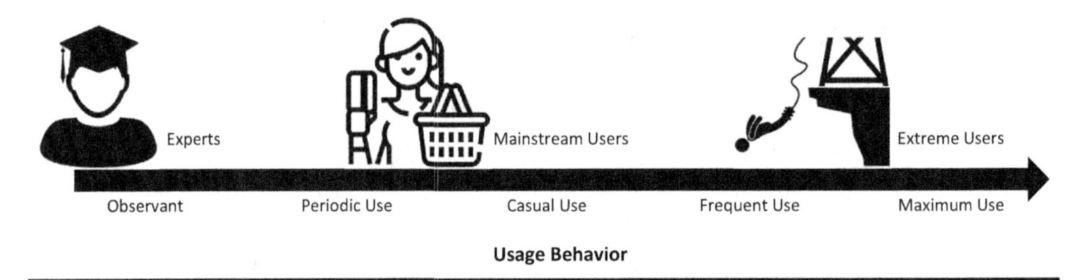

Figure 3.2 Product-use spectrum.

insights about how a product is used and experienced. The subcategories comprise a spectrum of end users each with their own unique insights. This "product-use spectrum" is summarized in Figure 3.2.

Experts

Experts are a good place to start. They provide a unique perspective that only they can provide. A perspective of an informed and knowledgeable outsider looking in. Usually when people think of experts, they think of scholars and academics. But the expert group is far more diverse than professors and researchers. An expert is anybody who has an intellectual expertise about a particular organization, operation, industry, or subject matter. Parents and grandparents can be experts about aspects of bringing up children. Religious clergy may possess expertise in volunteerism and community involvement. Community leaders, consultants, and educators can all contribute expertise in different settings. Likewise, particular occupations are not compartmentalized or pigeonholed as "only an expert." Who the experts are will depend on how the problem is scoped and characterized. As an example, a project aimed at improving the efficiency of a hospital may characterize nurses as an end user. Conversely, for a project aimed at improving patient experience during hospital visits, nurses can provide insights as healthcare experts. A university professor may be considered an expert in her field of research but is an end user for textbook publishers, online-learning management systems, and classroom designers.

The purpose of engaging with an expert is fairly straightforward. By talking to an expert, innovators can learn important information about a particular area of interest that they could not normally learn from an end user. A supply chain and logistics engineer will yield very different insights than a dock worker or truck driver. Experts may also have more historical knowledge about how the problem in question or current state has arisen or greater context about the environment, organization, occupation, or specific position. Generally, experts will not yield all or even most of the insights you desire. Because experts are not the end users, the questions they answer about end-user behavior and emotions are answered as an onlooker. The principal purpose of engaging with experts is to acquire additional context about the end-user group including their goals, challenges, and constraints.

Users

The second category of people to interact with are the users. Identifying a user is much more straightforward than identifying experts. Whereas an expert can be somebody who has intellectual knowledge about the product without actually having to use it, a user is somebody who personally interacts with the product. However, different insights can be obtained by understanding different classes within the user category. Therefore, users should be further categorized into one of two groups: mainstream users and extreme users.

Mainstream Users

Consider the age before the iPhone, when many people owned and used digital cameras. The mainstream user of the digital camera wasn't a professional photographer. Despite all the buttons and gadgets, and shutter speed, focus, and aperture settings, most digital camera owners only used the Zoom and flash settings. The mainstream users weren't using the full capabilities of the digital camera. Moreover, the behavior of the mainstream user was geared more toward sharing a photograph on social media than professional photographers who were preparing their photographs as works of art. Apple identified these mainstream behavior patterns, and to the chagrin of professional photographers, provided a watered-down digital camera built directly into the iPhone that enabled mainstream users to take and share photographs effortlessly. The iPhone camera did so well precisely because it was easy for the mainstream user to use.

Mainstream users, unlike extreme users, are the people you are designing a product or service for and were identified in the *Hoshin Kanri* phase of the Lean Innovation Cycle. They are the target audience whether that is defined by age, gender, lifestyle, or any other demographic that is relevant.

They are different from extreme users because they spend less time with the product and/or don't use all the capabilities of the product. The purpose of engaging with mainstream users is to understand how the product or service is likely to be used, including the environment, length of time, etc. The insights gained from these interactions will guide innovation efforts later on. The iPhone example is an extraordinary case of one of the eight wastes – extra processing. By understanding the behavior of mainstream users, iPhone developers removed many frivolous product features and focused more on the photo sharing. These decisions reduced the cost of the iPhone camera and heralded a new age of social media and dimly lit pictures of food.

Extreme Users

A much more common progression of innovation is that new features are added to an existing product in the market. With this type of progression, innovators cannot simply look at a product and decide what to remove, they must predict what customers will want in the future. For this challenge, innovators turn to extreme users.

Extreme users are users who spend an extended period of time with a product or service and have used all the product features and capabilities. Because these extreme users are using the product at its threshold, they provide insights about the direction innovation should take the product and what future demand will look like. These are insights the mainstream target audience simply does not possess. The extreme-user group is often very small in size and rarely the target audience of a product. Occasionally, manufacturers will create specialized, niche products targeted at the extreme-user group and any outgrowing communities. However, this is not the norm.

The extreme user and manufacturer partnership is an important one. The opportunity for manufacturers to learn from these extreme users is highly valuable and irreplaceable. This is why we see manufacturers like particularly high-performance sports brands, sponsor athletes, and teams. They're not just looking for brand recognition from the general public but rather want exclusive access to the insights of extreme users, which will generate new opportunities for existing product adaptations and new product lines.

The extreme users–manufacturer partnership isn't just limited to sports equipment either. Take for a moment a guitar equipment manufacturer that targets young males with modest disposable incomes to purchase their line of products. These mainstream consumers will likely transport the equipment often, either for playing shows or practice. These consumers might also be trying to emulate the sound of a guitar on their favorite rock album rather than trying to create their own distinctive sound of effect. These insights inform the guitar equipment manufacturer about the actual features of some of their products as well as design characteristics including the durability of the equipment as it is transported. Further, insights might inspire another product line of guitar equipment luggage and cases to ensure safe transport of the equipment. But none of these insights inform the guitar manufacturer about future features, proverbial bells and whistles that they should add to their products and if a new trend is emerging that requires additional product lines.

Conversely, consider the same guitar equipment manufacturer targeting their product toward a rock musician or music producer. This user group is vastly different than the mainstream consumer of guitars and their needs would reflect this. Extreme users are always looking for what is just beyond the horizon. For a rock star guitarist, it might be a new sound or a new effect or some particular aesthetic for a live performance. The extreme user of guitar equipment is not preoccupied with the transport of equipment so much as the uniqueness and novelty of the equipment. In particular, extreme users already have an idea of what they want next. This is their most illuminating attribute and is the reason innovators must engage with these extreme users. By understanding the needs of extreme users, innovators take the guesswork out of predicting the future direction of innovation.

With this extreme user in mind, it's not hard to look back and find many entrepreneurs started as extreme users themselves. Their presence shouldn't be surprising either. These extreme users-turned-entrepreneurs already had ample insights from their own experiences, frustrations, limitations, and challenges. Sticking with the guitar example, we see innovation as the product of end-user insights. Les Paul created one of the first electric guitars after identifying a desire for his acoustic to project louder and more sustained tone. For years, he had been trying to make a guitar that sustained the ring of his guitar strings without distortion or other changes, and found the options available to him in the market wanting [6].

Rock stars Brian May and Eddie Van Halen built their own guitars from scratch to produce a particular sound that they couldn't get from products in the marketplace [7, 8]. In these instances, these extreme users used their intimate knowledge of the product and environment to create novel products that immediately found a use in the marketplace. When engaging with extreme users, this is the intimate knowledge we hope to collect and leverage into actionable ideas to try and test.

The Adaptation Curve

Another way to think about the distinction between user groups is to consider the product adaptation curve. The curve, Figure 3.3, is probably familiar to you. It demonstrates a non-linear diffusion between ideas (or products) into the marketplace. First are the market innovators. It's important to specify that the "innovators" here refer to a particular consumer group. They are not innovators in the sense that they themselves are creating new products or are themselves entrepreneurs. They represent a very small fragment of the market. The size of this group is small and the ideas they take hold of are never guaranteed to gain market acceptance. These market innovators are the people who bought Plasma Screen TVs when they were $10,000 in the early 2000s. They may have also bought a laserdisc machine around the same time. To innovators, the technology itself is not as important as how they intertwine their self-identity with being a first to try or have something.

The next three sections are early adopters: the early majority and the late majority. Without belaboring the point, each group has its own identity and makes up a different proportion of the total market share. Finally, the laggards. These are consumers who are very late to market in accepting new technologies or products. If your grandparents just bought a DVD player

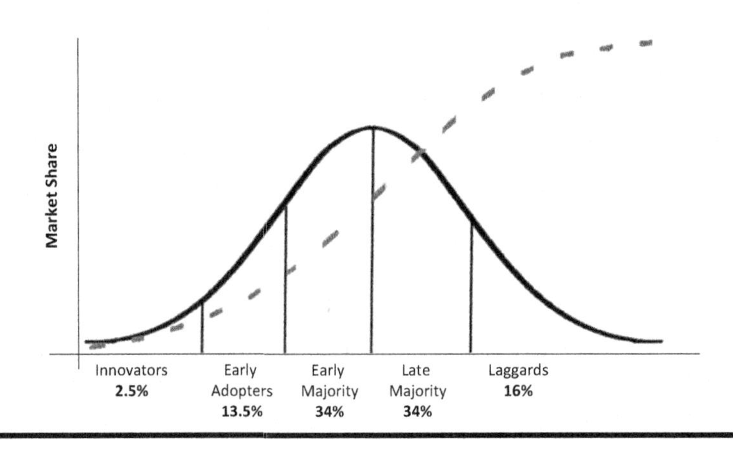

Figure 3.3 Market adaptation curve.

because they couldn't find a place that sells a VHS machine, you have successfully identified a market laggard.

The extreme users we engage with map quite nicely to the "market innovators" of the market adaptation curve. The mainstream users represent the majority of the curve in varying degrees. In a way, what the Lean Innovation Cycle aims to do is reverse engineer the product adaptation curve. This can be accomplished by understanding the needs and ideas of the extreme user group which will predict what ideas will take hold in the marketplace and expand these insights to the mainstream user – or the majority of the market that can benefit from the new ideas.

By thoughtfully considering who to observe, interact, and immerse ourselves with innovators and problem-solvers can identify particular and diverse opportunities for information and illumination on their journey toward meaningful innovation. The role experts play on this journey is important to understanding the context of the product or service and makes it possible to take a step back and see the particular design challenge from a higher level. The same is true for understanding the two categories of users. Mainstream users provide practical examples and information about how a particular product will be used. The extreme users, on the other hand, generate much more discussion about new ideas and potentialities. Both are important considerations in the world of innovation and product development. With a thorough understanding of who to interact with, we now turn our attention to answering how we ought to interact and fully immerse ourselves in their experiences.

Lean Innovation Gemba Methods

Interviews

One of the most straightforward and familiar ways to gain customer insights from experts, mainstream, and extreme users are interviews. Interviews have the added benefit of getting direct answers to specific questions, though conducting interviews also comes with its own risks and limitations. One such risk is that what people say and proclaim is often not what their behavior reflects. The immersion phase isn't about getting insights into what people want to believe or how they want to act, it's about finding out how people will actually behave. Another limitation of interviews is the lack of clarity that usually comes with respondents' answers. Journalists and interviewers walk a fine line between asking clarifying questions and derailing the conversation. If the interview respondent is consistently unclear in their responses there are only so many opportunities to clarify within the context of an interview. We'll see later how other immersive methods give us greater adaptability and opportunities for clarity.

As any journalist will tell you, interviewing is an art. It's not just about coming up with a list of questions you'd like to ask the interviewee. That's an interrogation. One objective every interviewer should have is to build rapport with their subject. By building rapport, interviewees become more relaxed and thoughtful in their responses, which in turn, produce deeper insights and move the conversation in a positive direction. There are a variety of methods for effective interviewing. Here are just a few novel ideas that align with the current discussion on immersion.

Interview on location. If possible, interview on location or in some place that adds to or facilitates discussion about the subject matter. If you're trying to gain insights about a coffee shop, conduct the interview at such a place. Further insights might be generated simply by changing the venue to a place that is directly in line with the experience you're interested in gaining insights about.

Use conversation starters. Conversation starters are scripted but natural questions that get the interviewee comfortable with talking to you about the subject. Conversation starters can serve to elicit insights from the interview respondent, but their primary purpose is to set up rapport for deeper insights later on in the discussion. Conducting an interview is more like chess than checkers. Conversation starters signal to the interviewer that it's safe to speculate and share their opinion. An example conversation starter question would be something like "What do you think about…" It's a surface-level question that leads the interviewee just enough to begin opening up. I also find that using negative questions and statements strongly engage people's critical thinking. Such questions would be something like "What would it mean to you if your favorite restaurant closed down?" This question elicits thoughts about why something is valuable in a different way. Rather than seeing opportunities for new ideas, it gets to the heart of why it's valuable in the first place and how consumer behavior would change with the privation of something they already value.

Find something you know is wrong, and ask them if it's correct. This is a great way to facilitate engagement from the interviewee and build rapport by making the interviewee feel like the expert. The method is simple. Ask a question you know is wrong. Perhaps, still at the coffee shop, you can ask if they're open 24 hours or if they have a drive-thru when it's clear that they aren't and they don't. Again, the purpose is not for this particular question to gain unique insight but to build rapport and make the subject of the interview more relaxed and confident in answering questions and internalize his or her role as the expert.

Gemba Observation

Interviews are great, but they should be used sparingly. While the insights we get from experts will likely be captured in their ideas expressed within the context of an interview, the benefits we get from extreme and mainstream users comes from studying their behavior. For this reason, we should not be content with just interviewing extreme and mainstream users but should strive to observe and understand their behaviors within the context of the product, environment, and experience.

To this end, one of the best practices for gaining customer insights is a good old-fashioned gemba. Go to the place where the end user is engaging with their product and begin to observe their behavior. Interject with questions about why they're doing things in a particular way or how they're making decisions, especially if they do anything unexpected or seemingly cumbersome or unnecessary. Record everything you see and hear exactly as you see and hear it. Also, jot down all your impressions about the environment or situation. All of this sounds more or less like a traditional gemba walk and in many ways it is. Perhaps the biggest add-on to human-centered immersion is the focus on the end-users' emotions. In the course of the gemba walk, make sure to capture their emotions. Be sure to record if they seem frustrated or pleased with an experience or result. These insights will be used later in the analyze phase to distill what is truly value added to the end user.

Peer-to-Peer Observation

There are limitations to simply observing the behavior of others all by your lonesome. Our knowledge is limited and we're bound to miss important details along the way. We don't know what we don't know. One of the best ways to mitigate this ignorance is to participate as the user themselves. If you have the opportunity to use the product or service, it's strongly recommended that you do, even for a short amount of time. We saw earlier the power these personal experiences have for extreme users-turned-entrepreneurs. But often, time constraints, training, safety concerns, and organized labor prevent us from fully participating in the experience of the end user. Nevertheless, we should still aim to gain more insight and expert observation for our efforts.

The peer-to-peer observation method allows us to do exactly this. Rather than superimposing ourselves into the experience of the end-user, we pull a user out of the process and allow them to watch the experience and behavior of another and comment on what they observe. This method allows for the user to dictate what they see and hear from the context of an insider. It's likely they'll see different things than the outside observer. The peer insider will also have added knowledge about *why* the user is doing something a certain way and the emotions that go along with the product experience. The peer-to-peer observation method creates an opportunity to obtain an insider's perspective of the end-user experience in real time and is an invaluable observational method to obtain meaningful customer insights.

Analogous Inspiration

This chapter started with an example of a police detective and how the methods employed by law enforcement ought to mirror those in innovation. People draw meaning and understanding from a variety of sources and forms. It's why storytelling, even in the 21st century (maybe especially in the 21st century) is still one of the most important skills to master. People make sense of the world through analogy. Too often, metaphor and analogy are thrown to the side in a crusade for unrelenting empiricism. But innovators ought to Lean into these allegorical tools.

The principle is straightforward. We shouldn't just limit the source of our insights to the experts, mainstream users, and extreme users but should actively search out inspiration wherever we can. This idea might give rise to qualms and make some feel uneasy. It may seem like we're abandoning our rigid framework of empirical observation and scientific problem-solving for a nebulous construction of liberal arts platitudes. Rest assured this is not the case and the principle of analogous inspiration is well founded outside of the design thinking framework.

One such example of using analogous inspiration in the context of innovation and problem-solving is a rigorous design problem-solving framework known as TRIZ. It is a Russian acronym for the Theory of Inventive Problem Solving. TRIZ was developed by Genrich Altshuller in 1946 after noticing patterns in the several thousands of patents he was studying [9]. While the particularities of TRIZ are fascinating, what concerns us is one of its main tenets. TRIZ posits that any particular problem has already been solved in some different context or application. TRIZ is a framework for decoupling a particular solution, to a more general solution, and then applying it to the relevant particular problem. And if further convincing is needed, it should be known that organizations, like Siemens, GM, P&G, BMW, Apple, and NASA, companies that heavily rely on innovative ideas and designs, all use this framework for innovative problem-solving – hardly the who's who of the liberal arts community.

Taiichi Ohno was a champion at finding inspiration from analogous sources. In his book *Workplace Management*, Taiichi Ohno tells the story of how the idea for *kanban* came about. *Kanban* is one of the fundamental tenets of the Lean methodology and ensures that downstream processes pull what is needed from upstream processes when they are needed. Taiichi Ohno explains that what inspired his idea for the *kanban* system was the US supermarket. The US supermarket is a place where consumers come to select the foods they want in the exact amount they need. No more. No less. This was a revolutionary idea in mid-20th century Japan where food was still delivered door to door and consumers had to forecast when the delivery man would come back again and if he would be carrying everything they wanted when he returned. The US supermarket system flipped this paradigm and created a system where the products are pulled from the supplier based on the exact needs of the customers. This inspired Taiichi Ohno and Toyota to do the same thing in their manufacturing facilities [10].

Taiichi Ohno also drew inspiration from one of his favorite desserts, a *Monaka* – something like a sweet bean pastry. Taiichi Ohno observed that pastry chefs would create the crust of the pastry ahead of time and only fill the pastries right before they were demanded by customers. This inspired what Ohno called the *Monaka* system for reducing the cost of die making by preparing the dies ahead of time and only cutting the final details once they were demanded [11].

The tradition of analogous inspiration extends well beyond the 20th century. Seemingly all of the geniuses of history were highly engaged in disciplines other than Science Technology Engineering and Math. The philosophers of ancient Greece, Leonardo Da Vinci, Isaac Newton and Ben Franklin, were in varying degrees all geniuses of technology, mathematics, and science. Yet these geniuses were not just harbingers of scientific advancement but were also champions of art, literature, and politics. They were effective at all of their endeavors because of the analogous inspiration they could draw from their many diverse backgrounds. This fundamental principle is echoed in the US university system today – unity through diversity.

The idea that art and science complement each other is something that has grown foreign in the 21st century. The point here is not to advocate for reading more Shakespeare in school but to acknowledge the benefit of seeking inspiration from everything – not just the empirical and evidential. The framework of the Lean Innovation Cycle does not shirk away from analogous inspiration, but rather, in the spirit of *yokoten*, capitalizes on the reality that analogous inspiration is and ought to be one more tool in the innovator's toolbox. Though innovation can emerge from genius or inspired brilliance, it occurs much more frequently in the context of small continuous improvements and new applications to old ideas – "Enlightened trial and error succeeds over the planning of the lone genius" [12].

The Usual Suspects: Focus Groups and Surveys

It may come as a surprise that two of the most popular means for procuring customer insights – focus groups and customer surveys – aren't part of the Lean Innovation Cycle's preferred methods for gaining customer insights. Rather, these two common methods for obtaining customer information go against much of what we've discussed in this chapter. Both focus groups and surveys rely neither on observing nor on immersing with the customer, product, or environment. Both focus groups and surveys rely on obtaining information based on what somebody *says* rather than what they *do*. It's akin to the familiar crime scene detective asking a responding officer for any ideas about the case rather than experiencing the crime scene for himself. It's cheaper, it's easier, it's less time-consuming, and it still comes from the customer, right? That should be enough for the C-suite upstairs.

But unfortunately, the cheaper, easier, less time-consuming route comes with a litany of trade-offs. To add insult to injury, just about all of these negative trade-offs are well known and documented, yet the siren song of easy customer insight entices marketing teams and innovators into its allure while ignoring the cold hard facts – these activities are fraught with errors.

There's really only one issue with focus groups and surveys – they're inaccurate. Surveys have a propensity to bias responses. Even if the questions are well constructed and don't lead a respondent to an answer, it's very unlikely that the results will represent the true sentiments of the respondent. In an effort to make the survey go smoother, respondents will try to be more agreeable than they actually may be (acquiescence bias). In an unconscious effort to save mental energy, respondents will answer questions in similar ways to previous questions (habituation bias). Most famously respondents seek to gain the approval of the surveyor by answering questions in the way they believe the survey responder would want or approve of (social desirability bias). Even outside the world of surveys and data collection, people regularly say things they don't actually mean and rarely practise. The phrase, do as I say not as I do, underscores this point in general, and is made even more acute when a respondent knows their response is being scrutinized, like say, when taking a survey.

Focus groups, to varying degrees, encounter many of the same obstacles and hurdles as survey methods. Focus groups have an added dynamic of a group setting which is intended to facilitate dialog about a particular idea within a group of people and capture what emerges from the discussion. However, groupthink can emerge as its own troubling phenomenon from these well-intentioned dialogs. Groupthink is similar to the habitual and acquiescence biases noted above. In an effort to reduce group tensions or save mental energy, the group will converge on an idea already presented rather than fully explore their own ideas and divergent possibilities. In short, because of groupthink, focus groups can produce the opposite of their intended effect. We have more to say about groupthink and ways to combat groupthink later on in Chapter 5.

The observational and immersive techniques outlined above should be preferred to the more common customer-feedback practices of surveys and focus groups. These Lean Innovation Gemba Methods are specifically designed to eliminate and mitigate these biases and phenomena. Particularly, the immersive techniques change the source of information from verbal testimony to empirical demonstration and allow for new insights to emerge and be followed.

Bringing It Back to the Lean Innovation Cycle

In all the chaos of discussing different observation and immersion methods, it's possible to lose sight of what should be the focus. Innovation is about delivering value to the end user by creating a new and novel experience. This phase, the gemba, is just one part of a greater framework for manifesting innovation. Even though the Lean Innovation Cycle started with the Hoshin Kanri phase of vision casting and policy deployment, it's this current phase, the gemba, which lays the foundation for all the subsequent phases. If it hasn't been said already, the reason this gemba phase is so vitally important is because the Lean Innovation Cycle is a framework based on empiricism. The traditional Lean framework relies on concrete observations, solutions, and results. Similarly, Human-Centered Design centers itself on letting the end user dictate what the end user wants. These two paradigms cannot be overstated. Without a thorough, diligent effort in the gemba, our efforts are reduced to nothing more than fancy tools based on hunches and misconceptions. The efforts will falter, and our organizations will be the worse for it.

As a word of caution, never rush the gemba stage of the Lean Innovation Cycle. In the world of Six Sigma, practitioners are introduced to the 80–20 rule; 80% of the problems will manifest in 20% of the data. In a similar way, I would urge you to make a goal to spend 80% of your time on the first two phases of the Lean Innovation Cycle. Anybody who has ever worked on a continuous improvement project – whether Lean or Six Sigma or something else – has felt that the projects are slow at first and then really start to take off. This is no coincidence. Continuous improvement is about clearly defining a problem and observing it in its current state before any "solutions" are generated. This tried-and-true approach allows for unbiased and empirical assessment of what is actually occurring in the problem area. The diligent fact finding in these projects' early stages eventually snowball into huge insights and high-leverage solutions.

The next phases of the cycle will introduce new tools and techniques for creating and testing innovative ideas. In these subsequent phases, there are no real-time constraints, and as you'll see, it may even be better to limit the amount of time spent in some of these phases. But what all these phases rely on is well-documented, well-researched, and mindfully-observed insights from the gemba.

Like everything else in this book, the tools are just another process. They're designed to take in inputs and produce outputs. Without a firm foundation from the gemba, these tools and processes will not produce the desired outputs for the simple reason that they never were given the necessary inputs. You won't get a good cup of coffee from a cheap coffee bean – regardless of how sophisticated the machine is. Be diligent, ensure that the gemba informs the rest of the activities in the Lean Innovation Cycle.

References

[1] "Ohno Circle". LeanSixSigmaDefinition.com website. https://www.leansixsigmadefinition.com/glossary/ohno-circle/
[2] IDEO. (2009). "Six Sigma and Design Thinking". *IDEO Design-Thinking Blog*. https://designthinking.ideo.com/blog/six-sigma-and-design-thinking
[3] IDEO. (2021). "About Ideo". IDEO. https://www.ideo.com/about
[4] IDEO. (2015). The Field Guide to Human-Centered Design. IDEO.
[5] Bonime, Western. (2020). "Human Centered Design Is Revolutionizing How We Respond To Emergencies Like COVID". *Forbes Magazine*. https://www.forbes.com/sites/westernbonime/2020/10/25/human-centered-design-is-revolutionizing-how-we-respond-to-emergencies/?sh=497d9b8f4c74
[6] Bacon, Tony. (2019). "An oral history of the Gibson Les Paul". *Guitar Magazine*. https://guitar.com/guides/essential-guide/the-oral-history-of-the-les-paul/
[7] Waksman, Steve. (2020). "The Astonishing Techniques That Made Eddie Van Halen A Guitar God". *National Public Radio*. https://www.npr.org/2020/10/10/922252577/the-astonishing-techniques-that-made-eddie-van-halen-a-guitar-god
[8] May, Brian. (2007). "The Red Special Story". *Brian May Guitars*. https://web.archive.org/web/20100209020916/http://brianmayguitars.co.uk/red-special-story
[9] Altshuller Institute. (2013). "What is TRIZ?". Altshuller Institute. https://www.aitriz.org/triz
[10] Ohno, Taiichi. (2013). *Workplace Management*. McGraw-Hill. pp. 67–69.
[11] Ohno, Taiichi. (2013). *Workplace Management*. McGraw-Hill. pp. 133–136.
[12] ABC Nightline (1999). "Reimagining the Shopping Cart". American Broadcast Channel. https://www.ideo.com/post/reimagining-the-shopping-cart.

Chapter 4

Customer-Driven Analysis

During the holiday season of 2005, Microsoft's Xbox released their new Xbox 360 console. For an entire year, the new video game system enjoyed an uncontested market. If a gamer wanted the newest games with the best graphics, the only option was the Xbox 360. Where was Sony and their new PlayStation console? Was Sony delayed because they were perfecting new graphics technologies that would delight their customers and leave Microsoft in the dust? No. Sony ran into manufacturing issues when a five-cent component needed to play Blu-ray disks became impossible to source [1]. Sony was so convinced that buyers of the new PlayStation 3 (PS3) console wanted, demanded, and expected integrated Blu-ray technology that they were willing to give Microsoft a 12-month head start to make sure their console delivered.

Meanwhile, as Sony was figuring out their production issues and planning a delayed release in November 2006, the Xbox 360, sans Blu-ray technology, was dominating an uncontested market. The head start was too much for the PS3. Sony was never able to recover the ground lost from the Blu-ray blunder. To date, the 3rd generation of PlayStation is the worst-selling video game console Sony ever produced [2]. The 3rd generation also saw the only time Microsoft's Xbox bested its main competitor [3].

If gamers really wanted the Blu-ray technology, why didn't they wait to buy the superior PS3? And once the PS3 entered the market, why wasn't it able to make up ground against the Xbox 360? The answer is simple enough: gamers really didn't care. They cared about the games, the

DOI: 10.4324/9781003206347-5

graphics, the online social experiences, the quicker loading screens. Blu-ray wasn't even on their radar. Sony's blunder wasn't that it ran into production issues. The blunder of the PS3 is that Sony gave away an entire generation of video game consoles for something their customers didn't care about!

The gemba is supposed to be our guiding force to avoid these types of blunders. Through interactions with the customer and firsthand experiences, innovation teams learn about the end-users' likes and dislikes, and empathize with their overall experience. But more reflection is still needed. The analyze phase allows us to prudently assess the lessons learned in our customer interactions and transform the gemba into the triumph and guiding light of our innovation efforts.

Consider for a moment a classic work of fiction. Classics can't be fully appreciated without a thoughtful reflection. Without careful consideration, Herman Melville's *Moby Dick* becomes a 1200-page tome about a whale with a genetic anomaly. And [spoiler] if you haven't figured it out by now, Edgar Allan Poe's "The Raven" isn't *really* about a raven. It's only upon dissecting the personification of Ahab's whale, the biblical allusions to Jonah, the social critiques and symbolism that it comes to light as a triumph of the written word. In the same way, gemba activities without deliberate, thoughtful contemplation are nearly a wasted effort.

The analyze phase creates a framework to thoughtfully reflect on the gemba. The goal of the phase is to obtain a focused understanding of the customer and identify all the parameters needed to develop a well-defined design problem. Specifically, three tools will be used to uncover three different insights. The Value Stream Customer Journey (VSCJ) Analysis will help identify non-value-added activities throughout the entire customer experience. The Kano Analysis will pinpoint new features that add novelty and augment the customer's satisfaction with a product. And finally, Quality Function Deployment (QFD) will illuminate what boundaries limit our ability to deliver customer value, the innovation frontier that ought to be challenged. It might get lost in the weeds of the analysis, but what's important to remember, is that through all of this, the ideas that were first espoused in the gemba is what is the driving force moving the analysis forward. To strain a metaphor, the analyze phase is a refinement process. The gemba is the crude oil. The purpose of the refiner is to distill all those interactions with the customer into a concise, meaningful insight called the Voice of the Customer. In time, the refined fuel will power the machine of innovation, in the ideation phase of the Lean Innovation Cycle.

The Customer Journey and Value Stream Mapping

One of the more thoughtful and holistic approaches to begin analyzing the gemba is by thinking about the whole customer experience, the whole "process" of using and interacting with a product. No product operates in a vacuum. In order to operate a product, an end user must undergo a series of steps before and after they actually interact with the product. The VSCJ Analysis brings together two analysis tools to holistically evaluate the user experience. First, the Value Stream Map (VSM). Widely used in Lean, the VSM helps Lean thinkers see waste. For the purposes of the VSCJ, the most important aspects of VSMs are the process steps, sequence, process times, and wait times. Also, and just like the VSM, the identification of waste will be a key feature of these analysis efforts. The second half of the VSCJ may be less familiar to Lean thinkers. Coming from a point of empathy, the Customer Journey Analysis uses the steps identified in the VSM and describes them in light of the customer experience [4].

Both are important for uncovering the end-user experience. One of the most powerful aspects of Lean is its ability to work congruently with different frameworks and tools. In so doing, it almost always augments both efforts. The purpose of the VSM is to identify and remove waste, but with the Customer Journey, we're now mindful of how the customer feels about that step in the process. With the VSCJ, innovators can remove *muda* from the process without damaging the customer experience. It may be to the customer's detriment to speed up the process, by eliminating a process step the end user finds most enjoyable.

Cleaning Up with the VSCJ

As an example, take the value stream/customer journey map in Figure 4.1. The diagram shows a stripped-down VSM for a familiar household activity, cleaning a hardwood floor. The VSM outlines eight steps in the process, indicates the time to accomplish each task, and signifies that there is no waiting time between each task. From start to finish, it takes nearly 40 minutes to clean the floor.

In addition to the VSM, the diagram also contains a customer journey map. Here it simply describes how the customer feels during each step in the process. In this case, and yes, I used myself as the test subject, none of

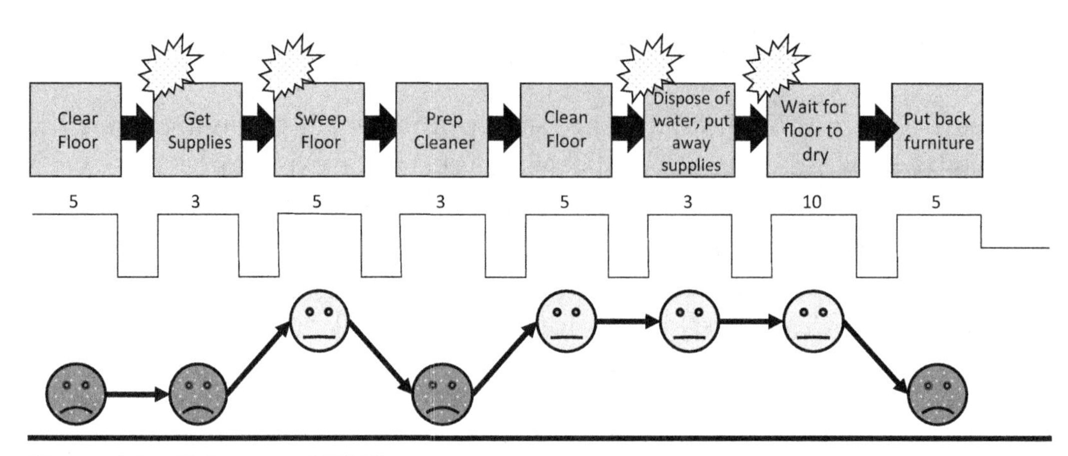

Figure 4.1 Unimproved VSCJ map.

the steps delivered any satisfaction. Sometimes life is like that. In half the steps, the end user was dissatisfied.

When cleaning my kitchen floor, I hated moving all the tables and chairs out of the way. As a Lean thinker, I was even more frustrated knowing that at the end of the process I would have to put them back again. I also hated getting the supplies. In my house, the liquid floor cleaner, bucket, and mop are kept downstairs. There is a lot of non-value-added travel up and down the stairs. After sweeping the floor, I had to prep the cleaning solution, which involved going into the bathroom, measuring out the floor cleaner, turning on the bathtub water, waiting for the water to heat up, filling up the bucket, turning off the water, and then, finally carrying the heavy bucket of water from the bathroom to the kitchen. I cleaned the floor, disposed of the water, put everything away, and then had to wait. Finally, once the floor was dry, I was able to put back my heavy, cumbersome furniture.

In addition to allowing me to vent about the frustrations of domestic cleaning, the VSM coupled with the customer journey diagram creates a qualitative and visual way to think about customer value. By specifying each step in the process and then describing the customer attitude at each of these steps, the VSCJ begets insights into which parts of the process is ripe for improvement and innovation. Calling to mind everything you saw and heard in the gemba will help make sense of these attitudes and the reasoning behind these attitudes. In this case, I really didn't mind filling the bucket with water or waiting for the water to heat up in the bathtub. What I hated was carrying the bucket from the bathtub back to the kitchen.

The VSCJ allows innovators to think about the whole customer experience, not just the product itself. The VSCJ begins to distill the data compiled from the gemba into a more concise and actionable Voice of the Customer. With the VSCJ in hand, innovators give themselves two levers to pull. The first is the traditional Lean route, which reduces the non-value-added activities in each of these steps. The added benefit of the customer journey is a greater context about what really is "value added." The second lever is to improve the customer experience within a particular step. By using the experiences and empathy gained from the gemba, Lean innovators can anticipate what drives the emotions and attitudes in each of the process steps. By changing the root causes of these attitudes, innovators can begin to improve the entire customer experience. This is all I'll say about this here but will return to this point in the chapter on ideation.

One of the best cases that demonstrates the VSCJ in action comes from Procter and Gamble. In 1994, P&G deployed a Hoshin Kanri strategy targeted at housewives in the home-cleaning products sector. In a specific project, an innovation team was interested in improving the floor cleaning experience. Probably because P&G is chiefly a chemical company, the initial focus of the innovation team was set on increasing the consumption of liquid cleaning detergent. However, after seeing the arduous process described above, they developed a new product, the Swiffer [5]. The new product eliminated a lot of the waste of movement and waiting. It combined the process of sweeping and washing the floor into one activity, and because the pads were not as soaked as a wet mop, it reduced the time waiting for the floor to dry. With Swiffer in hand, the process for cleaning the floor looks a bit different.

When Figures 4.1 and 4.2 are compared, it's easy to see that not everything in the process was changed. But what's noteworthy is that the

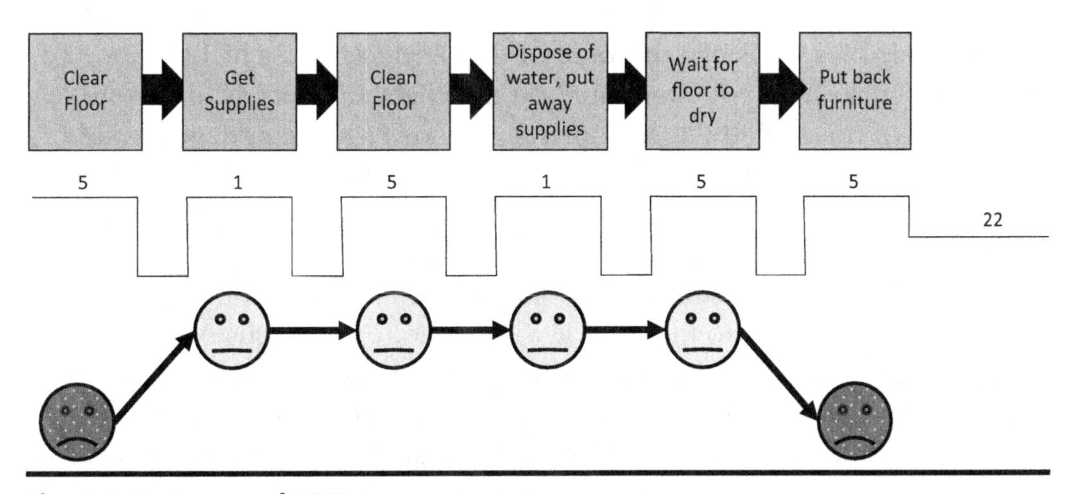

Figure 4.2 Improved VSCJ map.

innovation of the Swiffer grew out of the Lean elimination of waste and from sensitivity to the customer experience. In addition, the greatest improvements to the user experience didn't come from using the product itself. Rather, the improvements came from removing process steps that didn't interact with the product, like preparing the detergent solution and sweeping the floors, and expanding the scope of what the product does. The Swiffer sweeps *and* cleans. It is also self-contained. The end user doesn't have to get a bucket or wait for the water to get hot, add the cleaner, and dump the dirty water out.

Kano Analysis

The VSCJ is the best tool for the job in understanding the entirety of the customer experience. But often, innovators must understand the needs and values of the customers at a deeper level. To this end, we employ the Kano Analysis. Developed by Noriaki Kano in 1984, the Kano Model provides a way of understanding how different attributes of a product can satisfy the wants and needs of customers in very different ways, i.e. deliver value [6]. The Kano Model establishes a relationship between product performance and customer satisfaction. The first step to understanding the Kano Model is to visualize the relationship between product performance and customer satisfaction. For this, we employ the Kano Diagram. Constructing the diagram is a bit technical, so it's best to deconstruct it piece by piece.

The Kano Diagram is made up of two axes and creates a landscape where we see a relationship between customer satisfaction and product performance. The Y-axis measures customer satisfaction. The more satisfied a customer is by a particular attribute of the product, e.g. vehicle safety, the higher her satisfaction will be plotted on the chart. Conversely, the more dissatisfied or unsatisfied the customer is, the lower her satisfaction will be plotted. Different attributes of a product will deliver different levels of satisfaction to the customer. The X-axis is similar. It measures performance and allows us to visualize how well the vehicle performs across different product attributes. The better the product performs in an attribute, safety as an example, the further to the right it will be plotted. Like customer satisfaction, a single product will have many attributes, each with its own level of performance. By combining the satisfaction information (Y-axis) with the performance information (X-axis) for any product attribute we can visualize how satisfaction and performance relate to one another.

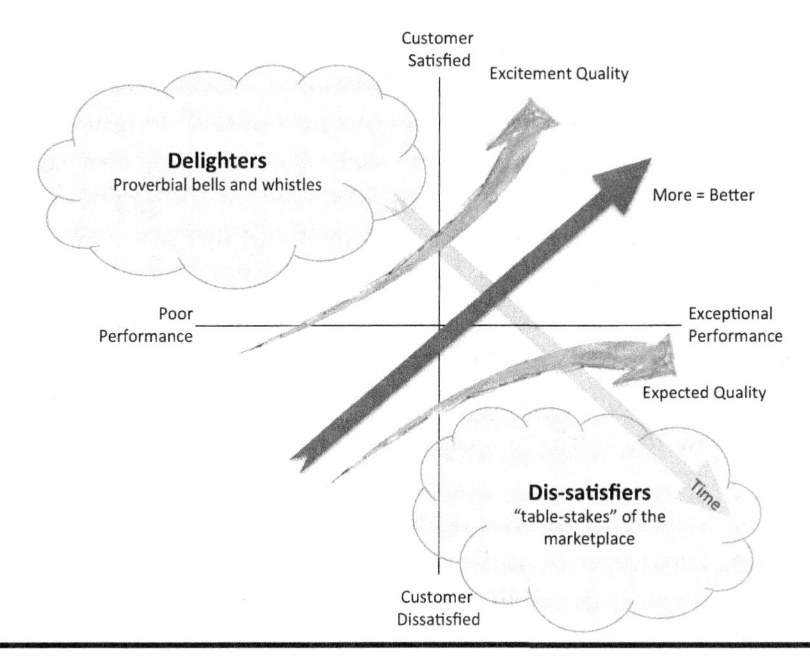

Figure 4.3 The Kano Diagram.

Finally, when this mapping exercise is applied across all of the product attributes product, patterns and trends begin to appear. The Kano Model generalizes these trends into three distinct areas which are depicted in Figure 4.3.

First, we have dissatisfiers. Think of dissatisfiers as table stakes or must-haves. These are characteristics that every customer expects. If a product does not possess these attributes, there's no market for the product. You won't find a new vehicle without A/C, power steering, windshield wipers, aligned axles, and an engine that starts every time you turn the key. Additionally, even when these things perform exceptionally well, we're likely not to notice or care. Car commercials won't mention with what careful precision they've engineered the car alarm or how crystal clear the windshield is. We may be much more dissatisfied if they *don't work* but since they are merely expectations, there is a ceiling to the satisfaction we as customers can derive from their performance.

Second, we have performance characteristics. The better the product delivers on these attributes the more satisfied a customer is. Products that advertise "more," "better," "cheaper," "faster," "stronger," "easier" all operate in this dimension. When these performance characteristics are plotted on the Kano Diagram, they form a positive linear relationship between the two axes. Performance begets satisfaction.

Finally, we have delighters. Delighters are your idiomatic bells and whistles. They provide a high level of customer satisfaction just by being a part of the product. James Bond gets all the coolest delighters: tire slashing hubcaps, poison darts, lasers, rockets, and an ejector seat. But for those of us without a license to kill, we're often delighted by a car that parks itself and looks forward to being delighted by autonomous vehicles in the future. Even if the autonomous features perform poorly (takes too long to park, breaks too hard, or jerks the car around without smooth acceleration) there is still a high level of customer delight and satisfaction just from the feature's inclusion in the product. Figure 4.4 demonstrates how the attributes of a new vehicle maps to the Kano Diagram.

The final dimension of the Kano Model is time. Time has a nasty little habit of making what is cool and exciting today the artifact of tomorrow. As time progresses, it pulls the delights and performance characteristics down into the "must-haves" of the market. For vehicles, fuel-economy expectations are vastly different than they were 30 years ago. Once the delights of top-end luxury vehicles, power windows, Bluetooth connectivity, and cruise control, now come standard in even the lowest-tier stock model of every automobile manufacturer.

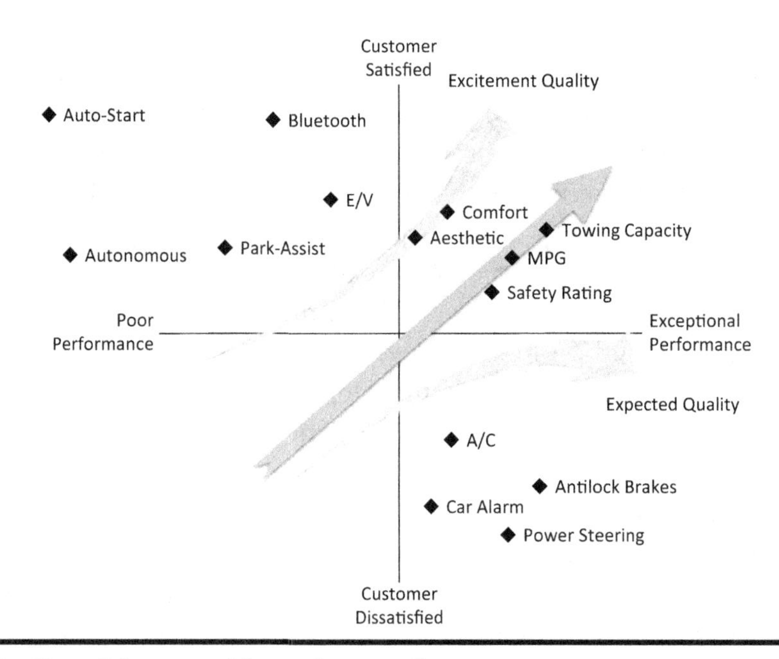

Figure 4.4 Kano Diagram with product attributes.

Kano's Key Points

From the Kano Model, we can take away a few key points that interest us as innovators. First, continuous improvement has its place in delivering customer value. That positive linear relationship we called "performance characteristics" is ripe for continuous improvement. Customers like faster, cheaper, easier, better products, and services. Continuous improvement delivers on these customer expectations. Organizations can deliver value simply by improving performance. Lean is already known as an excellent tool for performance improvement. Second, the "delights" are where the new and novel get created. No customer is expecting the inclusion of these novelties. Simply by being incorporated into the product they deliver a high level of customer satisfaction. These delighters are what evoke the emotions of novelty, newness, and innovation. Finally, where does the radically disruptive, sometimes destructive force of traditional innovation fit in? It doesn't. The products of tomorrow have their own Kano grid with their own must-haves, performance characteristics, and delights. Lean Innovation is focused on delivering delights to customers without disrupting an enterprise's ability to create and deliver customer value. Just one more reason why Lean is the perfect complement to traditional innovation efforts.

Kano in Action

The Kano Model might be all well and good for Dr. Kano, but how can innovators actually use it in the field to decipher customer expectations? How do innovators identify the product attributes customers want, let alone map them to an abstract diagram? To answer these questions, we have to return once again to the gemba.

Imagine an innovation team charged with designing a new home carpet cleaner for a major vacuum manufacturer. The team would start with the ethnography activities described in Chapter 3 and summarize the feedback from the customer into different customer requirements. In this example, things like cleaning of confined spaces, maneuverability, and weight are important requirements.

After the gemba, the innovation team begins the process of what I'll call the "Kano-method" for classifying customer requirements. Based on the customer requirements identified above, the team creates a survey crafted in a very particular way. The survey is formulated into a matched pair of survey questions. For a given requirement (e.g. cleaning confined spaces) a customer gets asked two questions about the carpet cleaner, one that framed it in terms of good performance: "The carpet cleaner is able to clean tight spaces." and another that framed it in terms of bad performance: "It is difficult for the carpet cleaner to clean corners and small closets." The survey respondent is asked to categorize how they feel about the statement (Like, Expect, Don't Care, Tolerate, Dislike). Similar to double-entry book-keeping for an accountant, the purpose of this is to verify the survey responses. The matched pairs make sure the customer really feels a certain way about a product's attributes.

In a sense, this is the final step of the gemba. The innovation team is still actively seeking insights about the customer experience directly from the customer. After this is completed, the team can move further into the Kano Analysis. Taking the survey responses, the innovation team maps the response pairs to a logical matrix, illustrated in Figure 4.5 where:

Q: Questionable – The response pairs were incongruent with one another.
P: Performance characteristics – The customer identifies this as a performance characteristic.
I: Indifferent – The customer is indifferent to this attribute.
M: Must-Have – The customer expects this as part of the product.
R: Reversal – The functionality of the product is the exact opposite of what was expected. (To the customer dysfunction = function).
A: Attractive – These attributes delight the customer.

I won't belabor you with describing the logic of each of the ratings in the matrix, it's not all that hard to think through. The matched pairs don't have to match exactly. If a respondent "Likes" a functional statement and "expects" a dysfunctional statement, this registers as "attractive." In other words, this would delight a customer. The innovation team tallies each respondent's rating for each product attribute and then assigns it a

		Dysfunctional				
		Like	Expect It	Don't Care	Live With	Dislike
Functional	Like	Q	A	A	A	P
	Expect It	R	I	I	I	M
	Don't Care	R	I	I	I	M
	Live With	R	I	I	I	M
	Dislike	R	R	R	R	Q

Figure 4.5 Kano logic table.

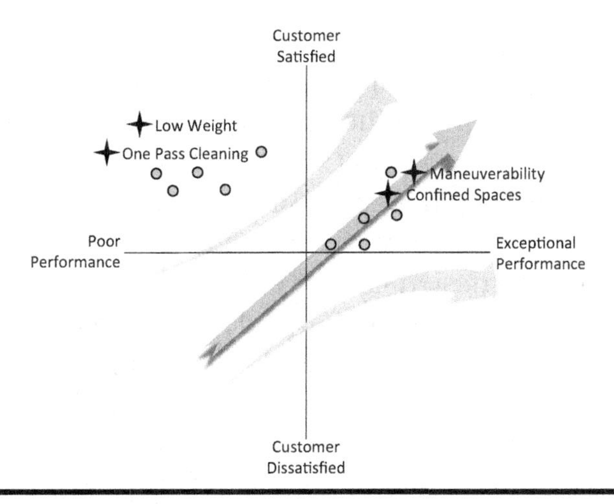

Figure 4.6 Survey-diagram matching of carpet cleaner.

dominant rating for the rating based on the tally count. Just like the Kano Diagram, the three ratings of interest are "Attractive," "Must-haves," and "Performance." For visual purposes these dominant ratings can be mapped to the Kano Diagram like in Figure 4.6.

For the innovation team, the final step of the Kano Analysis is simply to prioritize the different attributes for each rating. Oftentimes this is done by asking respondents to rank the importance level for each question in the matched-pair survey. This ensures that the innovation team considers the most important delights and performance attributes before the less important.

Quality Function Deployment

The final tool in the analyze phase toolbox is Quality Function Deployment (QFD). The purpose of QFD is twofold. First, like the Kano Model, it can be used to better understand what design characteristics will lead to greater customer satisfaction. Second, and in my estimation more profoundly, it can be used in challenging the status quo. QFD can illuminate the boundaries of our current paradigms and orient us to challenge these boundaries directly with incredible focus.

QFD has been a staple of Lean product development since its formulation in 1961. Also called matrix product planning and customer-driven engineering, the aim of QFD is congruent with all our efforts thus far – letting the customer pull the value through the innovation process. What's more, this analysis tool greatly speeds up the innovation process in a myriad of ways. First, it speeds up innovation by removing what doesn't matter to the customer. Just like the Kano Analysis, QFD is interested in what the customer says is important. The QFD structure eliminates the time spent on designing and engineering non-value-added components and features customers are indifferent toward. One corollary benefit to this is reduced complexity and design changes. Researchers have noted that Japanese firms that use QFD made fewer design changes than their American competitors, further reducing design and production startup costs [7]. Likewise, with a more streamlined design and less changes, QFD leads to a shorter time to market and a strategic first-mover advantage. Finally, QFD adds value for the enterprise itself. The structure of QFD creates a clear, standardized, and concise legacy of documentation. Businesses can use this documentation as a starting point for future iterations of the same product. The teams in charge of new innovations start on the shoulders of those that have come before, taking the lessons learned of the past and applying them from the future without having to do redundant and tiresome work.

The House of Quality

Like the Kano Model, QFD has its own play space, its own diagram where innovators map out their ideas and see the interactions between the Voice of the Customer and the product design. This space, illustrated in Figure 4.7, is called the House of Quality and it would be rude to keep you on the outside and not give you a tour.

Starting with the left, we have the customer requirements. This is the Voice of the Customer. The important characteristics that came through the gemba and the Kano Analysis should go here. For our carpet cleaning example, these would be descriptions like "easy to maneuver" and "cleans confined spaces." Like the front door of a house, the Voice of the Customer is always entryway and threshold into the House of Quality. Always start with identifying what the customer values.

Directly to the right of these descriptions is the relative importance of each customer requirement, this is a way to simply appreciate that not all of these features share the same level of importance. This information will be used later on when we make decisions related to what parts of the design we actually try to come up with new approaches for.

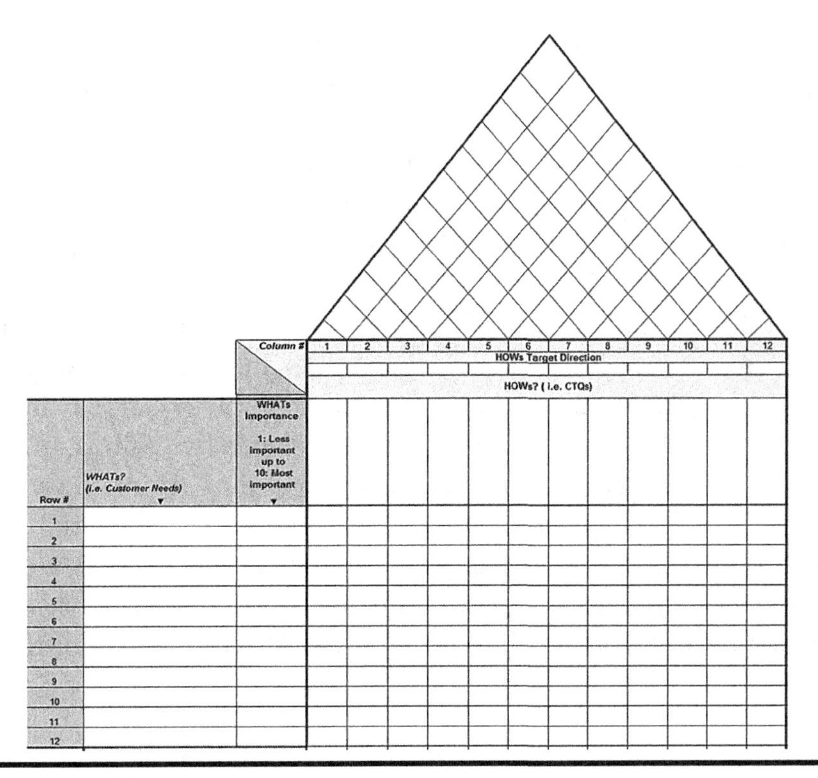

Figure 4.7 The House of Quality.

Skipping for a moment the main living space of the house, we'll move to the second storey. These are where the design and performance features are described. The carpet cleaner would have things like "weight," "sound," and maybe even "extra hose attachments." The point of this section of the House of Quality is to identify what performance characteristics and design components exist for the current product design. These should be added, independent of what relation they have to customer requirements.

Now back to the main floor. This is where the connections between the customer requirements and the design characteristics are made. The purpose of this room is to assess holistically how well a customer requirement maps to certain performance characteristics. As an example, the maneuverability requirement would strongly correlate to the "weight" design characteristic but have little correlation to how loud the cleaner was, "sound," or whether or not it has a modern aesthetic. This part of the house will look very familiar to anybody who has ever used a cause-and-effect matrix for process improvement.

Finally, the roof. This is the most interesting and insightful part of the House of Quality. Similar to the main floor we just toured, the purpose of the roof is to correlate different design aspects using the information acquired in the main floor assessment. However, whereas the main floor correlated the design aspects with the customer requirements, the roof seeks to identify correlations *between* the design components themselves. We might see that weight and durability are highly and positively correlated, but weight and maneuverability are negatively correlated, e.g. the heavier an object is, the harder it is to maneuver. What QFD users will see is that a number of trade-offs exist between what the customer requires and what the current product design can deliver. As an example, take a consumer tire for a vehicle. As shown in the fully-completed, albeit simplified, House of Quality in Figure 4.8, the customer desires five things: quiet ride, good gas mileage, longevity, cost, and safety/handling. Upon closer examination, desires of the customer, when plotted in the house matrix, shows the conflict between design and customer wants. A tire that has a quiet ride will use softer rubber and wear away quicker. A tire that lasts for 80,000 miles will sound like you're driving on the Flintstones' first set of tires.

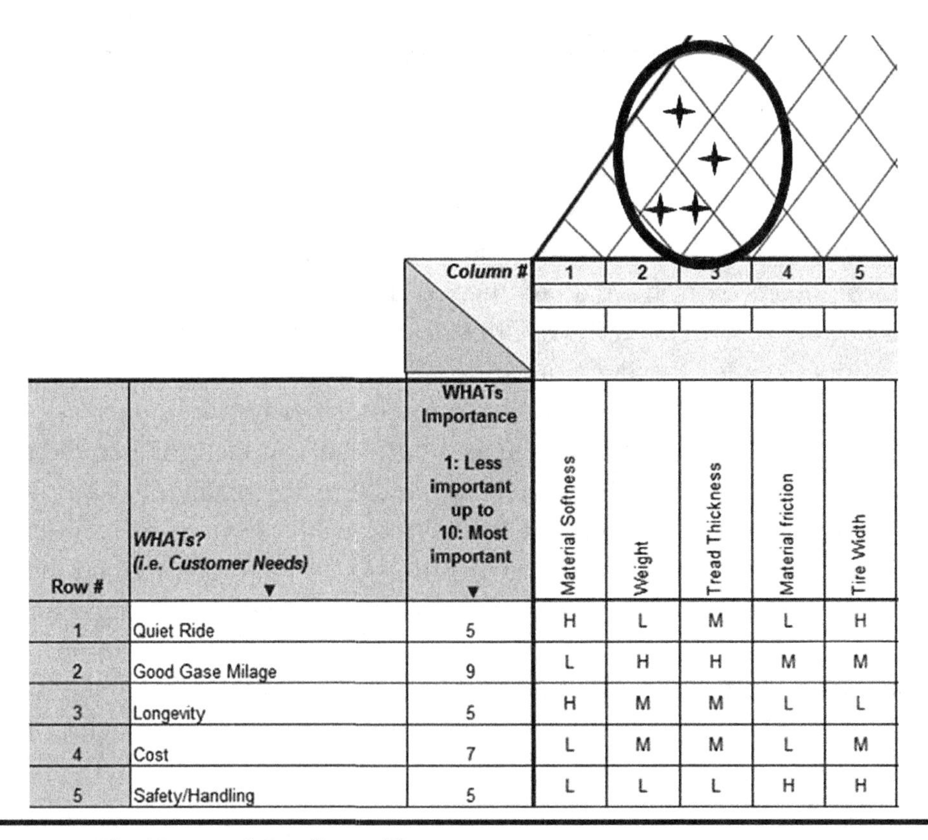

Figure 4.8 The House of Quality ceiling.

Good gas mileage usually means a lighter tire with less material, which leads to both a less comfortable ride and a shorter product lifespan.

The roof of the house also shows how the design considerations interact with one another, independent of anything the customer wants. In this instance, there are strong correlations for weight, for tread thickness, and for tire width. This strong correlation leads to a trade-off between good gas mileage (low weight) and a quiet ride (thick tread, wide tires). The design dictates the trade-offs a customer is going to face.

The Path to Innovation: QFD and Dominant Design

Like just about every other tool in the Lean toolbox, the main value-add of the House of Quality is that it provides focus. The House of Quality methodically structures design thinking around the product based on Voice of the Customer. It prioritizes the customers' needs. Most importantly, it allows the innovator to understand the design trade-offs between what the customer wants and what the current design can provide. The House of Quality becomes the key to unlocking innovative value for our customers. If a new design of process or product can reduce the trade-offs identified in the House of Quality, more value is delivered to the customer. This is innovation.

As an example of this mechanism in action, take the first iPhone. The first iPhone revolutionized the cell phone market and ushered in the era of the smartphone. It's so often venerated as the device that put the internet in our pocket, we often forget that we already had access to the internet and email before its release in 2007. Let me contend that the most innovative thing about the iPhone wasn't the software or the apps. The most innovative part of the iPhone was its physical design, particularly that the screen was the size of the phone for the first time ever. Clearly, this is something valuable to customers.

Just about every phone adheres to this "dominant design" that features no physical keyboard and a large touch screen. Why was Apple able to create this innovation where other dominant competitors, like Blackberry, couldn't? Up until this point, there was no dominant design for a cell phone. Cell phones could flip open like the Motorola Razr or slide open to reveal a keyboard or something else. In all of this, the conventional wisdom was that in order to text or type on a phone you either had to have a full keyboard or tirelessly type on the telephone keypad. Blackberry owes its early success to this paradigm. It was one of the first manufacturers to give consumers a full keyboard and a screen.

The obvious trade-off in this paradigm, as the House of Quality would reveal, is between cost, size, keyboard, and screen size. In order to have a phone with both a large screen and a keyboard, the manufacturer would have to make a very expensive, very large phone. Take away either the larger screen or full keyboard and the product loses its functionality. Customer satisfaction dwindles. These are the trade-offs Apple identified and exploited. By focusing on these design trade-offs, Apple's team got to work brainstorming ways to remove them. Their effort ultimately culminated in a phone that had a touch screen over its entire surface and used an on-screen keyboard in lieu of a mechanical one. This innovation led to other opportunities for autocorrecting and recommending words – reducing the time to send a message and increasing user satisfaction. It further reduced the complexity of phone. While Blackberry had upward of 40 buttons, the iPhone had five. The touch screen-centric design of the first iPhone shifted the paradigm of the cell phone industry and ushered in a new era with a new dominant design.

By following the approach of QFD and the House of Quality, innovators can focus on the boundaries of the current paradigm. This intense focus pulled by the Voice of the Customer is what allows innovators to make radical changes. Their efforts are highly impactful. The new approaches they come up with to remove or alter the trade-offs of design deliver radically new value propositions that delight the customer.

Congrats on finishing this chapter. The analyze phase of the Lean Innovation Cycle is undoubtedly the most technical step in the process. It began with the raw interactions and a few insights from the gemba activities of interacting with, interviewing, and observing end users. Through the use of the customer journey mapping activity, the Kano Analysis, and QFD, the analyze phase distilled these data into the Voice of the Customer. In turn, the analysis helped us make sense of the customer experience and helped us challenge the status quo whether it was through the process or the design of the product itself. Coming out of this analysis step are a few directional, concise design challenges that can make the product better. Going into the ideation phase, we know specifically what parts of the current process don't add value to the customer, which new features would add value, and where our current design constraints are for delivering more value to the customer. Imagine if this step was skipped. The rigor of this analyze phase has enriched our understanding, focused our thinking, and prepared us for the next step in the Lean Innovation Cycle, ideation.

References

[1] Barnett, B. (2019). "A $0.05 Component Delayed the PS3 – IGN Unfiltered". *IGN*. https://www.ign.com/articles/2019/11/18/a-005-component-delayed-the-ps3-a-ign-unfiltered
[2] Creststeel, E. (2016). "Xbox One Stagnates While PS4 Dominates: Can the Tables Turn?" *GameSkinny*. https://www.gameskinny.com/l3lrv/xbox-one-stagnates-while-ps4-dominates-can-the-tables-turn
[3] Orland, K. (2013). "Analysis: Xbox 360 poised to pass Wii in US sales by year's end". *Arstechnica*. https://arstechnica.com/gaming/2013/06/analysis-xbox-360-poised-to-pass-wii-in-us-sales-by-years-end/
[4] Richardson, A. (2010). "Using Customer Journey Maps to Improve Customer Experience". *Harvard Business Review*. https://hbr.org/2010/11/using-customer-journey-maps-to
[5] West, H. (2014). "A Chain of Innovation: The Creation of Swiffer". *Research Technology Management* 57, 3, 20–23.
[6] American Society for Quality. "What is the Kano Model". American Society for Quality. https://asq.org/quality-resources/kano-model
[7] Hauser, J., Clausing, D. (1988). "The House of Quality". *Harvard Business Review*. https://hbr.org/1988/05/the-house-of-quality

Chapter 5

Ideation

The Lean Innovation Cycle may seem puzzling at this point. Innovation is, necessarily, a creative process, and yet the analyze phase made creativity seem reductionistic. The analyze phase took the raw information of the gemba and distilled it into more refined insights. But at what cost? It may seem that the analyze phase has left us with a product that is too narrow and too constrained to sufficiently do anything creative with. But this is by design. The Lean Innovation Cycle works in an undulating way; the phases alternate between a convergence and divergence of scope and ideas. The Hoshin Kanri phase directs the purpose and focus of the innovation project, hence it focuses and converges our actions in a particular direction. The *gemba* phase allows the innovation team to explore different experiences and insights from experts, mainstream users, and extreme users. It diverges in the directions dictated by the experiences in the gemba. The analyze phase takes these raw insights and again converges on focused particularities about them. Now, in the ideation stage, our purpose is to once again generate divergent ideas, taking the outputs of the analyze phase as the new inputs. The ideation stage will help us answer the most important question of the Lean Innovation Cycle: How do we actually generate a solution?

Tools for the Job

The Lean Six Sigma community, for all of its abilities and contributions, has some tremendous blind spots. One of these blind spots is the ability to brainstorm and synthesize solutions to a problem, once the problem has

DOI: 10.4324/9781003206347-6

been clearly identified. With the exception of "removing waste" and a few other principles, there's not much in the LSS framework to guide us into our next stage in the Lean Innovation Cycle. If this gap exists for traditional process improvement experts, then it's a far greater gap when working outside of practitioners' wheelhouse, like when generating ideas for the creation of a new product or service. To make things more problematic, a lot of the solutions found in traditional Lean projects are reductive, not additive. Removing waste has generally become synonymous with adding value. "Standardize to Improve," has become a platitude for improvement based on the reduction of variability and variety. Lean practitioners have not sufficiently developed their innovation muscles. They lack systematic methodologies and tools for generating new additive ideas. In this chapter, new methods, borrowing heavily from the principles of Human-Centered Design, are introduced as a way of remedying this skills gap.

See a Snake...Kill a Snake

Recall that the analyze phase uses a wide variety of tools to help innovators pinpoint insights in the customer experience. The three tools that were presented, the Value Stream Customer Journey (VSCJ), the Kano Analysis, and Quality Function Deployment (QFD), all seek to uncover different insights into the end-user experience. The VSCJ uncovered emotional aspects of the end-user experience and provided more context in identifying what process steps are value-added and non-value-added. The Kano Analysis categorized how customers feel about features and performance characteristics of a product. QFD showed the design constraints of how the current need is being met through the dominant design. QFD's insights lie in its ability to illuminate some of the contradictions in consumer wants and design. At this point, you are the product or service expert. You and your team have studied the end users, their environment, and the product/service more than anybody else. And with this new expertise, you're allowed to take some artistic liberties within the framework.

There's an old quote from Businessman and Political Candidate Ross Perot that wholly applies to Lean: "If you see a snake, just kill it. Don't appoint a committee on snakes" [1]. It's a common-sense approach that should be applied to creating new ideas in innovation. If in the course of the Gemba or Analyze stage you identify some glaringly obvious part of the user experience that needs improvement, take care of it. While elegant tools can inform and guide our decision-making, sometimes all that's needed is an outside and informed perspective to see things in a different light. So while the tools presented in this stage of the Lean Innovation Cycle can help guide the idea-generation process, they are no substitutes for intuition and common sense. Feel free to deviate from the script if this is where intuition leads. It's far better to try an idea than idly pontificate on its merits. The chapter after this one focuses on the Kaizen phase of the Lean Innovation Cycle and present common ways to quickly try new ideas and monitor their effects.

Generate

Any innovation framework needs three things: a way to systematically generate new ideas, a way to evaluate the merits of these ideas, and a way to apply changes and adapt based on this evaluation. Without one of these facets, any innovation effort will founder either for lack of ingenuity, lack of value, or inadaptability. One of the best examples of this principle was already mentioned in Chapter 1. In his book, *The Lean Startup*, author Eric Ries introduces a way for cash-strapped startups to quickly learn from the market and adjust their products based on customer feedback. Ries proposes a Lean startup cycle which is comprised of three stages: Build, Measure, and Learn [2]. His proposed methodology is to develop a minimum viable product for a market, put it into the market, and then adapt the next iteration of the product based on the customer feedback. By learning from the market, startups avoid "leap of faith" products that may or may not be accepted by customers and can be costly if not devastating to startups [3]. It echoes the more general principles of generate, evaluate, and adapt. While slightly different than Ries's cycle, the purpose of the ideation stage is itself a framework and a set of tools to help guide innovators through a cycle of generating new ideas, assessing these ideas, and responding to the assessment.

As mentioned early, the Lean Innovation Cycle undulates from activities that help us converge on a particular problem or demographic, and then diverge into different possibilities and fields of influence and experience. Similarly, the ideation stage is itself a framework of generation, evaluation, and adaptation, it also possesses these same undulating characteristics of convergence and divergence. The diverging steps provide a space to explore new possibilities and new ideas while the converging steps help us make sense of the new ideas and insights as they are revealed and generated. Finally, whittling down the possibilities to the most plausible to implement. With this in mind, the first step in the ideation phase is to converge even further on our insights from the analyze phase and take an inventory of the outputs.

Facilitation of the Ideation Phase

Before jumping into the tools that help foster creative thinking that leads to innovation, it's important to pay particular attention to the atmosphere surrounding these activities. There is no scientific formula for coming up with good ideas. It's an intangible skill that can't be reduced to formulae or methods. And yet, it feels like some companies have it down to a science. Titans of innovation like Apple, 3M, Procter and Gamble, just to name a few, have dominated their industries for years because of the products they've created. It's uncanny how these companies, along with many others, can systematically come up with new ideas year after year. But if the ideation phase is predominately creative, the mechanism for idea generation lies within the mind itself, like a black box. And like a black box, its combination is unknown to us. So how is it that the perennial innovators are able to crack the combination so frequently? The formula for cracking the combination isn't reliant on exceptional intelligence but is rather reliant on the right environment. By benchmarking off of industry leaders and research, we're able to learn quite a bit about how to create environments that make for effective ideation and crack the black box of creativity over and over again.

Facilitating the Ideation Session

Truly novel and new ideas come from effective and collaborative brainstorming sessions. The job of an innovation team leader, then, is to create an environment that is welcoming to the kind of divergent and unorthodox thinking needed in brainstorming while still providing structure and cohesion. Only once the team feels comfortable with the creative space will they let their walls down and really dig into their creative ideas.

The most important aspect of a healthy ideation atmosphere is creating an environment of deferred judgment. The purpose of ideation is not to generate a bunch of good ideas. Rather, its purpose is to generate a lot of

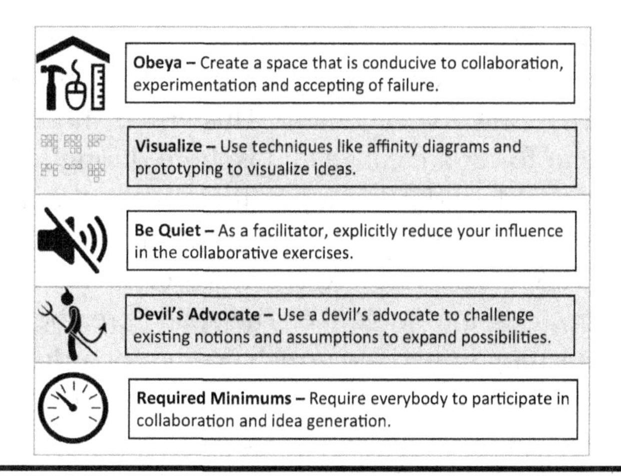

Figure 5.1 Summary of facilitation techniques.

ideas, some of which are good, some of which will inspire other good ideas, and some of which happen to be bad. By letting a free flow of ideas permeate from the collaboration of the team members, more novel ideas spring forth. After all, there's no way of telling if an idea is good or not until after it's been generated, and evaluating the merits of an idea as it's being generated is a hindrance to the creative process. If ideas are concurrently generated and evaluated it stifles the creative spirit of the team. Team members will be preoccupied with generating "good ideas" that gain acceptance in the group rather than focusing on novel ways to generate new solutions. As a rule, be diligent in safeguarding the environment of deferred judgment during the brainstorming phase of ideation. A summary of all these techniques is provided in Figure 5.1.

Obeya for Ideation

Consider also that, because brainstorming is such a collaborative and interpersonal process, the physical space of where these activities are conducted matters. In Chapter 2, we paid particular attention to the *Obeya* or war room. The room is a space that acts as a signal to the entire team. By entering the *Obeya*, the team is reoriented to their goals and objectives. The *Obeya* creates a safe space for Lean thinkers to use and discuss their tools and methods that may not get as much traction in other parts of the enterprise. And while this is good for Lean, it can be stifling and confusing for brainstorming and creative collaboration. Because brainstorming is about generating new ideas and thinking in new ways, it's also helpful to explore these ideas in a new space. In a way similar to how the *Obeya* signals a structured Lean approach to solving problems, a new space that is conducive to collaborative team efforts can signal to the team the importance of changing things up, if only for a moment. This visual and physical difference will continue to foster a creative atmosphere during ideation.

The ideation *Obeya* should be set up with collaboration in mind. The Ukrop Studio, a design thinking and innovation studio at the College of William and Mary in Williamsburg VA, is an excellent example of what a brainstorming *Obeya* ought to look like. The space breathes a spirit of action. Rather than sitting in padded armchairs in a boardroom, the space has elevated tables for group collaboration, which promote movement as much as discussion. The walls are unfinished and without drywall, look to the ceiling and you can see the plumbing and electrical running overhead. The façade is incomplete. The studio is unfinished by design. The unfinished look is a way of signaling to the users of the space that it's okay to not have the perfect or most polished idea. In fact, it's better that way. The small but powerful signal promotes innovators to keep trying new things. There is no finish line in a creative space. The studio is also supplied with a myriad of supplies and resources. There are whiteboards, sticky notes, playdough, construction paper, magic markers, and duct tape for innovators to use to help facilitate the ideation process through low-resolution prototyping. If you can create your own innovation studio, take these details in mind and benchmark design thinking studios like the Ukrop Studio to create your ideal brainstorming *Obeya*. If it's not possible to have complete control of the room, make it a point to procure the supplies and adapt the space you do have available to the ideas outlined here.

Facilitate through Affinity Diagramming

With the *Obeya* location selected and the creative atmosphere protected, it's time to turn our attention to the actual nuts and bolts of an effective brainstorming session. As mentioned, the goal of the facilitator is to protect the creative atmosphere and create a structure for these ideas to be shared and discussed. One of the best ways of creating this structure comes from the Lean tradition; Affinity diagrams. Affinity diagramming is a very visual, low-tech and hands-on way for teams to share ideas and collaborate. The essence is simply to write down an idea on a sticky note and then post the sticky note on some highly visible canvas, such as a wall, or whiteboard, or table. However, there are a few differences between the best practices of Lean affinity diagramming and affinity diagramming's use in brainstorming.

For one, usually in Lean, the sticky notes are categorized. Either the sticky notes will be color coordinated or they'll be placed on some tool like a fishbone diagram or priority matrix. This approach has merits. The goal with these methods is usually to hammer in on a process mindset and help a cross-functional team understand how their proposed solutions fit into the work already completed. But even these distinctions between process steps have some form of judgment and evaluation which, at this point, should be avoided as much as possible. I've even seen the approach backfire. A team that sees one step in the process littered with kaizen ideas will naturally try to even out the process map by coming up with solutions for other process steps. In effect their making a distinction that one process step is "complete" and the others still need work. This is not desirable.

Another best practice that is often not observed in Lean Six Sigma affinity diagramming is vocalization. Ideas are usually put onto a canvas, silently, as to not disturb other team members from formulating these ideas. But this is misguided. Idea generation doesn't work like this. Instead, it should be a best practice to have each person vocalize each new idea as it is added to the canvas. This helps facilitate a fun, unguarded collaborative environment, and it engages more than one sense. Now instead of people silently reading ideas on sticky notes, people are fully immersed in a market of ideas in free exchange.

Finally, Lean is all about formulating workable ideas in the affinity diagramming process. This also is misguided. Ideation doesn't work like this. The sticky notes don't have to be potential solutions. They can be and should be statements that provoke further thought. "The customer cares more about the experience of using the product than the product itself." They can be questions that invite people to see things in a different way. "What would the solution look like if the cost of material was 5 times as much?" There are many more best practices to successfully facilitate a brainstorming session, here are just a couple that are the most important and substantially influential in the ideation process.

Groupthink

In Chapter 3, I mentioned some dangers associated with working in groups. As an example, focus groups promise the opportunity to learn from diverse perspectives but often don't yield desired insights and suffer from groupthink. Groupthink is a phenomenon that occurs in group settings and is characterized by feelings of cohesiveness, alignment of ideas, and little to no conflict. All of these things may sound desirable, and in most circumstances, they are. But the purpose of ideation is divergence as much as convergence. There should be conflict, competing and differing ideas and perspectives. Groupthink becomes a cancer to creative efforts. Luckily there are ways to reduce the effects of groupthink.

Be Quiet!

When groupthink occurs, members of the group usually converge on a dominant voice. This dominant voice can be the person who speaks the loudest, the person who is most insistent in their ideas, or the person who speaks more often. And in the midst of all of these factors, everybody is still acutely aware of organizational hierarchy. Generally speaking, if the facilitator or leader of the team gives voice to his or her concerns during collaborative sessions, the rest of the group will fall in line with their ideas. With this in mind, one of the best tactics for facilitating brainstorming sessions and fostering a safe space for creativity is simply to be quiet! Feel free to continue facilitating the conversation, but don't posit any of your own ideas or opinions. Make the absence of your voice conspicuous before the brainstorming session starts. Announce to everybody in the group what your role is limited to. Maybe even give them a bell to hit if you step over the line. Doing so will remove the awkwardness of your silence and empower the group with the confidence and responsibility to actively contribute to the creative discussion. It will also demonstrate your own willingness to sacrifice your opinions for the good of the operation and team, thereby fostering an even safer space for collaboration and free exchange of ideas.

Devil's Advocate

Another tried-and-true method for avoiding groupthink is to ensure there is a dissenting voice within the group, the familiar Devil's Advocate. By ensuring there is a dissenting voice in the group, you are ensuring that not everybody will converge on the same way of seeing things. But the Devil's Advocate is an approach that requires the utmost delicacy. Without the greatest care, this perennial contrarian can detract from the creative environment and remove the feeling of deferred judgment. Therefore, it's beneficial to lessen the hostility and contrarian nature of the person in this position. Rather than having the Devil's Advocate poke holes in a proposed solution, they can ask "What if..." questions that change the paradigm and force greater divergent creativity from the group to handle the new circumstance.

To facilitate a creative discussion with a Devil's Advocate requires a few more housekeeping notes. The Devil's Advocate should be clearly identified before the start of the brainstorming session, and everybody should clearly understand the role of the Devil's Advocate. Likewise, the advocate should also understand their role. They need not interject a "what-if statement" after each idea. Rather, the Devil's Advocate should be conscious of the direction the conversation is taking and posit well-positioned questions with the purpose of redirecting the conversation, rather than tearing down an idea. Finally, the Devil's Advocate should be randomly selected for each brainstorming session. Studies have shown that when a Devil's Advocate is used, even when the team knows that this is an assigned role, there are still negative feelings projected onto this person from the rest of the team. By changing up who will play the Devil's Advocate, the group leader can mitigate these effects, thereby preserving the morale of the entire team and diffusing frustrations and negative emotions that may otherwise be directed at just one person.

Required Minimums

Groupthink can also emerge, not just from convergence on a particular idea, but also from the exclusion of somebody's voice. This is so common it's cliché. In almost every group, there will be somebody who doesn't feel comfortable contributing to the open dialog of the conversation, whether that is truly an open dialog, or an affinity diagram exercise, or more directed "*how might we?*" statements, which will be discussed momentarily. Everybody in the group is there for a reason and that reason is to share their ideas. Facilitation leaders must anticipate that this will happen and make efforts to prevent it. You can't simply call somebody out for being too shy 45 minutes into a brainstorming session. It will not have the desired positive effect. Like most everything else in managing a team, it's about setting proper structure and expectations ahead of time. Clearly indicate to the team that everybody will be expected and required to participate in some quantity. Creating a structure of a minimum number of cards for an affinity diagram or "how might we?" statement is a great way to ensure everybody is sufficiently giving voice to their ideas.

Some facilitators will limit the number of ideas other people contribute to the conversation. It's a tempting idea. Every member will be responsible for five ideas. But this stifles creativity and should be avoided. The outspoken participant who would likely produce 20 ideas will be vexed with what ideas to propose. As they judge their own ideas to select which they should propose the spirit of deferred judgment starts to come undone. Furthermore, because the environment is one of deferred judgment, most of the ideas will probably not be good ideas. Indeed, that's even a part of the process. We cannot expect, without some sort of discrimination of ideas, that the first five ideas of each member will be the best. Rather, we rely on quantity over quality because quantity has a quality all its own. The purpose should always be to empower people to produce more and set a minimum standard without worrying about who may be contributing more than their fair share to the conversation.

Tools and Methods for the Ideation Space

The discussion on facilitation was a necessary bit of housekeeping before we turn our attention to the tools. It allows us to think critically about how the tools should be applied as well as in what setting they will yield the best results. The physical and emotional environments as well as how the facilitation is conducted, i.e. affinity diagramming are significant factors in how we ought to proceed in the Lean Innovation Cycle. Now, armed with the insights gemba distilled through the analyze phase, we're ready to proceed in churning them into novel ideas.

Find Themes and Create Insight Statements

A good place to start in the ideation phase is to reflect on the analyze phase. Look for themes in the collected insights in all your hard work so far. From a Lean point of view, it's often the case that innovators will see reoccurring issues with a particular aspect of a product design or with a particular step in the user experience/process. On the other hand, the themes may be more nebulous. Themes won't be specific to a step in the user experience or particular to a feature of a product. For instance, when designing a porta john, the analyze phase yielded themes of cleanliness, privacy, and reliability. There's nothing about these themes that say anything about the product features themselves. And yet these themes led to designing a toilet paper holder that holds more paper, a hand sanitizing station, and elevating the porta john to make the user feel less vulnerable to their surroundings.

Another way to reflect on the analyze phase and consolidate the insights is to clearly articulate "insight statements" about some of the themes uncovered. The insight statements should *not* be about the design of the product. Rather the insight statements should clearly articulate the feelings and experiences of the end user. For instance, in the floor cleaner example from the VSCJ tool in Chapter 4, the end user was troubled with all of the wasted motion of preparing the product before use. The theme here might be "Wasted Motion" or "Long Prep." This theme might lead to insight statements such as "The end user wants a product that takes less time to prepare." Or "The end user is forced to transport the heavy bucket of water and cleaning product to the work location." Because these insight statements are directed toward the customer they further refine and articulate their wants, desires, and experiences when working with the product. In this particular case, both the desire for a more streamlined preparation and the frustration of transporting the heavy bucket shine through. With the themes stated and the insight statements generated, the first converging step of the ideation phase is completed, and we move to the first diverging stage in the ideation phase, brainstorming.

"How Might We?" Statements

One of the biggest trends in shaping an open and collaborative environment, free from judgment and open to failure comes from Silicon Valley. "How Might We" statements have transformed how people discuss and present ideas during brainstorming. The phrase "How Might We" at the beginning of idea statements and questions helps frame ideation in a way that is deferred of judgment and open to possibilities. The question is not about capabilities "Can we…" and it's not about whether we ought to do something "Should we…" Instead, it's more subtle and suggestive. The HMW statement frames an idea as a possibility and invites everybody else to consider it for the time being, nothing more or less.

How might our statements serve two purposes? The first is straightforward. It provides a vehicle for participants in the brainstorming session to share their ideas with the entire group. Second, it reinforces the environment of a safe space to fail, try new things, and broaden the scope of ideas. To this end, HMW statements don't need to all be serious concrete ideas. In fact, it's important that they're not. Rather, present ideas in metaphor or construct an analogy. Seek inspiration from a quote, and then try to apply the quote to the current topic. Write something down that's so out there that it can't possibly make sense. These strategies will further create an environment where others in the group let their guard down and feel freer to tap into their creative side. The reason we collaborate is because the ideas of another will likely spark another idea in somebody else. For this reason, the ideas contained within the HMW statements don't have to make complete sense, for they may hold the ability to inspire greater ideas.

Visualize

Another key tenant of a successful brainstorming effort is to push you and your team to be visual. Ideas don't pop into our heads as fully constructed, syntactically correct sentences. They pop into our heads in a vague and nebulous kind of way and are later translated to a complete sentence and thought. But sometimes we can lose meaning in translation. Instead, draw pictures, make a collage from magazines, or cut out a shape from construction paper. Push the team to break from the social norms of presenting all of their ideas through language. Allowing the team to create visualizations propels creativity and fosters the creative environment you're cultivating.

Similarly, it's important to consider what the team is visualizing. Rather than directing the team to focus solely on what an idea looks like, have them consider other attributes. As a facilitator, asking leading questions about what feelings the idea is supposed to evoke, or the idea relates to other ideas, stakeholders, or established products or services is a great way to generate new ideas from different perspectives.

Prototyping

One of the most important, if not the most important concepts in the ideation phase is prototyping. Prototyping has long been part of the creative process, but recently frameworks like Design Thinking have emphasized prototyping far more than in the past. Prototyping, to give a definition, is a process of creating a sample or model of a product that allows for quick and inexpensive construction and quick evaluation. From a Lean perspective, prototyping may seem like Non-Value-Added activities and rework. Why can't we just design the product right the first time? I would encourage Lean purists such as these, that prototyping is a lot more like the Plan-Do-Check-Act (PDCA) cycle. The purpose of prototyping is to fail fast to succeed sooner and to learn a lot from a little. The prototyping methods recommended here allow innovators to achieve these results while mitigating the risks of costs and time.

Low Resolution

Frank Gehry is a world-renowned architect. *Vanity Fair's* 2010 World Architecture Survey dubbed him "the most important architect of our age." He has been given 19 honorary degrees and 25 awards, spanning five decades, for his contributions to architecture and design. If there's something to be learned about ideation, innovation, and creativity, Frank Gehry can teach us. Frank Gehry does not attribute his success to intellectual genius or pristine education. Instead, Gehry attributes his success to the way he prototypes his designs. And Gehry is very particular about ensuring that his prototypes are all very low resolution.

Most people are familiar with the scaled models of architectural designs. They're usually 1:36 size models of a proposed construction. They are, as it were, very refined prototypes of what a building will look like once fully constructed. But step into Gehry's office and you won't see these buildings in miniature. You'll see very rough constructions of paper, metal, cardboard, plastic and Styrofoam. None of these prototypes resemble any of Gehry's finished work, but they allow him to play with the ideas he's generated [4]. By creating cheap prototypes of ideas and concepts, rather than buildings, Gehry is able to assess and evaluate his ideas and quickly reorient these features based on the assessment of the low-resolution prototype. By playing with these low-resolution models of his ideas, he's able to expend his energy in adapting concepts and ideas, rather than crafting a higher-resolution model of a still fuzzy concept.

Low-resolution prototypes should sound familiar to anybody who's written a paper or published a book. Gehry's innovation process looks a lot like the traditional writing process we learned back in school. By starting with outlines and working through rough drafts, 2nd drafts, and sometimes later, the final draft, creative writers are able to quickly jot down their ideas about characters and stories before they have to worry about proper syntax and grammar.

Prototyping concepts aren't just limited to the design of a product or the creative writing process. Animation studios like Pixar have been using storyboards to quickly get feedback from moviegoers and creative professionals. They use storyboards to crowdsource feedback about how to tell and construct a story and crafting how the characters should look.

Conversely, and as its own anecdote, Paramount Studios produced 2020 *Sonic the Hedgehog* movie received a myriad of negative feedback of how the animated title character, Sonic, appeared on screen. As the director of the movie, Jeff Fowler, tweeted:

> Thank you for the support. And the criticism. The message is loud and clear… you aren't happy with the design & you want changes. It's going to happen. Everyone at Paramount & Sega are fully committed to making this character the BEST he can be…[5].

Specifically, people hated Sonic's smile. It delayed the release of the movie to 2020 which later affected its runtime due to the pandemic. Not to mention it cost the studio millions of dollars to retroactively reanimate the movie to remove his unpopular pearly whites [6].

These examples ought to serve us as signposts for our own innovation efforts. During the ideation phase, the prototypes should still be very rough and of low resolution. The purpose of the prototypes is not to create a representation of a nebulous idea, it is to create another mechanism for further refinement, evaluation and adaptation of the idea. Prototyping extends the half-life of the creative phase in the process. And while we've seen how prototypes should be built and what they're used for, we still haven't answered questions about who they're used for and how they should be used.

Don't Lead the User

One of my favorite examples of prototyping comes from the comedian Chris Rock. Chris Rock is one of the most popular comedians in the world but it might surprise you to learn that he routinely "bombs" on stage all over LA [7]. In the small clubs of LA, Chris Rock is prototyping. He's trying out new material with small crowds and low-risk settings. What's also interesting about Rock's approach is how he performs his new material. He walks on stage with very low energy and delivers each joke as flat as possible. There's no emotion, no inflection in his voice, no comedic timing. He brings a notepad up on stage and writes down how the crowd responds, and then carries on to flatly deliver another joke. Many nights Chris Rock, one of the world's most popular comedians, walks off stage without making a single person laugh.

Rock's prototyping takes courage. Nobody likes to fail. But for Rock, he knows that the poor delivery is an essential part of the creative process. Innovators ought to learn something from this. First, Chris Rock is taking his prototypes, his jokes, to the end users. In his case, an audience at a comedy club. This is an important part of Chris's creative process because he lets the users decide which jokes are good and which ones need more work or need to be scrapped altogether. This allows Chris to curate a 45-minute stand-up routine that kills in every town when he finally goes on tour and the stakes are higher.

Second, Chris Rock isn't acting as a salesman. He coldly and flatly delivers his jokes, not to get a laugh, but to ensure that the content of the joke really is a good joke. If a comedian can get even the slightest laugh without adding in comedic timing, and inflection, and gesticulations, just think what a world-class comedian can get out of the joke when adding all of these back in. But it's also important that these embellishments don't muddle the audience's response when he's prototyping. This is true for innovators as well. When testing out a prototype with an end user, it's important not to try and sell them on the prototype. The prototype is not for sale. The more up-talk and sales tactics that surround the prototype, the more the user testing the prototype will be persuaded. Their true feelings will be diminished and muddled with your insistence on the prototype's merits. Rather, like Chris Rock, flatly explain what the purpose of the prototype is and what its features will be. Diligently observe how the end user interacts with and reacts to the prototype.

Fail Fast to Learn Fast

In a lot of ways, the ideation process mirrors the Shewhart Cycle – PDCA. Endowed with the tools of insight statements and low-resolution prototypes, innovators can quickly identify a possible solution, construct a low-resolution prototype, test the prototype, and then evaluate what worked and what needs to be improved. What's most important in this endeavor is to make the customer the focal point of the process. It does us no good to evaluate the prototypes we designed! Whether it's the check stage of the Shewhart Cycle or the measure phase of the Lean Startup Cycle, these should be the anchor points of the ideation stage. As important as deferred judgment and creative space is, it's imperative that we not be afraid of the criticisms we gain from the end users.

This is the purpose of the ideation stage. We're armed with tools and mechanisms to take the feedback from the users and swiftly adapt the design closer to their liking. To teeter between feedback and criticisms and creativity and deferred balance becomes a balancing act for any innovator. I would further admonish innovators to keep a spirit of play alive throughout the ideation process. Allow the atmosphere to get silly. Make fun of ourselves and let our barriers come down. The creative process thrives in this environment. It's only by failing fast that we'll succeed sooner.

References

[1] Perot, T.M.R. (1988). "The GM System is Like a Blanket of Fog." *Forbes Magazine*. https://archive.fortune.com/magazines/fortune/fortune_archive/1988/02/15/70199/index.htm

[2] Ries, E. (2011). *The Lean Startup: How Today's Entrepreneurs Use Continuous Innovation to Create Radically Successful Businesses*. Currency New York (Random House LLC). New York, NY. p. 75.

[3] Ries, E. (2011). *The Lean Startup: How Today's Entrepreneurs Use Continuous Innovation to Create Radically Successful Businesses*. Currency New York (Random House LLC). New York, NY. p. 76.

[4] Sims. P. (2011). *Little Bets: How Breakthrough Ideas Emerge from Small Discoveries*. Free Press (Simon & Schuster Inc.). New York, NY. pp. 54–55.

[5] Fowler, J. (2019). "Tweet from May 2, 2019". Twitter. https://twitter.com/fowltown/status/1124056098925944832?ref_src=twsrc%5Etfw%7Ctwcamp%5Etweetembed%7Ctwterm%5E1124056098925944832%7Ctwgr%5E%7Ctwcon%5Es1_&ref_url=https%3A%2F%2Fwww.theguardian.com%2Ffilm%2F2019%2Fmay%2F03%2Fsonic-the-hedgehog-movie-trailer-criticism

[6] Pulver, A. (2019). "Sonic the Hedgehog movie to be redesigned after criticism of trailer". *The Guardian*. https://www.theguardian.com/film/2019/may/03/sonic-the-hedgehog-movie-trailer-criticism.

[7] Sims, P. (2011). *Little Bets: How Breakthrough Ideas Emerge from Small Discoveries*. Free Press (Simon & Schuster Inc.). New York, NY. pp. 1–3.

Chapter 6

Kaizen

The last step in the Lean Innovation Cycle is appropriately the kaizen or implementation stage. Directed by the strategy of the Hoshin Kanri, the raw insights from the gemba, and the distillation of the analyze phase, the innovation team synthesized precise and specific ideas for innovation. At long last, this kaizen stage of the Lean Innovation Cycle is concerned with bringing the ideas generated from the previous stages of the framework to the end-user. In so doing, we must consider two distinctly different challenges to achieve this goal: getting a product to market (development) and what to do once the product or service has been introduced.

Thus far, the content of the book has been focused on synthesizing the concepts and design of an innovation. Little if any thought has been given to the steps it takes to deliver a real tangible product or service to the end-user. Now, fittingly in the kaizen stage, these considerations are brought to mind in order to ensure that the work thus far accomplished in the Lean Innovation Cycle is not in vain but is executed as effectively and efficiently as possible. The kaizen phase of the Lean Innovation Cycle needs to consider technical, concrete ideas and tools to improve the efficacy of bringing the product to market as well as study ways the innovation team can acquire and adapt to real market insights as the end-user interacts with the finished product for the first time.

Additionally, once the product or service is in the marketplace, it's helpful to think of it as an interconnected system between the product itself, and its deployment, including promotional factors such as branding, pricing, and advertising. This is an important paradigm for receiving the

DOI: 10.4324/9781003206347-7

feedback from the end-user. The end-user may be completely satisfied with the product but have qualms about how the product is portrayed in advertisements, priced, or even the product availability. A pristine product design that can't be manufactured is as good to the end-user as a horrible design. Now, by thinking of the innovation as a product-delivery system, we also have more levers to pull to improve the value realized by the end-user. We needn't reinvent the wheel and change the design of the product if some improvement closer to the customer will suffice. The product-delivery system is irreversibly married.

Concurrent Development

With almost all of the hard work of the Lean Innovation Cycle behind, the last thing you would want is for the product to suffer because of poor execution. But unfortunately, no matter how well the product or service delivers value to the customer, it can get derailed for reasons that are well outside of the scope of product design. Early on, we saw how speed to market can affect end-user's perceptions about a product or brand and create a first-mover advantage. Still, despite how good the "quality" of the product is, the ability to manufacture quality within the process, i.e. reduce defects and rework, is likewise important for delivering value to the end-user in a cost-conscious and effective way. Therefore, we should not just be content with a framework and toolbox to originate and design novelties and innovations but should also be highly proficient in the techniques that allow for efficient and effective delivery of these innovations. Concurrent development is one of these techniques.

Concurrent development is an intuitive and yet relatively new method for preparing a product or service for market. If firms aren't using concurrent development, they're using sequential development. In sequential development, product development tasks such as concept, design, process engineering, and product production are performed in series – one after the other. Concurrent development, also called producibility engineering and simultaneous engineering, is different. Concurrent development is a process that ensures all the key stakeholders are incorporated early on in the design and development process and throughout the product life cycle [1]. So as product designers are crafting the specifications of the product, production managers can add input about how the limitations of how product assemblies and finished products would be stored in inventory or manufactured in the manufacturing setting rather than being handed a set of finished drawings that they had no input in creating.

This is beneficial for at least three reasons. First, with all of the preparation for manufacture and delivery of the product happening at the same time as product development and design, the lead time to bring the target to market is greatly shortened. There are fewer handoffs and less waiting time, an all too common form of waste. Second, by garnering the insights of the delivery arm of the organization, opportunities for cost savings and improved quality are multiplied. Manufacturing personnel are able to identify which parts are more difficult to machine and what failure modes are common on the equipment. These insights may lead designers to remove parts of the product that are no longer needed, thereby reducing costs or designing a way around problematic manufacturing equipment and decreasing the lead time. Finally, because concurrent development involves such a collaborative work environment, issues are identified and corrected sooner [2]. As Figure 6.1 demonstrates, design changes to the product come much sooner in the development cycle leading to further reduced costs and on-time project delivery.

I saw the detrimental effects of sequential development when I was working with a large tire company. Product development had created a new

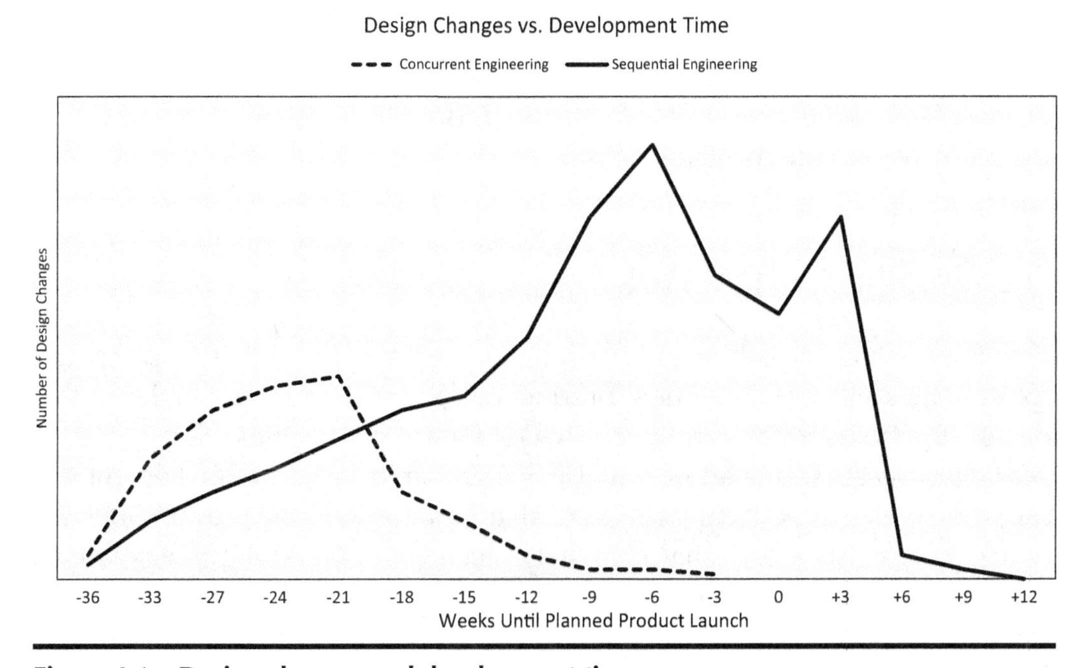

Figure 6.1 Design changes and development time.

tire that would be fitted on large rimmed wheels (mostly for SUVs). It was only once the product development process, along with the sale commitments and forecasts, were completely finished that the production control department was informed that they would be required to produce these tires. Unfortunately, the machines were incapable of producing these products. The company had sold tires it couldn't make! To alleviate this mess, swarms of project managers and process engineers were sent to the production facility. They quickly developed new tooling to modify existing machines. Rushing this tooling development was expensive and it took resources away from other parts of the business. Once the tooling was developed, it had to be machined and delivered. The rush orders of this tooling from the machine shops increased costs as did expedited freight. And the manufacturing facility lost untold thousands of dollars from the unplanned downtime of machines while they were refitted with the new tooling. The travel costs for the countless flights, hotel rooms, rental cars, and meals of the managers and engineers were a mere drop in the bucket.

While it's unlikely that having a manufacturing representative in the early stages of product engineering would have prevented all of this disruption from happening, we were still going to make those tires after all, the detrimental impacts would have been greatly mitigated through concurrent development. Getting wind of the sales plan, the company could have started the machine modifications sooner, reducing the development costs and losses in production facility downtime. Likewise, Sales and Operations Planning could have worked with the original equipment manufacturers to adjust delivery schedules and total demand. But with sequential development, it was too little too late.

Crashing the Critical Path

Crashing the critical path is another intuitive, technical tool that helps speed up the time it takes to get a new product or service to market. Similar to the idea of "the bottleneck" introduced by Goldratt in his business novel, *The Goal*, the critical path is an idea that has its roots in project management. The principle of the critical path states that in a complex project of different stages, there exists a path that ultimately dictates the time the project will be able to be completed. By decreasing the time it takes to maneuver through this path, the project lead time can be reduced. Figure 6.2 shows the critical and non-critical paths of a book publishing process.

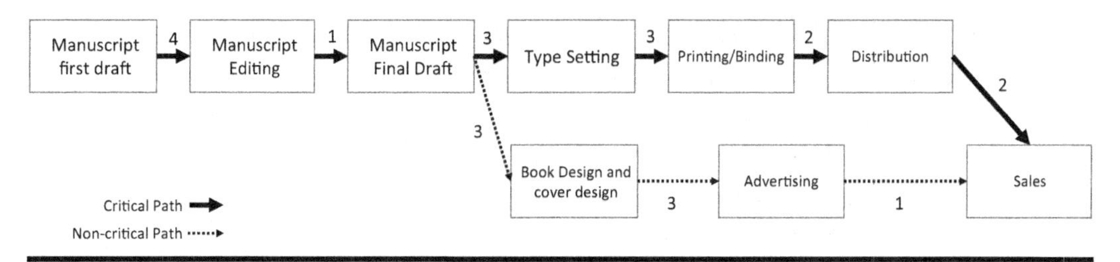

Figure 6.2 Example of the critical path mapping.

There are four, straightforward steps to crashing the critical path. First, is visualizing and mapping out the process flow. To just about every reader remotely familiar with Lean, this should feel like a very familiar, comfortable and logical first step. Just like in value stream mapping, the purpose of this first step is to clearly identify and understand how different parts of the implementation plan depend on one another as well as help visualize the flow. Once this flow is understood, the next step in crashing the critical path is to quantify the time it takes to complete each step. Unlike value stream mapping, the wait times and processing times needn't be separated out. We're not interested in what is and isn't value added. Rather, the wait times and the processing times of each step can be treated as the same step in the project plan. There is nothing groundbreaking to this, but it provides a firm basis for understanding the current state of project implementation. Third, identify the critical path. The critical path is the sequence of steps that determines the minimum time to complete the process [3]. As an example, in Figure 6.2, the critical path is a long sequence of seven stages in the book publishing process. Finally, the last step is to determine which steps in the critical path can and should be "crashed." Crashed is a way of saying, throw resources at it until the processing or lead time is reduced. These resources usually look like dollar bills but can take several forms including overtime, air freight, and employing additional experts and consultants. In my experience with the tire company, once the challenges became clear, the project managers correctly determined that the development, manufacture, delivery, and installation of the machine modifications constituted the critical path to producing the new tire design. This is why the plant was quickly flooded with these extra resources of engineers and project managers. They were crashing the critical path. There are all kinds of ways an organization can justify what stage(s) should be crashed, but as a high-level rule of thumb, focus on the stages with the longest processing time, lead time, or greatest reduction for additional resources.

By determining all the stages that are included in the critical path of the product creation and delivery, you can prioritize what stages in the critical path should be given more resources that will ultimately speed up the process of getting a new innovation to market. For instance, in Figure 6.2, by adding additional resources to the typesetting step in the process, the publishing house could decrease the entire critical path and cut down the overall time to market. Conversely, while adding additional resources to advertising may have its own justification and cost-benefit, it will not speed up the time it takes the new publication to market.

PDCA

Now with a technical understanding of tips and tools that support the Lean Innovation Cycle in bringing a product to market, it's important to consider an overall framework for understanding how these tools support the Lean Innovation Cycle and specifically support the kaizen phase of the cycle. Moreover, it's important to be concerned with using the kaizen phase to learn, grow, and improve your team's innovation efforts along with actually delivering the innovation to the end-user. Now that the end-user has the finished product, there is great opportunity to continue learning, just as with prototyping in the ideation phase.

In Lean, we have a standard, scientific method for implementing improvements. The Shewhart Cycle, also called the Deming Circle or the Plan-Do-Check-Act cycle, is a way to scientifically study a process by consciously changing inputs to the process, observing the results, and making decisions based on these responses. Even though this paradigm was created in heavy industry, it is still applicable to introducing a product to market.

First, let's recall how the Plan-Do-Check-Act cycle works within normal process improvement. Process improvements and countermeasures are first determined and prioritized, usually based on their projected impact and ease of implementation (PLAN). Next, these countermeasures are introduced into the process, one at a time (DO). As each countermeasure is introduced, the continuous improvement team observes the effect of the countermeasure in terms of their Key Performance Indicators (KPIs) – quality, capacity, cycle time, etc. (CHECK). If the results of the process are improved, the countermeasure becomes part of the new standard process. If the countermeasure does not create the desired effect, it is either tweaked and tested again or it is abandoned altogether (ACT). Then, the cycle starts over again by identifying and trying out new opportunities to improve. Taking this procedure as a best practice, the Lean Innovation Cycle does not deviate far from it when introducing a new product or service into the marketplace.

Plan	Plan how the product will be introduced. Advertisements, promotions, price point, seasonality.
Do	Execute the plan.
Check	Get feedback from customers – likes, dislikes, promotion, etc.
Act	Assess viability of Check-phase countermeasures and prioritize.

In my own work, I've used a template for rigid PDCA experimentation, reflection, and reaction. My template paints a picture of how following the PDCA method should be implemented; it is structured, thoughtful, and organized. The template starts by identifying the KPIs that are tied to a desired outcome. Next, variables (process inputs) are identified that will be changed as I conduct different trials, just like a well-designed scientific experiment. However, the name of the game is pragmatism. Unlike a truly scientific experiment, I'm not interested in quantifying with statistical certainty the impact of these variables. Rather, I'm simply aiming to observe if adding or removing these variables move the needle and in what direction. It's quasi-experimentation. Finally, I update the results, study the results for discernable insights, and reflectively make changes based on these reflections. Figure 6.3 is an example of the template in use. With "personal fitness" as the theme of my goals, the template directs me to understand both the positive and negative impacts of each variable introduced in the trials as well as any other difficulties that arose that might not have been part of the experiment, logistical issues, as an example. Again, it's quasi-experimentation. While I've planned out what variables I'm interested in tweaking, I'm not opposed to learning and implementing other lessons along the way.

There are, however, some differences between the PDCA approach in continuous improvement and the PDCA approach in innovation. The biggest of which is in the CHECK stage of the PDCA cycle. In traditional manufacturing or operations, the countermeasure is put in place and the process reacts. It follows a natural, physical law. Adjustments to pressure settings, machine alignments, and routine maintenance all elicit some consistent response to the changes. In service operations, wait times, line lengths, and service time follow a similar law known as Little's law [4]. In both

P	Variables		Healthy Meal Plans Process	5S Pantry – Remove NVA foods	List on Fridge – Visual Management	Practice New Warmup Plan	Track miles on iPhone + Coached warmup	Runners Watch
	Observations		3	1	5 (Daily)	6 (Days)	7(Miles) 2 Days	10 (Miles) 2 Days
Metric	Base	Target	Trial #1	Trial #2	Trial #3	Trial #4	Trial #5	Trial #6
Increase VA Food Source in Pantry	50%	80%	60%	75%	90%	90%	100%	90%
Warm Up Plan Adherence	0%	100%			D	75%	100%	100%
Miles at Pace	0%	80%					50%	100%
What Worked Well?			Had standard (Plan) for healthy options	Learned wife was shopping by visual. Made space easier to see VA.	Simple and visual list. Easier to update real time.	Could see value in stretching before run. Felt looser during start of run.	Had alerts from app on or off pace.	Nailed may pace. Felt loose and capable. Had lots of energy.
C What Did not work Well?			Did not follow standard completely. Looked at pantry for missing items.	Threw a lot of food out. Wasted Money. Change management for family.	Rely solely on manual updates. Not don't, no food to replace.	Not sure if I was performing to standard. Cut corners during prep.	Had a clunky device. Not easy to run with . Lost connectivity to app when out of range.	Added costs of equipment.
What should be done differently with the next trial? A			Coach / Train and observe new standards	Make visual management on Fridge.	Reinforce new process/standard with team.	Pull on coach and team to observe practice	Buy GPS watch.	Nothing – sustain for 3 months. Track visuals, and reinforce standards.

Figure 6.3 PDCA template for quasi-experimentation.

manufacturing and service operations, countermeasures create a direct effect that is easily measurable in the data. Unfortunately, end-user reactions to products and services don't work the same way. If the data we're interested in is sales, then the sales metrics may tell you if the product is popular, i.e. effectively delivering value, but the data might provide little explanatory value about *what* needs to be changed. In order for the PDCA cycle to work, we need to take it a step further. Once again, going to the gemba, just like in the prototyping stage is important. Capturing end-user sentiments as they interact with the finished product for the first time will reveal greater insights and direct further opportunities. These insights can be used to tweak the existing product design, pricing, and advertising as well as inform design of new innovations and product lifecycle adaptations.

Agile

The PDCA method for implementing a new product design or service is a novel approach for using the Lean toolbox to further the efforts of sales and marketing. But it's not alone. In the world of software development computer, programmers have been using similar ideas and principles to improve their ability to quickly develop working high value-added software. Software developers aren't just desk jockeys writing code for 40 hours a week. They are designers. And because they're designers, they have a leg up on traditional Lean process improvement professionals. They design very technical products that directly solve or mitigate a customer problem. This solutions-based framework is a high value-added product which, from a Lean perspective, is why software and computers have been the dominant disruptive force in the world for the last 50 years. Moreover, despite the common tropes, software developers are acutely aware of the human and end-user elements inherent in using their software. "Front-end developers" have become specialists in creating systems that are intuitive and easy to use for the end-users. These efforts to be mindful of the end-user in the software development process have even created new jobs such as human-factors engineers and user-experience (UX) designers. They all have ample experience in delivering a product to the customer and responding to their needs. And with these things in mind, the consortium of continuous improvement professionals ought to look mindfully at the principles surrounding how they develop and deliver their products to the end-user.

A not-so-quiet revolution has been going on in the world of software development that shares many of the same ideas and principles as we find within Lean. Agile was first developed in 2001 by Mike Beedle and 16 other authors as a set of values and principles to guide the development and delivery of software to customers [5]. Since its creation some 20 years ago, the principles of Agile have greatly transformed the way software is developed, delivered, and enriched. Startups, tech giants, and every other sized software company use Agile principles as the dominant paradigm in designing and delivering digital products and software services. The 12 Principles presented in Beedle's *Agile Manifesto* that began this transformation are as follows:

Our highest priority is to satisfy the customer through early and continuous delivery of valuable product.	Working software is the primary measure of progress.
Welcome changing requirements, even late in development. Agile processes harness change for the customer's competitive advantage.	Agile processes promote sustainable development. The sponsors, developers, and users should be able to maintain a constant pace indefinitely.
Deliver working software frequently, from a couple of weeks to a couple of months, with a preference for the shorter timescale.	Continuous attention to technical excellence and good design enhances agility.

Business people and developers must work together daily throughout the project. Build projects around motivated individuals.	Simplicity – the art of maximizing the amount of work not done – is essential.
Give them the environment and support they need and trust them to get the job done.	The best architectures, requirements, and designs emerge from self-organizing teams.
The most efficient and effective method of conveying information to and within a development team is face-to-face conversation.	At regular intervals, the team reflects on how to become more effective, then tunes and adjusts its behavior accordingly [6].

In addition to these principles, the Agile Manifesto defines four core values that are fundamental to its philosophy. These values include valuing individuals and interpersonal interactions over processes and tools, creating working software over comprehensive documentation, customer collaboration over contract negotiation, and responding to change over following a plan [7]. These values create a dichotomy between competing interests and present a roadmap for prioritizing options and determining trade-offs.

By and large, the principles are congruent to the overall thrust of the Lean Innovation Cycle. The Lean Innovation Cycle demands that the customer pull the value from the innovation and demonstrates the collaborative spirit Agile infers. The value of creating a workable product that is readily able to add value to the customer, what Agile calls "working software" is paramount to the spirit of the Lean Innovation Cycle as well as traditional Lean. It's true that comprehensive documentation, like standard operating procedures and documented processes, are important to organizations but it's also clear that these are only as good as the value they add to the customer; they should not be means in and of themselves. Without an unrelenting determination for delivering value directly to the customer, any product design, software, or otherwise is doomed to founder in the bureaucratic mess of paperwork and documentation before the customer can realize value from the product.

Likewise, ideas such as customer value, respect for people, and continuous improvement permeate the principles of Agile. "Pursuit of technical excellence" is continuous improvement and the kaizen by any other name. While the principles of Agile are harmonious with the principles and framework of Lean, Agile contains a few novel ideas and principles that are worthy of diving deeper into and including in the wider multidisciplinary framework of the Lean Innovation Cycle. They are "Working software is the primary measure of progress" and "At regular intervals, the team reflects on how to become more effective, then tunes and adjusts its behavior accordingly."

First the working software. This Agile principle is elegant in its simplicity. Recall from Chapter 2 the discussion about Key Performance Indicators. Selecting the appropriate indicator is critical to successful execution of strategy and tracking the KPI is essential for accountability. Agile tackles both of these considerations by defining the KPI as working software. It's not the number of lines of code, the number of variables defined in the program, or the number of hours spent writing and testing the software. These indicators may be incongruent with other Agile principles and detract from the primary goal – delivering working software to the customer. The KPI aligns the principles with the work.

Next is the principle of cadence and reflection. This principle contains two ideas that are both worth considering for the Lean Innovation Team. First, Agile insists on a defined structure that creates what I like to call a *cadence of accountability*. This principle creates a consistent tempo that the design team can work toward. The team knows their goals (working software) and when they are expected to deliver the goal by (cadence). Taken together, they create a clear standard for the software design to work toward. Again, Agile introduces an idea that the consortium of Lean practitioners can learn a lot from defined, periodic reviews. Too often, the savings of Six Sigma projects will erode away as improvements aren't administered properly or the process changes with time. The control phase in the DMAIC framework is supposed to address these issues but often the control plan is completed and filed away without being consulted ever again. Similarly, Lean, when administered as an operational philosophy, relies on creating a new standard to sustain an improvement, and nothing more. The cadence of accountability that comes from the Agile principles demands a more structured and hands-on way to assess progress and ensure accountability.

In the previous chapter, we already made note of the Lean Startup Cycle which Eric Ries introduces in his book *The Lean Startup* [8]. While our focus in Chapter 5 was to introduce the general mechanism for learning from end users, his startup loop becomes even more applicable when discussing after action reviews. Recall that Ries's startup cycle has three stages – Build, Measure, and Learn. Of all the stages the learn stage is the most important. By introducing a product to market and hearing how to improve the product directly from the customer, entrepreneurs are able to gain a competitive advantage by delivering superior value, defined directly from the customers' mouths. But this cycle is chiefly predicated on the after action review, what Ries calls the "Learn" stage.

This principle espouses a structure that's not merely focused on going forward at all costs. It also considers how we got here and if we want to take the same path next time. This cadence of accountability is interested in making sure things are getting done and the project is progressing, of course, but also presents an occasion to learn, adapt, and continuously improve the team's operations as it rapidly designs and delivers the finished product. After action reviews are one of the hallmarks of high-performing teams and by including the after-action review as part of standard operation with specific timetables, deliverables, and occasions for performing these reviews, the software design teams are able to improve themselves with astonishing success.

Both the Lean Startup Cycle and the principles of Agile mean a great deal for innovation teams. The principles of PDCA and Agile allow innovators and implementers the ability to define and redefine value directly from the feedback of the customers.

What Happened to My Tools?

You may be wondering why this chapter has focused so specifically on the Plan-Do-Check-Act cycle as the chief framework for introducing an innovation to the marketplace. Lean practitioners who are also familiar with Six Sigma methods will be wondering where the control plans, FMEAs, and statistical process controls are. In process improvement projects, these ensure that the process innovations are impactful in achieving the project goals and moving the organizational KPIs. These concerns are well-founded and rational. But while these control methods are well-suited and effective for processes, they unfortunately lose their potency when applied to delivering a new product or service to the end-user. One of the chief reasons for this loss of effectiveness is the difficulty in identifying a key performance indicator that is truly congruent with the implementation and delivery. Recall that once we get to the kaizen stage of the Lean Innovation Cycle, the product and the implementation are inexplicably linked. Marketplace KPIs like sales volume and revenue don't necessarily tell the whole story and won't provide direction on how to respond to unfavorable circumstances by themselves.

Moreover, the statistical tools in the Six Sigma toolbox presuppose conditions that don't really apply to delivering a new innovation. Control charts, control plans, and capability analysis all seek to describe a steady state of affairs. The control chart method works because we're looking to detect process changes. Capability analysis is a way to quantify how capable a *stable* process is of achieving specific results. The Ppk statistic generated in these analyses is especially concerned with long-term viability of process capability [9]. Control plans are put in place so that things don't change, or if they do, we know how to bring the process back into standard. All of this is contrary to the spirit of the kaizen stage of the Lean Innovation Cycle. If we're successful in creating and delivering a product or service that truly adds value and is desired by the target customer, the last thing we should expect is stability. Instead, we should see growth. We should see an increase in all those KPIs – sales, revenue, market share etc.

This underlies another distinction and it's kind of the point of the kaizen phase. We need to learn and improve while we bring a product to market. The PDCA framework allows us not only to control the kaizen stage but enables a reactivity and agility that cannot be realized through the statistical tools already described. The familiar PDCA slope diagram, Figure 6.4, demonstrates this paradigm. The standards are our controls to prevent backsliding and undoing the work we've already done, but the Shewhart Cycle is the mechanism by which we climb the slope of continuous improvement, obtaining knowledge and realizing growth for the organization. It should be no surprise to Lean veterans that the Plan-Do-Check-Act Shewhart Cycle is the workhorse of the kaizen phase.

The last thing I ought to mention is that the kaizen stage is the last phase of the Lean Innovation Cycle. The Lean Innovation Cycle is itself a PDCA

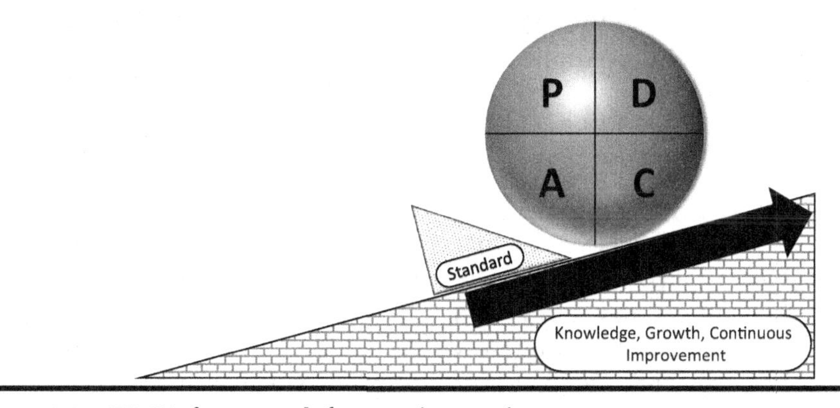

Figure 6.4 PDCA framework for continuous improvement.

framework of sorts. It starts from the planning stages of the Hoshin Kanri, works through the do and check phases of the Gemba, analyze and ideation phases, and finally implements the innovation in the Act phase of the cycle. Fittingly then, this Act phase ought to inform the next iteration of the Lean Innovation Cycle. Starting again, with the Hoshin Kanri the innovation team and organization ought to take what has been learned in the subsequent iteration and react to change, refine the customer, redefine goals, and realign the efforts of the innovation team to the new knowledge that was generated.

The Lean Innovation Cycle is a process to learn from the end-user and methodically, yet creatively, synthesize new ways to bring value to the end user which finally culminates in the actual process of delivering these newly synthesized ideas to the customer in the form of products and services. The Lean Innovation Cycle is customer-driven. It is deeply focused and unflinchingly resolute on understanding what the end-user values and how to increase user satisfaction by augmenting the product, service, environment, or experience. It is the attentive focus on defining and delivering customer value that has always been at the heart and center of Lean. And yet, even in such a highly concentrated framework, the approach of the Lean Innovation Cycle offers something more than analytical scientific reductionism. The Lean Innovation Cycle, with its multidisciplinary approach, takes the best practices of Human-Centered Design, Agile, Six Sigma, and many other disciplines to offer a dynamic and creative approach to synthesizing ideas and realizing opportunities, all with the end-user in mind. Now, with a deeper understanding of the Lean Innovation Cycle, the attention of the book turns from the technical dissection of the framework, to painting with broader strokes for the organization. In turn, questions such as "how does using the Lean Innovation Cycle support sustainable innovation, impact internal capabilities, impact strategy, and create and sustain competitive advantage?" and more will be answered.

References

[1] Hunter, J. S. (1988). "Statistics and Quality: It's Only the Beginning." *American Society for Quality*. https://asq.org/statistics/2011/11/continuous-improvement/statistics-and-quality-its-only-a-beginning.pdf

[2] Lightman, Jason. (2019). "Breaking down the walls of product design with concurrent development". *Fictive Website*. https://www.fictiv.com/articles/breaking-down-the-walls-of-product-design-with-concurrent-engineering

[3] Kramer, S. et al. (2006). "Understanding the basics of CPM calculations What is scheduling software really telling you?" Project Management Institute. https://www.pmi.org/learning/library/critical-path-method-calculations-scheduling-8040
[4] "Little's Law". Kanban Zone Website. https://kanbanzone.com/littles-law/
[5] Highsmith, J. (2001). "History: The Agile Manifesto". *Agile Manifesto Website.* https://agilemanifesto.org/history.html
[6] Beedle, M. et al. (2001). "Agile Manifesto". *Agile Manifesto Website.* https://agilemanifesto.org/principles.html
[7] Eby, Kate. (2016). "Comprehensive Guide to the Agile Manifesto". *Smartsheet Website.* https://www.smartsheet.com/comprehensive-guide-values-principles-agile-manifesto
[8] Ries, E. (2011). *The Lean Startup: How Today's Entrepreneurs Use Continuous Innovation to Create Radically Successful Businesses.* Currency New York (Random House LLC). New York, NY. p. 75.
[9] Minitab Blog Editor. (2016). "Process Capability Statistics: Cpk vs. Ppk." *Minitab Website.* https://blog.minitab.com/en/process-capability-statistics-cpk-vs-ppk

Chapter 7

Differences between Approaches to Innovation

In the Introduction of this book, I briefly defined what innovation is and painted a shallow picture of the differences between contemporary, what might be called traditional, approaches and efforts toward innovation and efforts of Lean Innovation. In this chapter, the aim is to further elaborate on these differences and how they fit into a greater framework for understanding innovation. Moreover, these distinctions between Lean Innovation and traditional innovation will provide a basis for understanding the benefits of the Lean Innovation Cycle in future chapters. In so doing, the Lean Innovation Cycle demonstrates as conducive to innovation at differing levels of complexity while the traditional approaches are aimed at a narrower objective of technology-based innovation. Moreover, it will also be demonstrated that the Lean Innovation Cycle can deliver on its goals more consistently and predictably than its traditional counterpart. This commentary will provide fuel for further development of ideas regarding issues of organizational sustainability and competitive advantage.

Before beginning this dissection, recall a few ideas already discussed at the beginning of this book. First, innovation is a business activity. Its essence is not a new technology or a new product or service by itself, though innovation certainly can, and often does, manifest itself in this way. Second, the Lean Innovation Cycle has been defined as the method by which we achieve innovation in alignment with the goals and values of the business. The Hoshin Kanri phase of the Lean Innovation Cycle made sure

DOI: 10.4324/9781003206347-8

of this. Additionally, the Lean Innovation Cycle *pulls* the information it needs directly from the end-users to ensure that the innovation efforts of the organization are efficient and effective in delivering real value.

Levels of Innovation

With innovation redefined, I want to reintroduce with a little more rigor, the different levels of innovation. In order to understand the differences between the different approaches to innovation, a more intimate understanding of what innovation is and the different ways it manifests itself is needed.

Recall that the TRIZ community, which practises specialized tools in technical brainstorming and innovation, has categorized innovation into five different levels, which has been illustrated in Figure 7.1 [1]. Level one innovation is the most remedial. It constitutes a simple improvement to an existing technical system. When we think of traditional Lean we think of many activities and small improvements which in turn create a big impact. Each of these improvements is in a sense level one innovation. They don't revolutionize an existing system or process but make a definite positive impact.

Level two innovation is defined as an activity that resolves technical contradictions within a physical system. Technical phraseology aside, these types of innovation are also found within the purview of Lean. Single-Minute Exchange of Dies (SMED) is a great example of this in action. The contradiction is between time and the activity. By speeding up the change-over through various methods the improvement team effectively eliminates or at least reduces the contradiction between downtime and flexibility. SMED further resolves other contradictions within the physical system – like

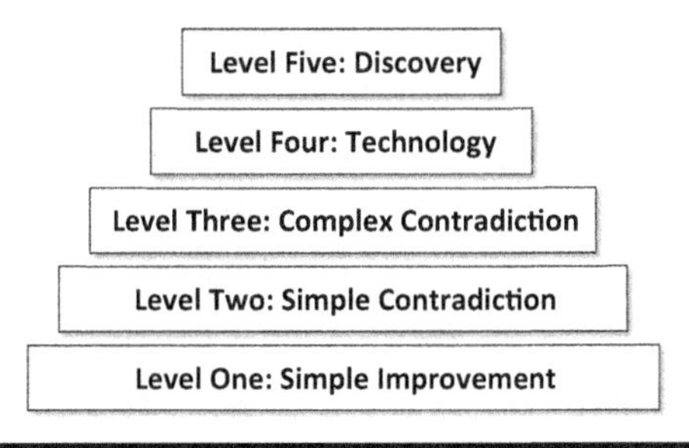

Figure 7.1 Levels of innovation.

running smaller lots with more changeover to reduce inventory and balancing lots rather than scheduling long production runs to reduce the changeover downtime.

In both cases of level one and level two innovation, the impact of these innovations is muted in their scope and impact. This might hurt the pride of Lean practitioners but in the grand scheme of a business or industry the individual impacts of these innovations are quite small. Each innovation resolves a specific, well-defined issue that only has an impact on their immediate context (i.e. a production facility, a hospital intake process). Moreover, these types of innovation require a relatively small amount of knowledge. In both cases, having particular knowledge about the system or the industry is all that is needed to find a solution to the issues.

Here it's important to see that Lean as a process-improvement strategy and operational philosophy is an effective avenue in enacting level one and two innovations. Lean relies heavily on the gemba, the operators or the front-end-users of a system/product/service. They are the process experts, who reliably have knowledge of the system, though not much more. I've heard Lean explained as "A ditch dug one inch deep but five miles long." It's a way of expressing that each improvement will be small and limited in impact but that the real impact of Lean is realized when these small improvements are administered several times over. The larger impact of Lean affecting more than just the immediate system emerges as a sum of all the small efforts taken together. The whole is greater than the sum of its parts. The symphony comes together.

Moving up the ladder of innovation, level three innovation is a lot like level two, but more so. It resolves a technical contradiction in a system but pushes the boundaries of knowledge to areas not readily available to industry and systems experts. What is most characteristic of this third level of innovation is that the solution to contradictions come from knowledge of other industries and sciences. With tough problems, it's not possible to come up with the solution by ourselves. Outsiders with different acumen and expertise must be consulted to find a solution. Analogous inspiration must be found in other industries and sciences.

Lean has a familiar mechanism for finding this kind of exterior knowledge. The Japanese call it *yokoten*, we English speakers call it benchmarking. Benchmarking is a deliberate way of learning from experts with different backgrounds and knowledge than what you, your organization, or your industry possess. Other people in other industries have encountered and solved different problems that may be directly or at least analogously relevant to the issues you are currently facing.

Regarding benchmarking, Hewlett Packard (HP) provides a great case study. Faced with variable and uncertain demand patterns for some of their products, HP sought to learn from others who already experienced this kind of volatility in their industry. Textile and soft goods (clothing) have some of the most volatile demand patterns of any industry. What styles and colors will be popular next fall is highly uncertain and impossible to predict. Textile manufacturers face a tough trade-off between large production runs with the risk of producing unwanted inventory but having enough stock and a lower unit price or small production runs with a higher price and risk of running out of inventory. HP found itself in a similar problem in producing its printers with different functions and features.

HP found Benetton, an Indian manufacturer of textiles, and began benchmarking. Benetton's supply chain strategy was radically different from HP's. Benetton shipped unfinished, undyed products to their distribution centers. Once the seasonal trends were identified, the distribution centers could dye the clothing to match the desires of the customers with less shipping and only a minor delay. This demonstrates a fantastic use of pull vs. push Lean thinking and HP took note.

With the Benetton benchmark in mind, HP redesigned their supply chain as well as the computer printers themselves. HP developed and shipped generic printers to the distribution centers which would later add the finishing touches and product features based on customer feedback and demand. By adhering to a best practice in a different industry, HP was able to reduce inventory, free up working capital, and improve their product offerings to the customer [2].

This advantage of using benchmarking in innovation rests in the ability for one organization to leverage the experiences of other organizations who have greater acumen and experience with different solutions to solve problems. It is the deeper knowledge of particular problems, reframed in a different context, which yields the innovative insights. Six Sigma methods are a great example of this principle in action. Using Six Sigma methods, practitioners take a business problem, turn it into a mathematical problem, solve the mathematical problem, and then transform the mathematical solution back into a business solution. Six Sigma makes a habit of deliberately framing the business problem in a way that compels the problem-solvers (level three innovators) to pull knowledge from other areas of knowledge to solve the problem, namely statistics. Using Six Sigma is a level three innovation.

It is only at the fourth level of innovation where the advent of new technologies as part of innovation is demonstrated. In fact, level four innovation is defined *as* a new technological development. Rather than solving existing problems within a complex system (e.g. manufacturing plant) the new technology, the new innovation, improves the system by its own merits and virtues. Human labor is replaced by the steam engine. Typewriters give way to a system of word processors and computers. As another example, take the microwave. Surely, the speed of preparing food has always been in the front of chefs' minds for millennia. But with the new technology of the microwave, the "system" of preparing food by convection oven and stove top was radically altered. The new technology, by virtue of its existence added value, in this case reduced preparation time, to the system.

The microwave example demonstrates another important aspect of level four innovation. The knowledge required to achieve this level of innovation requires knowledge from different fields of science, similar to level three innovation, but more so. The microwave was developed as an offshoot of RADAR technologies in World War II which was on the cutting edge of human technology and highly confidential, to say the least [3]. Even the most experienced chef couldn't have developed this technological innovation which is now a staple in every American home. Technologically based innovation relies on divergent scientific ideas.

Finally, the fifth level of innovation is really far outside the purview of most business functions and entails the discovery of a new principle or phenomenon. This is essentially akin to scientific advancement or revolution. Examples abound throughout history, but one recent and demonstrative example has been the discovery of nuclear fission. In the late 19th century, physicists were beginning to understand fundamental forces of the atom as well as some atoms' propensity to expel neutrons in what is now known as a form of "radioactive decay" [4]. Eventually, these phenomena and a few other laws, like critical mass, gave way to nuclear physics and engineering. By understanding nuclear physics and how to capture the energy released from splitting an atom, scientists and nuclear engineers have been able to harness this level five innovation in a myriad of ways including clean energy and weaponry. Suffice it to say, that level five innovations have extreme impacts with a scope enveloping all of mankind. But the frequency and reliability of producing a level five innovation require huge capital and expertise in the physical sciences.

Let me pause here to reflect on these levels of innovation. What level of innovation do our modern and contemporary ideas about innovation fall? Only in level four is innovation defined by the advent of a new technology. This categorization should help us start drawing lines in the sandbox. Traditional innovation efforts seek to create level four innovations within an organization whereas the Lean Innovation Cycle is oriented to identifying existing problems or emerging problems that the end-users have.

It might also be worthwhile to ask, at which levels of innovation should businesses aim to realize? How should they spend their resources and efforts in pursuit of innovation? To pursue level five innovation is probably outside the realm of possibilities for most organizations except for research laboratories. Level one innovations may be easy to come by, but their scope and impact might not be impactful enough for the vision of the business. Level four innovation promises stepwise growth and market impact which can be alluring but requires an infusion of outside knowledge that hardly seems consistent or sustainable for an organization. Where should we begin?

Benchmarking provides some insight. We should first identify where innovation is actually happening. The first three levels of innovation provide the lion's share of all technological and business innovations. In his research, Genrich Altshuller, founder of the innovation framework TRIZ, found that 77% of filed patents were either level one or level two forms of innovation [5]. This trend occurs not because organizations are not willing to make bigger impacts through technological innovations and scientific discoveries but because these higher levels of innovation are more resource intensive. Figure 7.2 demonstrates the principle. As we move up the ladder of innovation, the cost associated with each innovation as well as the body of knowledge required increases. If organizations are to pursue innovation as a sustainable strategy of obtaining and maintaining competitive advantage, they must resolve to increase their understanding of how innovation occurs and how frequently different types of innovation occur. In particular,

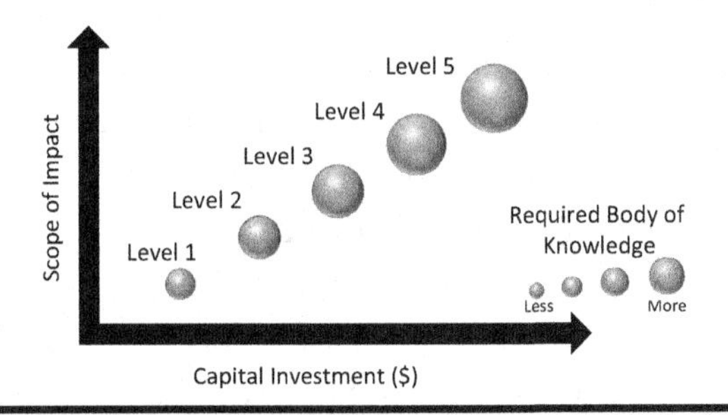

Figure 7.2 Levels of innovation: scope, impact, and requisite knowledge.

organizations must understand the chief differences between traditional innovation efforts and the effects of the Lean Innovation Cycle. It's only through this understanding that businesses can charter an innovation strategy that is tailored to their needs and is truly sustainable and impactful.

Technology Focused vs. Customer Problem Focused

If you can't tell by now, the biggest distinction between the Lean Innovation Cycle and traditional innovation lies in the pursuit of technology. Traditional approaches to innovation assiduously focus on the development of technology as a means of novelty and invention. When people talk about "innovation," it is almost always in the context of a new technology or application of a technology. And this should guide our understanding of the traditional approach. When businesses say they are focused on innovation, what they mean is that they are focused on developing in-house technology or acquiring new technologies that deliver value to their customers. The strategic aim of these approaches has already been documented in the Introduction but bear repeating: By developing and acquiring new technologies, companies are able to realize stepwise increases in their own capabilities to make, distribute, and/or sell products. Moreover, new technologies that are focused toward the end-user promise huge growth in the form of new market segments, greater market penetration, or other intangible advantages.

Conversely, the Lean Innovation Cycle seeks to discover solutions to contradictions and from the end-users themselves. In light of the levels of innovation just discussed, the Lean Innovation Cycle as a model is suitably fit for realizing the first three levels of innovation. The tools of asking experts, mainstream users, expert users, and seeking analogous inspiration all work to expand our knowledge and allow the creation of solutions to the problems without having to, quite literally, reinvent the wheel. Moreover, the tools of the analyze phase help bring these contradictions to light. By way of the Lean Innovation Cycle, we are attentively working through a process to identify what the opportunities of innovation are and designing a solution to these problems.

Because the Lean Innovation Cycle is a mechanism for identifying contradictions and creating solutions for these contradictions, it isn't an all-in-one tool for achieving all levels of innovation. In particular, the Lean Innovation Cycle is not effective in innovating through scientific discovery or technological development. There's nothing wrong with putting your hammer down to unscrew a screw and such is the case with higher levels of innovation. Different problems require different solutions. The Lean Innovation Cycle will deliver consistent and sustainable value but only when used and aimed properly. One of the particular reasons why the Lean Innovation Cycle cannot achieve higher levels of innovation is because of the body of knowledge that is required to attain these levels. Both level five and level four innovations require external knowledge in a way that the Lean Innovation Cycle is not well suited to help obtain or exploit. Rather the Lean Innovation Cycle is much better adept at *pulling* information from end users and experts. The burden of knowledge required for higher levels of innovation makes it clear that there is a trade-off between frequency, consistency, and impact.

More to the point, the Lean Innovation Cycle is better at identifying and resolving "contradictions" in the end-user experience. These contradictions are the design challenges we saw throughout the deep dive of the cycle. Particularly in the analyze phase, we used the Kano Diagram and Quality Function Deployment to see how user desires often conflict with one another. A car loaded down with safety equipment will have worse gas mileage, but a consumer wants both a fuel-efficient and safe car. A passenger car tire that produces a quieter ride means using softer rubber and won't last as long. Yet the customer wants both a quiet ride and a long-lasting tire. The frontier of innovation lies in disentangling these contradictions. Creating a car that is safe without resorting to heavy safety equipment, for instance, decouples the contradiction between weight, safety and fuel efficiency. The resolution of these contradictions always creates an impactful innovation that the end-user enjoys and delights in because the end-user's desires are already at the limit of existing product capabilities, the innovation frontier.

It should also be noted that in identifying and resolving these contradictions, it's the users themselves who are describing and explaining the issues. This helps innovators in two ways. First, by letting the users define the challenges they want to be solved or the limits they're encountering, it avoids wasted time and effort spent on grasping at straws or trying to push a new idea onto the customer. With a user-defined design problem, the innovator will deliver a valuable solution every time. Second, a user-defined problem helps to quickly resolve the most fundamental challenge in problem-solving: defining the problem. In just about every problem-solving methodology, you must start by understanding the problem that is to be solved. This is true in Lean, Six Sigma, Design-Thinking, and a litany of other frameworks. Unanimously, projects and problem-solving frameworks start with planning and scoping the activities and processes in question. The need to understand and define the design challenge is a fundamental truism that can't be avoided. The Lean Innovation Cycle puts the impetus to define these challenges on the end user in order to ensure alignment between innovation efforts and delivering actual value to the end user.

Levels One and Two and the Lean Innovation Cycle

Having the end user define the limits of their own experience allows innovators to target these design problems as contradictions to the end-user experience and realize what the TRIZ community calls level three innovation. But this isn't to say that the lower levels of innovation with smaller scope and impact should be brushed aside and deemed unworthy of our time. We already saw that three out of every four innovations occur at these two levels. We shouldn't fight this reality. Rather, by integrating the Lean Innovation Cycle, along with the traditional disciplines of Lean, we ought to build a well-oiled machine of producing many lower-level innovations that, collectively and with time, emerge into an impactful improvement to the customer. Quantity has a quality all its own.

This underlies a familiar point for Lean practitioners. The summation of many small improvements with small impact is able to create a large, sustainable impact on the customer. The analysis and impact of each individual improvement does not need to be groundbreaking. What matters is that some activity is getting done. I once carried out a Lean transformation for a property & casualty claims organization. They were looking to improve how they selected candidates for their call center operation. There was no groundbreaking milestone of the project, no one activity that I could point to and say, "That's what made the difference." Rather, it was the multitude of small improvements to their process that made the difference. Things like aligning management on what they wanted from a candidate, developing success profiles, changing the process flow, and standardizing interviews all contributed to small impacts that aggregated in less rejected candidates and a shorter lead time to fill an open position. Remember that innovation is a business activity that delivers value to the customer. In this case, by affecting many small changes internally, the claims department was able to deliver better service to the customer. Per the new success profile, the new call center hires were selected for their interpersonal savvy and were better communicators. Because the lead time to fill an open position was less, this meant the call center was operating near full capacity more often and realizes less wait times for the end-user/consumer. Small internal improvements yielded a truly valuable impact to each and every customer in terms of their customer experience and the time spent on the phone.

Because the Lean Innovation Cycle is first and foremost a Lean framework, it should be no surprise to see that it has all the ingredients it needs to create a smooth operating machine that spits out small improvements and innovations, frequently and consistently. It's unrelentingly gemba focused, it shares a bias toward acting by employing the PDCA Shewhart Cycle for implementing new ideas, and its primary focus is always about adding value to the final customer. All of these components are needed to establish a mechanism for consistent improvements.

This is not the place to go into the intricacies of setting up a kaizen submittal system in any detail but suffice it to say that this tenet of traditional Lean is perfectly aligned with the Lean Innovation and the Lean innovation team is perfectly situated to administer these low-level innovations, what we would traditionally call kaizens. By integrating a systematic system to have internal, direct end users identify and elevate problems to be solved, the Lean innovation team can round out a two-prong approach for delivering innovation for the organization. These internal kaizens work as an operational philosophy of continuous improvement while the projects following the robust framework of the Lean Innovation Cycle act as a larger lever, a project approach to make an acute impact and deliver innovations directed either to internal customers or external customers.

One disadvantage that comes from this approach is that we as innovators lose some agency in directing what value will actually be delivered to the customer. The summation of all these small improvements has an impact on the direct and indirect end-users but it's hard to say what will emerge from the effort. Confidently, we can say that with these types of activities we see an increase in process reliability, removal of rework, and reduced times to deliver products to market, all of which have discernable valuable impacts to the customer.

Process Innovation

This topic above anticipates another point that needs discussing – namely process innovation. So far, this entire book has been defining innovation, more or less, as a business activity that creates a product or service that the "end-user" derives value from. Our definition has taken the end-user to be something very narrow, akin to the consumer or customer. But this need not be the case. The end-user does not need to be external to the organization. The reality is that innovation efforts can be directed internally as well as externally. Value can be delivered in both of these directions by focusing on improvements and innovations within an organization itself.

As an example, one place where internal or process innovation is most prominent is within the world of supply-chain management. Supply-chain management has recently become one of the principal focuses of many top organizations [6]. The ability to deliver products faster, cut down inventory, reduce overhead, and build resilience in sourcing materials has implications for just about every industry and customer whether they are a final consumer or a customer getting materials from a supplier to manufacture and sell as something new altogether.

From a traditional standpoint of technological innovation, the investments have been staggering – barcode technology, RFID tracking, and even the use of augmented reality, robots, and drones have transformed organizations' abilities to effectively and efficiently manage their supply chains. And all of these technologies have nothing to say about the other innovations in route optimization, warehouse and factory location planning, contingency planning, safety, and other logistical, less physical, innovations.

If innovation is occurring within businesses' supply chains and other processes, how then should we think of and define the end-user? The end-user is anybody who is affected by an innovation – a stakeholder as it were. When considering any one of the supply-chain innovations mentioned, many different end-users come into focus. Workers in the supply chain become end-users of the new technologies and processes that are created and must be adhered to. Meanwhile, the customer or consumer would also be an end-user because the changes to the process will likely affect the output of the process which the consumer/customer is chiefly concerned with. Therefore, the end-user of internal, process-based innovations can be thought of as two separate groups: direct and indirect. Direct end-users are the individuals who are working in the process itself. Their daily job is directly affected by changes in the process. The customer at the end of the process becomes the indirect end-user because the changes in the process will indirectly affect him or her. Changes to a business process will affect the output, be it quality, cost, consistency, customer experience, or something else. The customer is indirectly impacted by changes to the process by means of the process output.

Traditional Innovation

But why can't traditional innovation accomplish all of this and more? Why can't the approaches taken by traditional innovation realize the more modest levels of innovation? The truth is, it can. Traditional, technological innovation actually plays a much greater role in improving internal capabilities than it does in affecting the end-user. Chapter 10 discusses this in more detail, but suffice it to say that many technological innovations are not aimed at the end-users, but are aimed at reducing costs through the value chain.

Regarding traditional innovation in the marketplace, however, it has already been noted that traditional innovations are mostly focused on developing a new technology that can be exploited for growth in the forms of new customer segments or increased market share. It doesn't have the pull of taking from the customers but is rather focused on what internal capabilities can be exploited to deliver a new product or service. Technology isn't always the solution to adding value. Sometimes a customer can get more value out of the resolution of a contradiction than a new device. When you're a hammer all you see is nails.

A prime example of this is how, for the past 10 years or so, we've been putting touch screens in automobiles. Touch screens feel cool, modern, and look sexy. They make dashboards with buttons seem clunky and antiquated. But consider what a consumer would want in a vehicle – comfort, gas mileage, and of course safety. We're inundated with warnings and Public Service Announcements about texting while driving and the dangers of distracted driving which makes the idea of touch screens even wholly misaligned with customer wants and expectations around safety [7]. Thinking about this another way, if it's such an improvement, why hasn't the US Air Force put touch screens in their F-18s?

To say it differently, there is a contradiction between aesthetic and safety. Thankfully, the misstep is already being remedied by benchmarking the technologies in the fighter jets. Heads-up displays (HUDs), where dashboard options are displayed on the windshield, rather than a dashboard panel, are becoming commonplace in new and luxury vehicles [8]. This is far from new technology, the US Navy had precursors to the technology before World War II but developed the initial prototypes as early as the mid-1950s, which supposes we've known about the benefits of not having to switch focus between panel instruments and the skies very shortly after we started flying [9]. I assume the same is true for automobiles. The HUD solution delivers much more value because it truly resolves the contradiction between safety and a desire for modern aesthetic. By becoming too focused on technology as an end in itself, product designers and innovators have made missteps in pushing a square peg in a round hole.

The Risks of Technology-Led Innovation

Traditional approaches to innovation also come with a certain amount of risk. This is partly the thrill of working in innovation and why innovation and entrepreneurship have become so tightly intertwined. High risk, high reward. There are at least three principal risks that you run in pursuit of developing a new technology. The first risk is that the technology is never developed. A new innovative technology that is long in development or hasn't gotten all of the bugs worked out of it can be given the axe because of the exceedingly long development or budgetary overspend. But the development can also be shelved for reasons not related to the technology development activities themselves. Macroeconomic trends and changes can greatly affect an organization's or even a whole industry's priorities. In the 2010s, when crude oil prices were skyrocketing, oil companies were spending billions to develop new technologies to extract oil in more inhospitable places – namely the tar sands of Canada and Siberia. When the crude oil price swung back the other way all of these projects were abandoned because they were no longer economically viable [10]. They would not return a profit at the going rate of crude oil. The point here is not to make a value statement on their activities and whether or not they should have pursued green technology or something else. The point is that some risk factors are wholly outside of your control.

The risks in developing technology also come with risking the fallacy of the sunk cost. The fallacy of the sunk cost is when an organization pursues the completion of a project (or developing technology) even when the writing is on the wall that the opportunity no longer exists. To use the previous example, if the oil companies continued developing tar sands extraction technology even after the price of crude oil dropped, just to finish the project or develop the new method of oil extraction, they'd be operating within this paradigm.

Finally, there is the risk of competitors. In technology, development is not a game you play in a vacuum. At every turn, you're trying to beat your competitor to the market and adapt to what your competitors are offering at the same time. And they're doing the same thing to you. Competitors pose a real risk to innovation at all levels but especially when pursuing an innovative new technology.

The principal and most devastating risk a competitor poses is that they develop a new technology faster than you do and gain the intellectual property, brand power, first-mover advantage, and everything else that comes along with it while you're stuck with a large expenditure. But even if you're the first to develop a new technology and bring it to market, there is the risk of imitation from your competitors. If you've ever watched the TV show *Shark Tank*, you know what I'm talking about. In addition to sales, profitability, and the company valuation, the Sharks are constantly assessing new products and inventions not just based on how easy it is to mimic and reproduce. Even intellectual property like a utility patent is not enough to ensure the Sharks that the product is safe from competitors, including substitute goods. This threat is also an ever-present threat in Chinese trade and commerce. In China, it's common for the government to initiate forced technology transfers (FTTs) where companies hand over their technical drawings and methods of manufacture to China in order to produce goods in China and distribute to the huge domestic Chinese market [11]. In the presence of competitors, the development of a new technology does not guarantee the competitive edge you seek.

Conclusion

The levels of innovation provide a fantastic foundation for understanding the landscape of innovation and how different approaches to solving problems and inventing solutions lead to divergent levels of impact and scope. The lower levels demonstrate simple improvements that are limited in scope and impact. But knowing what we know from the Lean body of knowledge, the aggregate of many of these small level one innovations can have a huge impact on an organization and its customer base. Higher levels of innovation yield solutions to simple and complex contradictions. Examples of these contradictions abound in our daily lives and consumer products. Speed and quality, comfort and affordability, amount of information, and ease of understanding are all in conflict with one another. Value is delivered when a solution to these conflicts is found.

Higher up on, technology and scientific discovery promise greater impact but do so with less reliability and consistency. Innovation at these higher levels has greater challenges than the lower levels. The burden of knowledge needed to attain novel technologies and discover new phenomena cannot be overstated. Likewise, the risks of seeing innovation efforts come to fruition increase with scope and impact.

To this end, the Lean Innovation Cycle is a useful tool to frequently and consistently deliver the lower levels of innovation. It is a not all-in-one tool for all levels of innovation but has a specific role to play in an organization's innovation strategy. In the upcoming chapters, its ability to create sustainable innovation through multigenerational product design and consistent, focused innovations that add value to targeted end-users is demonstrated.

References

[1] Souchkov, V. (2007). "The 5 levels of solutions explained". *The TRIZ Journal.* https://triz-journal.com/differentiating-among-the-five-levels-of-solutions/

[2] Venugopal, G., Venkataraghavan, G. S. (2007). "Cross Industry Benchmarking". *The Economic Times.* https://economictimes.indiatimes.com/cross-industry-benchmarking/articleshow/2251955.cms?from=mdr

[3] Ackerman, A. (2016). "A Brief History of the microwave oven". *IEEE Spectrum Magazine.* https://spectrum.ieee.org/tech-history/space-age/a-brief-history-of-the-microwave-oven

[4] "Radioactive Decay". (2021). United States Nuclear Regulatory Commission. https://www.nrc.gov/reading-rm/basic-ref/glossary/radioactive-decay.html

[5] Shulyak, L. (1998). "Introduction to TRIZ". The Altshuller Institute for TRIZ Studies. https://www.aitriz.org/articles/40p_triz.pdf

[6] Banker, S. (2021). "Supply Chain Talent is More Important than Ever". *Forbes Magazine.* https://www.forbes.com/sites/stevebanker/2021/03/10/supply-chain-talent-is-more-important-than-ever/?sh=1a618b605e19

[7] Gilboy, J. (2021). "Why I'm Done Pretending Touchscreen Infotainment Isn't a Stupid, Hazardous Fad". *The Drive.* https://www.thedrive.com/tech/39304/why-im-done-pretending-touchscreen-infotainment-isnt-a-stupid-hazardous-fad

[8] Glon, R. (2021). "The best head-up displays (HUDs) for 2021". *Digital Trends Website.* https://www.digitaltrends.com/cars/best-head-up-displays/

[9] Popular Mechanics. (1955). "Windshield TV Screen To Aid Blind Flying". *Popular Mechanics.* March 1955, p. 101.

[10] Orland, K. (2020). "Teck cancellation in Alberta may signal the end of oil sands mining". *World Oil Magazine.* https://www.worldoil.com/news/2020/2/25/teck-cancellation-in-alberta-may-signal-the-end-of-oil-sands-mining

[11] Prud'homme, D. et al. (2018). ""Forced technology transfer" policies: Workings in China and strategic implications". *Technological Forecasting and Social Change* 134, 150–168. https://www.sciencedirect.com/science/article/abs/pii/S0040162517304602

Chapter 8

Sustainable Innovation

One of the most important advantages of creating a culture of Lean Innovation through the Lean Innovation Cycle is that it allows businesses to operate within a framework that produces innovation in a sustainable way. This is important for any business that wants to make innovation part of their DNA or espouse innovation as part of their culture and values. As should already be clear, and what this chapter continues to demonstrate, a big technological boon, to open up new markets and greater revenue can be hoped on to propel a business forward but will lack the ability to do so with regularity, predictability, or consistency. Conversely, the Lean Innovation Cycle is a method toward sustainable innovation. The Lean Innovation Cycle works to support and build a culture of perpetual innovation and novelty. In particular, the sustainable advantages of the Lean Innovation Cycle manifest themselves in two important ways. First, it provides a mechanism for extending product lifecycles through the development of multigenerational product design. Second, the Lean Innovation Cycle allows a firm to achieve innovation while mitigating disruption to the organization.

Multigenerational Products

As just mentioned, by using the Lean Innovation Cycle and the tools within the framework, businesses can extend the product life cycles of some of their product offerings through a tactic called Multi generational Product Planning (MGPP). Multigenerational products are products that are designed

DOI: 10.4324/9781003206347-9

to encompass multiple iterations of the product with new features and add-ons that enhance the user experience, deliver more value, and importantly for the company, extend the life of a particular product. To clarify, "life" here refers to the amount of time the product can be seen attractive in the marketplace, not the actual usable life of any one particular product itself. To further the point, take toothpastes as an example of multigenerational products in action. There are a million and one different types of toothpastes each with its own concoction of breath strips, flavors, whitening, cavity protection, baking soda, fluoride, sensitivity, and colors, none of which extends the life of a particular tube of toothpaste, but all of which extend the viability of the product line in the marketplace. By adding all kinds of novelties and add-ons, a manufacturer is able to keep the product engaging, new, and exciting for the customer. And all of these new features don't change the core of a product or how the product is used. With each of these iterations, the end-user is squeezing some sort of paste out of a plastic tube, putting it on their toothbrush and scrubbing their teeth clean. Neither the core product nor the process is fundamentally changed.

It might also be interesting to think about why there aren't hundreds of different types of toothpastes in the marketplace at once. With all these add-ons constantly being brought to market, why can I only get five or six different types at the supermarket? The reason is Multi generational Product Plans incorporate a plan for discontinuing older iterations of the product. Go into a grocery store and try to find "Crest" without any of the add-ons or upsells. You won't be able to. As Figure 8.1 demonstrates, this tactic helps prolong the life of the product line by reducing the chance customers become complacent with a particular product. The customer is constantly buying the newest add-ons because the older product iterations have stopped being produced. And even while each new iteration has a shortened lifecycle, it creates a sustainable value proposition for the producer that keeps the customer engaged and satisfied.

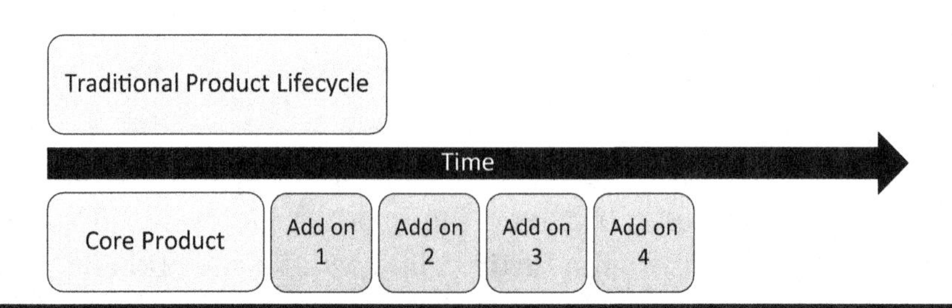

Figure 8.1 Extending product lifecycles.

Multigenerational products are not a strategy unto themselves but fit into a greater market and product strategy that is dictated by the Hoshin Kanri. The overall product mix and product line strategy are already determined as part of the organization's Hoshin Kanri. Who should be targeted in the market, what this market segment values, and how we should meet the needs of this market segment in terms of product or service is a whole different strategic animal. Aligning to this strategy, the MGPP becomes the tactics for carrying out these parts of the greater Hoshin Kanri. This supports sustainability for the business. In order for an organization to be sustainable, it must remain true to its core strategy and beliefs while also extending itself to deliver more and more value to its stakeholders.

Pertinent to sustainability is how multigenerational products help create sustainability and how the Lean Innovation Cycle can effectively identify the options available to a multigenerational product and map the course the MGPP should take. The most important takeaway is that multigenerational products extend the product life of a product line but do so without fundamental changes to the product or the market. As new iterations of the product enter the market, they target the same market segment as before, but add enhanced value propositions, the proverbial bells and whistles that keep the customer excited and engaged with essentially the same product. Recall the Kano Diagram from Chapter 4. The breath strips, cavity protection, and other add-ons are what "delights" the customer into buying the product, even if the key performance attributes remain relatively unchanged. Moreover, by targeting the same customer segment with a different product the normal risk of product introduction is greatly reduced. Issues such as market diffusion, brand alignment, and customer loyalty are virtually non-existent, especially since part of MGPP is to remove older products with established loyalty that would otherwise act as substitutes to the newly introduced product. The newest generation of the product continues and builds loyalty to the brand, not the product, which simply put, is a much better place to be.

The other great sustainable advantage of multigenerational product development is its ability to shorten product development time. In a world with fickle customer demands, disruptive social movements, and complex global dynamics, agility has become a differentiator in every industry and for all organizations. And there's nothing more important to agility than the ability to quickly bring a new product to market, or switch out and replace an existing offering that has gone out of vogue. One way that MGPP speeds up product design, and thus speed to market, is by limiting the scope of a

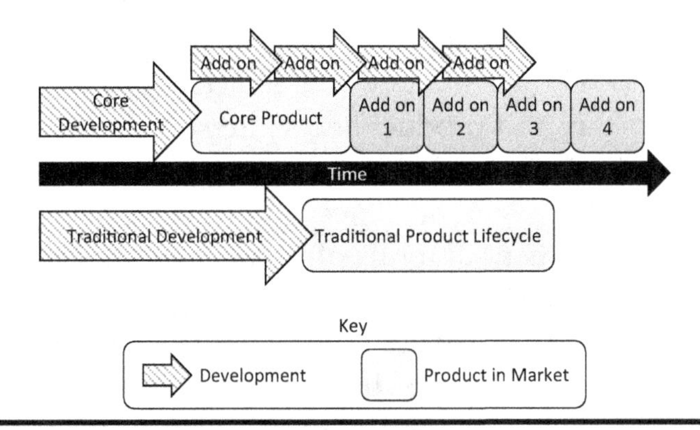

Figure 8.2 Comparison of development timeline.

product [1]. By planning to add product features later on in the product life cycle, the design team can narrow their focus on the core of the product and thus produce a more streamlined and higher quality base model. With each new product iteration, the development process is further reduced, because instead of having to start the development of a product from scratch, they can start with the quality base model or latest iteration. Figure 8.2 demonstrates this phenomenon. In the figure, the core product is able to be put to market faster than traditional approaches. Subsequently, many add-ons can be developed with much shorter development cycles creating a queue of innovations waiting to be put to market.

This concept of base model iteration brings us back to the important concept of Dominant Design. As you may recall from Chapter 4, dominant design is the existing paradigm of the product design. When discussing the Quality Function Deployment (QFD) tool we saw how the iPhone broke with the dominant design paradigm of a physical number pad or keyboard and created an on-screen touch screen keyboard that allowed the phone screen itself to be much bigger, and thus create a device more conducive to a multimedia experience and ushered in a new era of technological interaction. For our purposes here, we're not interested in breaking from the dominant design but rather iterating around the design as the base model to speed up development. Take a men's razor, for example. The dominant design of a men's razor is essentially two parts: a handle and a blade cartridge which attaches to the handle. But how many iterations have companies like Gillette and even the low-cost disrupters come up with? Comfortable grips, three blades, five blades, comfort strips, the flexball for better contour, anything and everything to extend the life cycle, all iterating around a single, primitive dominant design.

Lean Innovation Cycle Tools Applied to MGPPs

The final opportunity of the multigenerational product is its ability to facilitate the incremental development of the products as well as orchestrate the cannibalization of existing products before competitors can. How many flavors of toothpaste do you think the Crest brand manager is sitting on right now? How many other razor prototypes do you think Gillette has ready to go? Because the speed of development is so short in comparison to the life of a particular product iteration, the introduction and cannibalization of product offerings can be planned out months if not years in advance before they're put into action. Moreover, as the market environment changes, the product plan can be changed with little disruption or cost from the development, manufacture, or market position of the product.

Probably the most conspicuous way the Lean Innovation Cycle supports the tactics of MGPPs is through some of the tools already discussed in the analyze phase. In particular, Kano Analysis and QFD. First the Kano Analysis. Recall that the Kano Analysis is built on the theory that product attributes fall into three categories – either performance characteristics, expectations, or delights. The Kano Diagram (Figure 4.3) demonstrates the relationship between how well these attributes perform and how much satisfaction the customer gets from them. For our purposes here, it's not important to recount every detail about the Kano Model but draw attention specifically to the delights portion of the model. The delights are so named because, simply by virtue of their addition to the product, the customer derives high levels of satisfaction. The delights don't even have to perform to all that well. Their inclusion in the product is novelty enough. The product becomes reinvigorated, refreshed, and unique. And it's these characteristics which make them perfect candidates for multigenerational iterations or add-ons. The core of the product remains unchanged, while the delights identified from the Kano Analysis reinvigorate the product with new life.

The time component of the Kano Model also explains a lot about the nature of executing a MGPP. The MGPP anticipates the termination of a product offering well before demand for the product abates. The Kano framework illuminates why this is the preferred strategy. In the Kano framework, customer demands are always in motion. What delights a customer today will become the customer expectation tomorrow. Once-unique product attributes like remote start vehicles, electric windows, and mobile phone syncing technologies now come standard on all new vehicles. With this fluctuation of customer demand in mind, the MGPP tactics make sense for an incumbent organization to keep one step ahead of the customer demands and competitors by anticipating new customer expectations.

The other tool that was introduced in Chapter 4 that is important to MGPP is QFD. Recall that in Chapter 4 QFD was used to uncover design contradictions between the wants and needs of the end-user and the design of the product. Now with more knowledge about the different levels of innovation from the previous chapter, we can see how this application leaves us well-poised to tackle the complex design contractions indicative of type-3 innovation. But more to the topic at hand, QFD is also instructive as it relates to MGPP because it helps us define the scope and value of the current dominant design of a product.

Figure 8.3 was originally introduced in Chapter 4 and shows the relationship between technical aspects of a consumer tire (i.e. weight, material softness, etc.) and five different customer dimensions (quiet ride, good gas mileage, longevity, etc.). Whereas before this "House of Quality" was instructive for identifying the contradictions between the wants of a customer and the technical ways those wants were realized, the House of Quality can now be used to illuminate the scope of the dominant design or

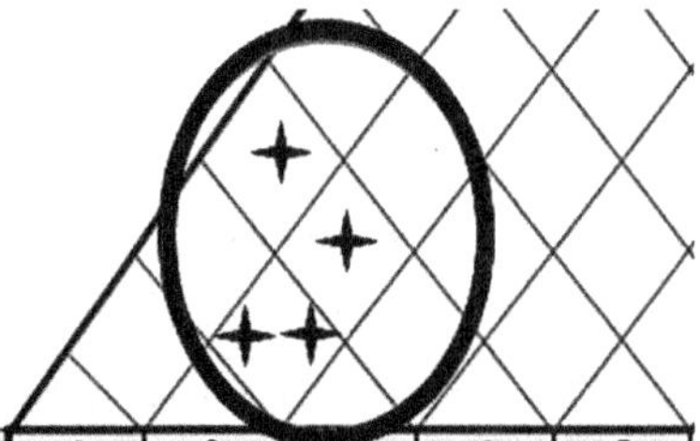

		Column #	1	2	3	4	5
Row #	*WHATs?* *(i.e. Customer Needs)* ▼	WHATs Importance 1: Less important up to 10: Most important ▼	Material Softness	Weight	Tread Thickness	Material friction	Tire Width
1	Quiet Ride	5	H	L	M	L	H
2	Good Gase Milage	9	L	H	H	M	M
3	Longevity	5	H	M	M	L	L
4	Cost	7	L	M	M	L	M
5	Safety/Handling	5	L	L	L	H	H

Figure 8.3 House of Quality ceiling.

the base model of a multigenerational product. The consumer tire example illustrates that in order to deliver on what customer wants we must balance the technical components of our product. When contradictions exist, any increase in one technical area may decrease the performance of a customer want (i.e. increasing the tread width to improve the comfort, safety, and handling, but at the expense of cost and gas mileage).

This is important for MGPP because it allows us to understand what the customer wants and expects from the product, and thus what add-ons or small alterations can be pursued later on in future generations of a product. For instance, a tire company may have a product line for small sedan vehicles. Starting with the base model, innovators can create future product generations by increasing the tread width of the tire thereby greatly improving the tire handling and the road noise while only having a modest impact on the cost. Since this plan would come as the product was maturing, the loyal consumer coming back for the 2nd or 3rd set of the same tires will be less cost sensitive than with a new product line of tire.

From the QFD we can take as a general rule that we have three levels to pull which will always yield us products that delight the customer and therefore increase the lifecycle of a multigenerational product. I've called these levers the (a) product aesthetic, (b) superfluous items, and (c) functional additions. Aesthetics are the most straightforward of the three options in creating multigenerational products. By changing the look and feel of a product (or its packaging), the products are rejuvenated simply because they look different than they did before. If in innovation novelty is the name of the game, then there's something to be said for the simple reality that we like an old product or brand with a new modern feel. But while changing the aesthetics is the easiest "delight" to implement, it is also the option that gets the least mileage out of the change. The product is substantially the same, and as such, the value proposition to the end-user has not substantially changed. The bump in excitement from change in the aesthetic will quickly dissipate when the next shiny object comes along.

But as more complexities are added on the customer value and product life increase as well. The next option for multigenerational items, superfluous items, is case and point. These items add value by being over-the-top add-ons that improve the performance of a product in many adjacent areas of customer value but only improve the core product performance to a marginal degree. Men's razors are a great example. Three-blade cartridges, five-blade cartridges, a comfort strip, three comfort strips, and flexball handles all improve the auxiliary performance characteristics of the razor, be it closeness of shave or comfort to the product end-user. But the core value and performance of the razor, be it safety, time to shave, useful life of a cartridge, the need for some sort of shaving cream, or the razor's effectiveness in cutting hair all have not changed. But because there is some concrete and measurable improvement in value, even auxiliary value, the addition of superfluous features to a product will add value beyond sheer novelty and are able to markedly extend the life of a product.

Men's razors are a great cautionary tale in multigenerational products as well. In recent years, many of the incumbents in the men's razor industry have been usurped by small subscription service razor manufacturers who offer stripped-down versions of the product for significantly less cost. The superfluous items mentioned above ultimately don't change the functionality of the product. As such, they can create a quagmire of opportunity for industry leaders and incumbents. By exploiting the benefits of superfluous features, companies can realize the ample opportunities within multigenerational innovation and prolonged product life. But with these opportunities come the risk of creating a product that isn't worth the cost. While industry incumbents continued to increase the price of refills by adding the superfluous items to them, they left the door wide open for a competitor to offer drastically reduced prices while still providing the same core value proposition to industry customers. After all, the Kano framework identifies delights as "nice to have" not, "worth the extra money."

Finally, the last option for realizing the delights of multigenerational products is creating some add-on that delivers new or improved functionality to the product. Unlike aesthetics and superfluous items, product add-ons are additions to existing products or product lines that improve or extend the core functionality of the product in a significant way. From a Kano perspective, they fall somewhere in the area between a complete delighter and a performance attribute. In Chapter 4, I briefly introduced a carpet-cleaner manufacturer who used the Kano Diagram to identify what features should be included in the next product model. Many of the features that customers wanted like "cleans in tight spaces" were revealed, through the QFD process, to require product additions to the carpet cleaner. These product additions add to the functionality of the current design of the carpet cleaner and therefore provide additional value to the customer. Detachable hoses allow the machine to clean tight spaces, curtains, and cushions, not just carpets. A hardwood brush extends the functionality to multiple surfaces around the house, not just rugs and carpets.

It's clear that functionality-extending add-ons deliver the most value to the customer and therefore will extend the life of the product further than either change to aesthetics or superfluous product additions. But of course, there is a trade-off. Functional add-ons take much more work in developing, both in identifying what add-ons the customer would actually value the most and the technical process of integrating these add-ons onto the existing model. As such, the best approach is to use all three options in MGPP. By following a balanced approach, a product can undergo minor changes like aesthetics while longer lead times for superfluous items and functional extensions are still in development.

MGPPs and the Service Industry

Despite all of the benefits multigenerational products can offer, the application of these concepts to the service industry are truncated and limited. At a high level, the service industry is about performance attributes. Better service means quicker service. Better service means less rework and defects. So the application of the multigenerational levers is narrow. Moreover, unless you're changing the actual service being offered, there's no need to terminate or cannibalize a delight once it's been added to the service process. There's no opportunity for these delights to be part of a constantly changing portfolio. Call-waiting music must have seen like such a nice little delight when it was introduced but now, following the flow of the Kano Diagram, it has since become the expectation. The newest delight for call centers is when the service center calls you back so you don't have to be tied to your phone for an unknown time. For a service industry organization, there's no reason to actively manage these features in a rotating portfolio.

Perhaps if there is a benchmark for delights in a service process it's in the Happiest Place on Earth, Walt Disney World. If you've been to Disney World, you'll notice a stark contrast between the designs of the queues compared to other amusement parks. The lines at Disney are almost always covered to keep the park visitors out of the hot Florida sun. Oftentimes there are games for the kids to play while they wait for a ride or animatronics along the concourse. All of these create a sense of superfluous novelty. While you'd prefer to wait less and just get on with the ride (performance characteristics) they provide a nice experience when your desired performance cannot be met [2].

Though the opportunities for adding delights in the service industry are quite limited, there is one delight particular to the service industry that can always be incorporated to the benefit of the end-user, Transparency. Have you ever been to an amusement park and decided not to wait in line because the projected wait time was too long? Or conversely, have you ever hung up your phone after waiting for over an hour to talk to somebody, and afraid of waiting even longer hung up the phone dejected? The information given doesn't just have to be about wait times either. Domino's received fantastic customer feedback after introducing the Pizza Tracker on its website and app in 2008 allowing customers to track how close their order was to completion, which helped Domino pass $1 Billion in online sales by early 2010 [3]. By adding transparency to a service process a service provider can always add value to the end user because it gives them insight into the process and allows them to make decisions based on the information.

At any rate, MGPPs are dependable ways to extend a product life cycle by generating economical innovations onto the core, dominant design of the product. The Lean Innovation Cycle is an attractive framework to use in support of this product strategy. The tools and theories included in the analyze phase of the cycle provide explanatory value for the MGPP tactics, like terminating a product offering, while also providing methods obtaining deeper insights into what product add-ons will deliver value to product end users.

Mitigating Organizational Disruption

Another way that the Lean Innovation Cycle helps support sustainable innovation is through its mitigation of disruptive change. Disruptive change is a necessary part of traditional innovation. As a firm pursues and realizes traditional innovations, new markets and opportunities open up. This in turn leads to further growth. But it's not all sunshine and roses. The new innovation, almost by definition, will be at least somewhat misaligned with the existing processes or values of the organization, and as such will create internal disruption that needs to be more thoughtfully managed.

First, take the internal processes of a firm. For new and small firms, people tend to just get things done. Startups thrive on the energy of wearing multiple hats. But as organizations mature, specialization sets in and tasks become more recurrent. At this point, people's motivation stops being the driving force of a firm's output, and standardization and processes become the guiding force of production and productivity. This evolution is important to understand because the existing processes of an organization aren't arbitrary. They reflect the collective knowledge and know-how, best practices, and capabilities of a firm. And these processes aren't just technical. Processes do not just reflect the knowledge of how to manufacture a product, or process accounts payable, or administer a medical treatment plan to a patient. It's also the organizational knowledge of knowing how to interact, coordinate, communicate, and execute within the firm as well as the decision-making processes at the top of the organization or down. A company's culture is built on the company's processes. So if a new innovation does not align with some or any of these processes, it signals that the firm doesn't know how to care for and manage the innovative opportunity and must therefore allocate resources to bring the innovation into the fold of the standard operating procedures of the business.

There are several ways to deal with the problem of misaligned organizational capabilities. The most straightforward and basic of which is to provide additional oversight to managing and integrating the innovation into existing processes. With extra oversight, specialization, care, and attention, existing organizational processes, or the innovation itself, can be slightly adapted to accommodate the other. The level of management oversight needed to integrate will differ depending on how disparate the new innovation is from the company's existing processes. But these differences are hard to decipher from the beginning. When Hewlett Packard started manufacturing ink-jet printers along with their laser-jet printers, they thought it would be a similar endeavor with little to no disruption to the business or extra management needed. But instead, HP found that the disruptive innovation had a slew of manufacturing and quality issues and as a result struggled to gain market share [4]. The existing processes and capabilities were not sufficient to tackle these challenges unique to the new technology. HP eventually moved the ink-jet manufacturing operations to a separate location with separate managers, communication channels, and resources to solve the unique problems posed by the new disruptive ink-jet printers.

It would be nice if the internal disruption new technology creates could always be solved by adding extra oversight, but it's not always the right tool for the job. Innovation cuts both ways, the more opportunity for growth the more disruptive it's going to be for your organization. That means sometimes extra oversight won't be enough. The next tool to consider when managing process misalignment is internal capability development. This of course falls best into the domain of learning and development. To adequately improve a firm's internal capabilities, learning and development would need to first identify the capabilities needed, determine how best to train employees to the new processes and standards, deploy the training, track the performance of the trainees to determine the efficacy of the training, and then of course make adjustments as needed.

As an example, take the digital transformation that has been ongoing for the last 20 years or so. Reports and studies have found that because of digital transformations workers have had to be "upskilled" to use new digital systems [5]. We also know that as technology continues to advance new jobs will be created that don't exist yet, and many of the jobs that are currently needed won't be around in another 30 years [6]. These macro-level trends demonstrate the principle that disruptive technology necessitates a response. Oftentimes the best response is to train and upskill workers or create new jobs and establish new norms, functions, capabilities, and processes.

Finally, new capabilities might be needed that can't be developed in house either because it's not cost-effective, has too long of a training lead time, the organizational labor force is not suited for the new work, or something else. If this is the case, and the innovation opportunity is still determined to be pursued, the only option is to acquire another organization with the needed processes and capabilities. This book is far too small to handle the complex topic of mergers and acquisitions, but suffice it to say that one of the chief reasons for acquiring another organization is the capabilities and processes. If this is the course of action taken, it's also important to consider that a full integration of organizations should be delayed, perhaps indefinitely, in order to realize the value of the acquired organization's capabilities vis-à-vis innovation.

I was recently talking with a friend who works for a Tier-1 auto supplier. The auto supplier makes the grills for almost all of the auto-manufacturing companies. They had recently bought a company that specializes in the production of automotive glass. This was a strategic move for the company. The automotive grill market seems to be heading toward commodity territory, where price is the most important factor over performance. In order to continue to grow, the company shifted toward a new product line entirely. What's important here is not the rationale behind the decision to take on a new product line. Instead, what's important is that this acquisition demonstrates that when innovation and growth are so distant from the current processes and organizational capabilities the only recourse is to purchase an existing organization that already has these capabilities developed. In this case, my friend's existing business had all the knowledge needed for steel heat treating, shaping, welding, and chrome plating, but had no capabilities regarding the manufacture of glass. To simply add managerial oversight to a new glass factory or try to upskill existing workers would have fallen short of what the company needed. The internal capabilities, processes, and collective knowledge are so disparate from the existing enterprise that acquisition was the only logical way to incorporate the new business line.

All that has been said about disruption and internal capabilities and processes can be said about values as well. If an innovation opportunity arises that is misaligned with the values of an organization, then the focus of the activities, attention, and care must shift to the people within the organization. And if this is the case, additional managerial oversight should be implemented. But whereas before the oversight was directed at harmonizing technology and process, the oversight should not be focused on managing priorities and coordinating groups of individuals to the new goals, activities, and opportunities presented by the innovation [7]. By way of example, a new medical device might yield a new opportunity for a medical device manufacturer. The new medical device might sell fewer units but with higher sticker prices and profit margins. The sales force, driven by high commissions on the higher sticker prices, might pursue the opportunities of the new technology and neglect the firm's existing customers and business lines. Conversely, if a new, high-quality design for a self-blunting hypodermic needle was developed the capabilities of the medical device manufacturer's sales force might already be well equipped to start selling these products, but without the right oversight and transition of values and priorities will lack the incentive to do so.

Likewise, new innovations might cause the organization to rethink their goals entirely. As such, the organizational structure of the firm and the stated values of the firm ought to be reviewed, reevaluated, and altered to fit its new mission. And finally, mergers and acquisitions still provide an opportunity to bring in an entire organization with a different structure, priorities, and values that might better realize the opportunity afforded by an innovation.

Suffice it to say that if a company wants to make innovation a pillar of their organization and a mainstay in their strategy they cannot do so merely through traditional innovation. The traditional approaches to innovation create the disruptive changes mentioned above and must be managed. An organization cannot survive if it has to keep retraining its workforce to new standards, altering its current standards and values to fit new opportunities or acquiring separate entities to realize new opportunities. Instead, the company ought to search for a way to innovate that mitigates these organizational disruptions.

The Lean Innovation Cycle is this needed approach to innovation that mitigates organizational disruption. The Lean Innovation Cycle is structured in such a way as to pursue innovations without greatly disrupting the existing processes, values, and culture of the business. In a word, sustainable innovation. The types of innovation that are pursued by the Lean Innovation Cycle aim not at stepwise growth and disruption, but concerted, methodical progress in delivering value to existing customers.

Keeping in line with the theme of internal disruption, one of the greatest advantages of sustainable innovation is that a firm can achieve growth while everything else, the communication, processes, and management, remains unaltered. In particular, regarding the way traditional innovation disrupts organizations through extra burdens on management to harmonize values or processes to the force of the new innovation. Sustainable innovation through the Lean Innovation Cycle works within the existing organizational structures and processes of the firm; there is no need for additional management. In fact, innovations can be retained within the original scope of functional ownership or the existing value stream. Multigenerational products certainly exemplify this principle. The scope of a product manager's work would become managing the several add-ons and iterations of a core product rather than merely the pricing and positioning of a new product.

And the multigenerational product also anticipates another added benefit of sustainable innovation – the positioning of value to the customer. We saw with MGPPs that the market segment is already expecting the company or brand to deliver a certain value proposition which reduces risks of product introduction and facilitates brand loyalty. But it also allows for adjacent diversification of the product mix. Who is going to trust Crest toothpaste but not Crest branded floss or Crest whitening strips? Because the new innovation of whitening strips is so closely related to customer ideas about oral care, and because the business processes, namely in this example consumer product manufacture and distribution, are not substantially changed, the customer feels comfortable buying the adjacent product – even though the products themselves of toothpaste, floss, and whitening strips share nothing in common.

A similar example can be given in the world of finance. In the late 1980s, Merrill Lynch introduced a cash management account which allowed customers to write checks against equity accounts. This was a sustainable innovation that grew out of their existing business processes. They already had all of the systems, infrastructure, and people in place to launch the product. They didn't need to hire new brokers or invest in new transactional systems. And it paid off big time. It's estimated that Merrill Lynch enjoyed a direct increase in revenue of about $78.4 M from the innovation as well as untold benefits of capturing commissions from customers bringing disparate parts of their business under the management of Merrill Lynch [7].

Sustainable innovation comes with better value to the customer. First generation innovations don't deliver higher value or higher profit margins and often have different cost structures than existing product lines [8]. This is why commercial spinoffs materialize. They allow for capitalization on an opportunity that may mature later on but that might not be palatable at the current margin level, especially if existing process and capability alignment will need to take the form of substantial investment in either capital assets or human capital. For reasons we've already discussed, namely shorter product development cycles, speed to market, less organizational disruption, market positioning, and customer expectation, sustainable innovation can realize greater gross profit margin.

Internal Capability Development through Sustainable Innovation

There's also a less tangible but equally important argument for sustainable innovation. It's better to grow organically and deliver increasing value to the end user by honing your craft than by seeking out new technologies and new markets. This isn't a business axiom I can point to and quote, but it just makes sense.

By pursuing innovation sustainably and fostering growth organically, a firm also develops a number of intangibles that can't be substituted by new technologies or new acquisitions. These intangibles grow out of the knowledge gained from interacting with familiar customers, familiar marketplaces, and familiar systems. Repetitive interactions with these fountains of knowledge allow for deeper understanding. This in turn illuminates more innovative possibilities. It's the principle of the Ohno Circle – more time spent on the gemba leads to better knowledge and better identification of where value is added and where it is not. And if the gemba is defined as where the work is being done, then we have ample opportunities to dive deep with customers, systems, and even ourselves as individuals and our teams.

Regarding the value in learning from the customer, I've already said a lot in this book that doesn't need to be rehashed and repeated any more than it has been. Pulling insights from the customer is key to success by any measure. Aligning the organization to what the customer values is critical to creating high impact innovations. At the fundamental level, this is the Lean ethos of *pull* from the customer. But Lean practitioners aren't the only ones who have noticed the benefits of this customer orientation. In the business classic *In Search of Excellence*, authors Tom Peters and Robert Waterman explicitly identify "closeness to customer" as a critical piece to building an excellent and successful business. They conclude that by orienting business activities to what customers value, even if it doesn't make hard economic sense, will later pay off in customer loyalty [9]. IBM was successful not just for their technology but for their service. McDonald's made a fast hamburger, but it was the attention to detail and cleanliness that brought customers back for more. There's nothing to say a company that is constantly disrupted by new technologies and disruptive innovations can't achieve this closeness to customers, but it certainly becomes an obstacle to overcome. It hurts more than helps. When managers are discussing mergers, acquisitions, new training programs, hiring campaigns, or additional oversight to curtail the disruption from a new innovation it's easy to see how the focus on the customer can drift into the background.

Another very important area for creating organic growth within a company comes from the individual employees themselves. In Peter Senge's book *The Fifth Discipline*, the author points out that as our economy shifts away from producing goods and into providing intellectual services, the mark of a healthy, thriving organization will be in how well they adapt and can change to new situations and dynamic surroundings, in a word, how well they learn [10]. We all are shifting to becoming what Senge calls "knowledge workers," purveyors, and communicants of the information and insights we possess. Senge goes on to describe that organizations can only learn if the people within the organizations can learn. In particular, the values of personal self-mastery, the ability to clarify visions and tolerate new ideas, team learning, the ability for groups or organizational subunits to grow together, and the ability to recognize and scrutinize assumptions about reality are all vital competencies in developing a healthy learning organization. Being able to learn at an individual level means being able to challenge and change ideas, assumptions, and visions that are deeply engrained in how we think. Through personal growth, the organization grows, and just like closeness to customers, it's not that an organization can't do if it's constantly disrupted, but the odds are stacked against it.

One of the opportunities for growth through knowledge is in how well firms understand the interconnectedness of the departments and people within an organization. What is sometimes called a system's thinking perspective, we can make improvements that improve internal performance and affect external customers by taking heed of how decisions in one part of the organization affect others elsewhere. Again, the *ethos* of Lean is present in the thought. Many small improvements to local systems create big improvements and value to the greater system, and eventually the end user. The purpose of systems thinking is to make sure we can see the forest through the trees. Organizations must ensure that parts of the whole, be it departments, or functions, or processes, do not distract from the bigger picture.

We've already seen an example of this sort of systems analysis in action. Recall from Chapter 6 the improvements that were made through restructuring the developmental flow using concurrent engineering. Development time was shortened, waste was removed from the product itself, and all the value got pushed to the end user who was able to enjoy a higher quality product sooner than would have otherwise been possible.

At a fundamental level, these principles all come back to organizational discipline. Sustainability is a discipline. Lean is an organizational, operational discipline. Stepwise growth is exciting. It leads to great opportunities and new horizons. But too much of it comes at the cost of losing sight of how your organization operates, becoming out of touch with what customers value, and allowing human capital to wither on the vine rather than achieve greater individual and collective growth. The thrust of sustainability in any application is about being disciplined. An organization that hopes to survive and thrive generations from now must be agile enough to adapt to new market conditions and definitions of customer value, but must also be disciplined enough to reel in their operations and remain focused on what is most important for their organization and their stakeholders. The Lean Innovation Cycle straddles both sides of this dichotomy. The primary gaze of the Lean Innovation Cycle is set on customer value and is highly responsive to stakeholder values. At the same time, it is also tempered in its approach toward new opportunities, favoring strong alignment to existing organizational values and structures and Hoshin Kanri strategy rather than pursuing misadventure in the brave new world of emerging technologies.

Conclusion

If an organization is seeking to be innovative as part of its culture or values it must think critically about what this means for the organization. The people, processes, capabilities, and structure will all be affected by this vision. The two approaches discussed in this book, traditional, technology-driven innovation and Lean Innovation, have vastly different effects on the organization. Traditional innovation provides for stepwise growth but severely disrupts the organization. A business should be mindful of more than just the pursuit of innovation as an objective. It should also have concrete ideas about how to harmonize new technologies with the existing processes, capabilities, and human capital within the organization.

Conversely, Lean Innovation is sustainable. Its pursuits, though much more modest in scope and force, allow for a company to be methodical and consistent in their march toward excellence through innovation. This chapter demonstrated how this Lean, sustainable innovation mitigates disruption within the organization in a variety of ways. First, we saw how MGPP can extend the product life cycle, shorten product development time, build customer loyalty, improve profit margin, and facilitate innovation. Moreover, the tools in the Lean Innovation Cycle, like the Kano Analysis and QFD are perfectly fitted for such an endeavor and explain why MGPPs work. Next, we saw how sustainable innovation reduces organizational disruption by keeping the innovations modest and self-contained within the existing departments, functions, or value streams. And finally, we saw the human side of sustainable innovation and how, at an individual level, less organizational disruption can result in personal growth, team advancement, and systems thinking which ultimately leads to a healthy learning organization.

Both types of innovation have their place and are valuable to organizations. In the next chapter, we take a final deep dive into where each approach feels most at home and delivers the greatest benefit to the organization. Technological boons are one-time phenomena that can't easily be replicated – certainly not on a consistent basis and leave the organization in a position that requires high adaptation. They are good for short-term plays. But if a company wants to make innovation part of its DNA, they need to have a plan to create sustainable innovation. The Lean Innovation Cycle provides a path forward.

References

[1] O'Connor, Paul (2019). "Multi-Generational Product Plan (MGPP) Vs. Product Line Strategy and Roadmap". *Adept Website.* https://adept-plm.com/multi-generational-product-plan-mgpp-vs-product-line-strategy-and-roadmap/

[2] Cortez, L., Close, K. (2020). "Designing experience: A Case Study of Disneyland's Lines". *Talking About Design Website.* https://talkingaboutdesign.com/designing-experience-a-case-study-of-disneylands-lines/

[3] Domino's Press Release. (2010). "Domino's Fan Favorite Pizza Tracker Now Makes Some Noise". *Domino's Press Release.* https://ir.dominos.com/news-releases/news-release-details/dominos-fan-favorite-pizza-tracker-now-makes-some-noise

[4] Fisher, L. (1996). "How Hewlett-Packard Runs Its Printer Division". *Tech and Innovation Magazine*, 1996, Issue 5. https://www.strategy-business.com/article/12217?gko=b6f97

[5] O'Donnell, J. (2020). "Digital transformation requires upskilling and reskilling". *Tech Target Website.* https://www.thepeoplespace.com/ideas/articles/upskilling-crucial-successful-digital-transformation-business

[6] Kelly, J. (2019). "Predictions For The Uncharted Job Market Of The Future" *Forbes Magazine.* https://www.forbes.com/sites/jackkelly/2019/02/27/predictions-for-the-dystopian-job-market-of-the-future/?sh=642bb1960574

[7] Clemons, E. et al. (1988). "The Merrill Lynch Cash Management Account Financial Service: A Case Study In Strategic Information Systems". Institute of Electrical and Electronics Engineers. https://www.computer.org/csdl/pds/api/csdl/proceedings/download-article/12OmNxdm4Cn/pdf

[8] Christensen, C., Overdorf, M. (2009). "Meeting the Challenge of Disruptive Change". Harvard Business Review One Point Article. http://innovbfa.viabloga.com/files/HBR___Christensen___meeting_the_challenge_of_disruptive_change___2009.pdf

[9] Waters, Peters. (1982). *In Search of Excellence Lessons from America's Best-Run Companies.*

[10] Senge, Peter. (2006). *The Fifth Discipline: The Art & Practice of the Learning Organization.* Currency, New York, NY.

Chapter 9

Innovation and Organizational Strategy

Over the last few chapters, the differences between traditional innovation and the Lean Innovation Cycle have been dissected in a variety of ways. First, we saw how traditional innovation is aimed at higher levels of innovation and is principally focused on advancements in technology. Conversely, the Lean Innovation Cycle is aimed at resolving contradictions, improving complex interactions between systems, or even simple systems improvements. These we called low-level innovations or "Lean Innovation" collectively. Second, we saw how the resulting differences between these two innovation paths can be distinguished. It was determined that technology-focused innovation comes with greater growth and impact but does so at the expense of consistency or predictability. This bled into the previous chapter's discussion on innovation sustainability. The biggest takeaway from these discussions is not a value statement about one type of innovation being better than the other but rather that both approaches to innovation work toward different objectives, and therefore, an organization should use the best tool for the job they have ahead of them. The aim of this chapter is to extend this principle further and to provide some support for how organizations can determine which innovation strategy is poised to best support their business. By joining tried-and-true strategy frameworks with these previously developed principles of innovation a landscape emerges that will help organizations determine the best innovation strategy to support the business as it faces pressing considerations internal to the firm and externally in the environment.

DOI: 10.4324/9781003206347-10

What Makes a Strategy a Winner?

There are many ways to gauge whether or not a business strategy is a good one or not. The Holy Grail of all business strategies is to find a strategy that produces and/or maintains a significant and sustainable competitive advantage for the firm. While we approach this topic in the next chapter, there are still other litmus tests an innovation strategy needs to pass in order to be deemed worthy of acceptance, adoption, and implementation. Particular to the present discussion is whether or not a proposed strategy is a good fit for the organization. Internally, the strategy should be aligned with the goals and objectives of the organization and should be something that the organization is capable of achieving and also structured to support. Externally, the business environment and a firm's competitive positioning in the business environment must be amenable to the strategy as well. A startup shouldn't be pursuing the same strategies as the *Fortune* 500 industry incumbent. A good strategic plan should exhibit a dynamic fit amid the external and internal aspects of the firm's overall situation. By using the frameworks outlined in this chapter, innovators will have a strong understanding of how the dynamics of the external competitive environment come together with the internal factors of an organization to direct the innovation strategy that is most advantageous for the firm.

Innovation Strategy Frameworks for the Competitive Environment

A good way to start this topic is through a simple, high-level framework known as the 5-Fs. The 5-Fs are characterizations of tactics that a firm might use to get the upper hand in a competitive marketplace or maintain the advantage over their rivals. Briefly, the 5-Fs of strategy are:

Frontal: Empowered position, leverage your advantage.
Flanking: Surprise competitors who have the advantage by going around them.
Fragment: Win by sacrificing or letting go of components from the total. Pull back to a more tenable position.
Fortify: Add resources (Capital, time, money) to gain an advantage.
Flee: Retreat and harvest for the future.

This framework is helpful for firms who are able to identify their competitive positioning and instructive to the extent that it helps this firm understand what strategies will support their organization and importantly what won't. By way of an example, a new entrant into the consumer electronics market could not begin competing against Apple in the smartphone market, a "frontal approach." Rather they are best situated to try to flank industry incumbents in a new product category and leverage their small size, and nimbleness. Likewise, other competitors with more resources may want to try to compete with the industry leader on smartphones, but since they don't have a true decisive advantage, it makes more sense to either add additional resources, fortify, or sell off aspects of their business to get better at their core business, similar to what GE has recently done [1].

The 5-Fs framework is also helpful in understanding where innovation fits into the organizational strategy and what type of innovation goes best with the style of strategy pursued by the firm. For instance, it wouldn't make sense to push for groundbreaking technical innovation while pursuing a "Fragment" strategy. Innovation must be subordinate to the organizational strategy, the Hoshin Kanri. You can't expect to be effective when half the organization is excited to innovate and grow while the other half is throwing assets overboard trying to stay afloat.

There must be a congruence between innovation and strategy. Taking the two types of innovation discussed in this book, we can create a model to guide which method of innovation is best supportive of the strategy. As Figure 9.1 below demonstrates, both the Frontal and Fragment strategies are best supported by a strategy of Lean Innovation. When you have an advantage, you press and extend that advantage. In this way, Lean Innovation is a good fit because it makes heavy use of existing product lines, customer segments, business functions, processes, and distribution channels. It exploits and continues the advantage already realized and does so without

Lean Innovation	Technological Innovation
Frontal Fragment	Flanking Fortify

Flee

Figure 9.1 5-Fs and innovation approaches.

adding a significant amount of uncertainty and risk. Likewise, the Fragment strategy is best supported for reasons already mentioned. The Lean Innovation Cycle helps an organization get better at the core of their business by pulling information from end-users and mitigating disruption to focus on getting better. By pursuing a Fragment strategy, a business can break away from auxiliary or expendable assets, and with the framework of the Lean Innovation Cycle the firm can continue to fine-tune the most fundamental core of the business.

Conversely, Lean Innovation does a poor job of supporting the Flanking and Fortify strategies. Both of these strategies look to find ways to usurp somebody else's advantage either by increasing material resources like manpower, time, or capital (Fortify), or by out-maneuvering a competitor with a new product or service (Flanking). Both of these strategies share themes we've already seen in technology-centered innovation. Namely, larger technological innovation takes more material resources, and the purpose of these innovations is to open new markets and opportunities for a firm, the very definition of the Flanking strategy.

Finally, a note about the Flee strategy. If an organization is fleeing from a marketplace, the firm is in duress. The business is either not turning a profit or is not adequately meeting the needs of its stakeholders. In this situation, it's not advisable to pursue innovation for the simple reason that there is too much change going on in the industry and organization. The Flee strategy is a very short-term strategy to mitigate losses. If the army is retreating let them retreat. After the execution of the Flee strategy, an organization will regroup and select one of the four longer-term strategies where innovation can play a larger contributing role in support of the organization.

It should be obvious that the 5-Fs framework is not a definitive, detailed mechanism for describing what an organization ought to do strategically, but it does do a good job of characterizing the actions a firm should take to pursue its organizational goals based on its competitive positioning in the marketplace. Unfortunately, it offers no tangible mechanism for determining what that competitive positioning is. In order for an organization to make use of the 5-Fs framework, or any strategy framework for that matter, it must bring in other strategic perspectives and make sense of the information contained in both. In this way, strategy formulation is like developing a new scientific theory – it makes sense of the data. The more frameworks that are analyzed, the more angles the business is scrutinized through, the more data we will have, leading to a more robust and correct strategy.

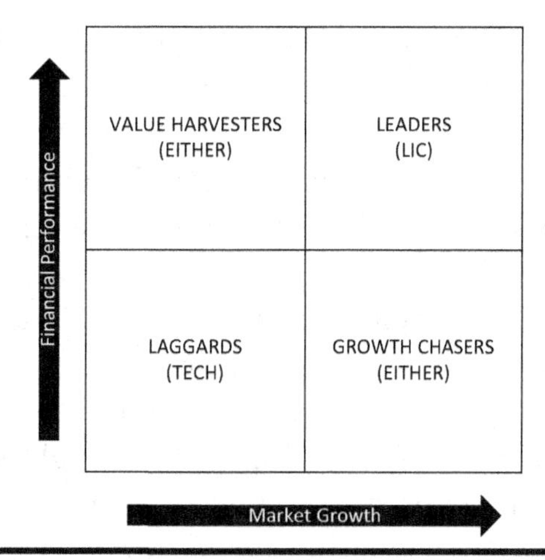

Figure 9.2 Growth performance matrix.

With this in mind, Figure 9.2 helps make sense of this competitive positioning. Figure 9.2 demonstrates how we can compare the industry standing of an organization on two dimensions: Market Growth and Financial Performance. Leaders are firms that have healthy financials while also experiencing high market growth. Since leaders are in a commanding position, they should choose the Lean Innovation strategy in pursuit of a Frontal strategy. Lean Innovation is a dominant strategy for the leader category; it will create a preferred outcome in all situations. Firms in the leader category have strong financial performance and growth which suggests a successful business model and product offerings which could be further extended and exploited through the Lean Innovation Cycle. Meanwhile, the risks ventured and advantages gained by pursuing stepwise technological innovation is unwarranted. The firm is already a market leader in terms of growth which suggests a strong top line and growing market share. Technological innovation adds a level of risk by way of organizational disruption or failure that could damage the brand and simply isn't needed to sustain the competitive advantage that a firm already maintains.

The Laggards are the exact opposite of the leaders and are experiencing poor financials and market growth. By all accounts, a firm that is a Laggard has a business model that is not working. As such, the Laggards are suited to technological innovation based solely on circumstance. A Laggard is in desperation. In order to survive, they must radically alter their value proposition either through a new business model or product/service offerings.

The other two categories are a mixed bag of either poor financial performance with high growth or vice versa. The Value Harvesters are organizations that compete on operational efficiency. While they haven't mustered high growth, these organizations still command high returns and profitability. Conversely for the Growth Chasers. Growth Chasers are oftentimes the category that startups fall into. They are focused more on obtaining clients and building a base of operation than anything else. As a result, they post modest, sometimes negative profits. Regarding the innovation strategy for these categories, it might be surprising that both innovation strategies should be considered viable options for them. It might seem like value harvesters *need* to focus on growth or that startups *need* to get better in the financial performance dimension. But the world just isn't that simple. As is discussed in more depth later on in this chapter, the innovation strategy for firms in either of these two categories will be dictated more by their internal initiatives, capabilities, and stakeholder interests than anything else. Their innovation strategies will be based much more on their identity of who they are and who want to be than anything else.

Internal Factors for Strategy

So far, the 5-s framework and the competitive positioning matrix has helped us characterize where the organization stands in its industry and characterized the strategic action a firm wants to make. However, strategy is not as simple as figuring out what you want to do and then doing it. The internal culture, processes, and capabilities of the organization also have a great effect on the type of strategies an organization is able to or willing to carry out. Some of the cultural norms, capabilities, and executive focus will strongly align with Technological Innovation and others will be better supported through the Lean Innovation Cycle. The trick is in deciphering which one is better where.

One of the biggest cultural determinants for innovation strategy selection will come down to what I call the Initiative Portfolio. The Initiative Portfolio is the high-level goals and thrusts of the organization. The initiative portfolio answers the question, "What is the organization focused on?" Is the organization interested in growing the top-line revenue or is it interested in the bottom-line profitability and results? Maybe it's a case-by-case basis of net operating income or return on investments for particular ventures and projects. Or maybe the organization is interested in improving the outlook of its balance sheet. In each of these cases, the business activity of innovation can support these initiatives or detract from these initiatives based on which course of innovation strategy the firm pursues.

This same method of inquiry can be carried out across many other domains relevant to the internal capabilities and stated goals of a firm. What the organization cares about and is focused on illuminates what strategies ought to be employed in support of these goals. Understanding whether an organization cares more about gaining market share, or acquiring new customers, or retaining customers, or realizing increased customer profitability is vitally important. These insights act like windows into how the organization thinks about their customers and provide knowledge into how the organization will proceed in support of its customer vision. The same can be said about stakeholder value. Understanding the goals of a business's stakeholders, i.e. increasing revenue, entering new markets, improving efficiency, increasing return on capital employed, or mitigating financial and operational risk can also inform and characterize the type of innovation strategy that ought to be used in support of their goals. Rather than belaboring the point with verbose commentary, Figure 9.3 summarizes the dichotomy of innovation strategies between several of these facets and how they support each organizational goal.

The reasoning for where each of these factors is positioned has by and large already been thoroughly discussed, so rather than beat a dead horse, I'll spare the commentary with one exception. In the Customer Focus swim lane, Lean Innovation is favored in almost all situations except for growth in

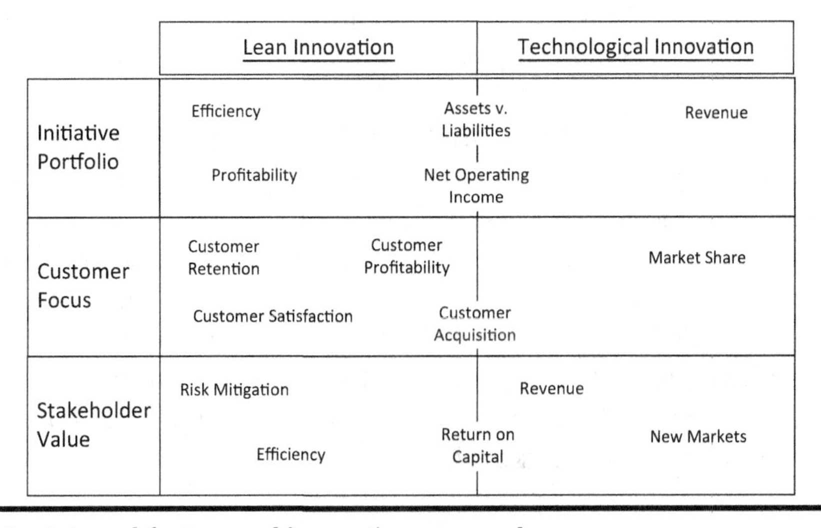

Figure 9.3 Internal factors and innovation approaches.

market share. Given what is known about the Lean Innovation Cycle, this shouldn't come as a surprise. Because there is a *pull* of information from the customer, the Lean Innovation Cycle is better positioned to leverage these insights into whatever goals the organization deems pertinent – retention, satisfaction, profitability, etc. Moreover, Chapter 8 on sustainable innovation clearly demonstrated that these expectations cannot be shared with new technologies or virgin product lines entering the marketplace for the first time. Rather, these technologies come with the expectation of increased market share but less marginal profit and deferred customer satisfaction through later iterations and newer models [2]. Furthermore, in the upcoming chapter, the Lean Innovation Cycle will be demonstrated as an invaluable tool to achieving competitive advantage through customer captivity vis-à-vis customer feedback and engagement.

By considering their own initiative portfolio and mapping them to the same table as I have in Figure 9.3, organizational leaders can start to get a feel for which strategy innovation strategy better supports their own goals, and in turn, which innovation strategy will be supported by the organization itself.

Product Profiles Based on Innovation Strategy

Thus far I have introduced many frameworks and profiles that assist in thinking about organizational strategy through abstraction. But what these have been missing is a more in-depth profile about the products and services that are developed through the different avenues of innovation themselves. The following framework helps characterize the type of product/services that result from different approaches to innovation. For this, I turn to a very popular strategy tool called the Product Portfolio Matrix or the Boston Consulting Group (BCG) Matrix. As you might have guessed, the Product Portfolio Matrix was developed by the BCG over 50 years ago in 1968. It was created to help the BCG's clients make decisions about their products and lines of business. These decisions usually entailed managing priorities, especially around things like capital investment, workforce planning, and marketing [3]. The Product Portfolio Matrix characterizes business lines and products into four categories based on two dimensions: existing market share and growth. Figure 9.4 depicts the matrix.

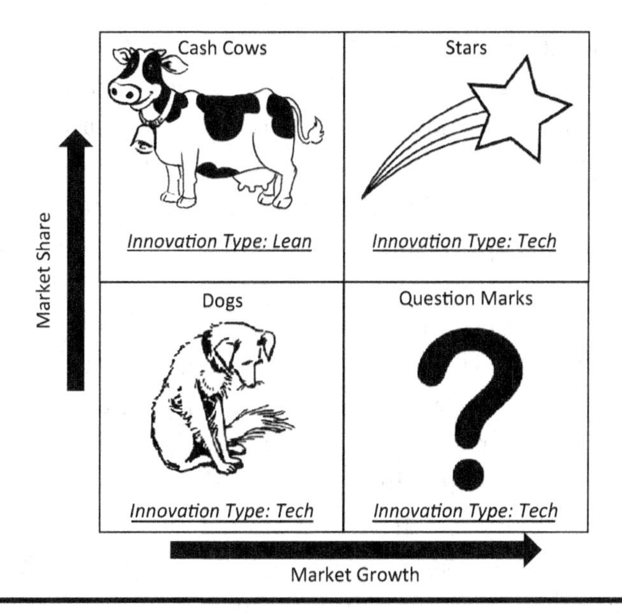

Figure 9.4 Product Portfolio Matrix and innovation.

The simple 2x2 matrix demonstrates different caricatures of product performance. Their categorization is fairly straightforward and a detailed explanation of each of these is not needed. But suffice it to say that a product commanding a large share of a growing market is best for business and has the most opportunities; high market share, and low growth still reaps financial returns; high growth with low market share still leaves questions about the product's viability; and products with no market share and no growth need to be taken out behind the shed.

I've also added a small addition to this Product Portfolio Matrix. Historically, the Product Portfolio Matrix has been used to look at an existing portfolio, and then once each product has been categorized into one of the four groupings of cows, stars, dogs, or question marks, the organization is able to make better informed decisions about how to allocate resources to particular product lines. But the BCG Matrix alone provides little explanatory value regarding how an organization can proactively shape their product portfolio. By thinking specifically about the effects of different innovation strategies, we can gain additional insight into how an organization comes to its current state product portfolio to begin with.

Obviously, businesses would like to produce nothing but stars every time. Wouldn't it be nice if each time a new innovation was created and put into market the end result was high demand and large market share? Unfortunately, this ideal cannot be realized with any precision or consistency. As such, an organization needs to incorporate the principles of innovation strategy in its business plans. By understanding how different innovation strategies will lead to different outcomes, the organization can shape their product portfolio to capitalize on opportunities while mitigating risk.

In Figure 9.4, I assigned an "innovation type" to each square in the Product Portfolio Matrix. This is to identify the avenues of development that a product takes to become either a cash cow or dog or star or question mark. This concept requires a bit of explanation but the general idea is that high reward only comes with high risk. In order to create star product performers, an organization will not be able to play it safe. All technological innovations start off as question marks. Nobody is putting heavy capital investment in crowded markets with little growth and where gaining market share means taking it from a powerful industry incumbent. Technological innovations are always targeted at high growth opportunities. In a sense, a technological innovation is by definition always a high growth question mark. Over time, these technological question marks will either grow to become stars or fail to gain hold and become dogs. It might not be clear why this is inevitable, but with a little explanation, this life cycle becomes clear. In a competitive marketplace, when high growth opportunities are present, competitors aren't just waiting around for the firm to try out new innovations. They're actively pursuing their own innovations to take the same coveted high growth market share and produce stars of their own. This is a zero-sum game. Both can't be winners. If one firm's technological innovation in a high growth market fails to take hold, it will be usurped by a competitor who will kick competitors out of the market entirely. No growth. No market share. A dog.

Lean Innovation from a product portfolio perspective is a little bit more of an enigma. Unlike technological innovation with its dogs and stars, Lean Innovation has a deterministic life cycle. Even though it can be applied in very different market circumstances, products successfully developed through Lean Innovation always grow into cash cows. First, Lean Innovation can be applied to an aging star. As a star starts to age, it inevitably becomes a cash cow. The market growth slows, but the product still retains high market share. Lean Innovation can be applied to these cash cows to extend the product life cycle in the myriad of ways we've already talked about, such as Multigenerational Products.

Additionally, the Lean Innovation Cycle also helps uncover those next great opportunities right on the horizon of a product's dominant design, and for that reason, the Lean Innovation Cycle can jump straight to a high market share, low growth space. Once again, take the recently disrupted men's razor industry as an example. A small innovation – product delivery, coupled with bare-bones product design is quite demonstrative of Lean Innovation. Having existed for centuries, the men's razor industry is anything but a high growth space. But the subscription delivery services were still able to take substantial market share from the incumbents through a Lean Innovation of the business model that entailed very little risk in terms of capital investment, product design, or labor.

What product outcomes, and therefore innovation strategy, an organization should select is married to the concepts already discussed in this chapter; the product portfolio a firm creates for itself should be a conscious, thoughtful action that is aligned to the rest of its goals. For instance, an organization that is in dire straits financially might want a star product but wouldn't be able to stomach the risk of producing a dog. Therefore, it might choose to pursue smaller innovations to take market share in the more mature markets. Meanwhile, the organization that is facing financial hardships is probably not too focused on growing their business but, to return to the 5-Fs from earlier, is most likely to be pursuing a Fragment strategy – offsetting their less profitable assets in order to achieve greater profitability in the near-term.

External Circumstances that Dictate Different Innovation Strategies

In addition to the internal factors that a firm must weigh to determine which innovation strategy best supports the goals of an organization, there are several external factors that a business must consider as well. These external factors go far beyond the usual topic of supply and demand, scarcity and surplus. Economic recessions, unemployment, and inflation all absolutely reduce the buying power of the consumer and therefore economic consumption which will have a direct impact on an innovation's ability to grow, gain market acceptance, and deliver all the promises that coincide with a successful innovation. But there are still other factors that are just as important and often go unnoticed.

One of the most important of these factors is the prevailing monetary policy of the marketplace. Monetary policy is different than a nation's fiscal policy. Many thick leather-bound books have been written dealing with the intricacies of monetary policy which I'm going to attempt to summarize in a short pithy paragraph. Rather than deciding what the government spends money on, the monetary policy, administered by the Federal Reserve (Fed) in the United States, dictates how much money there is in the economy. The Fed does this through changing the monetary incentive landscape. By changing federal interest rates, the Fed either encourages or discourages individuals and companies from spending money. Take right now, in 2021, the federal interest rates are and have been very low for several months. Why? The government, which has been trying to stimulate the economy since before the Coronavirus pandemic, wants people to spend money, so by not giving any interest on cash in the bank or low interest rates on mortgages, there is a relatively high incentive to employ money elsewhere in the economy – either in investments or mortgages or some other way to employ your money to realize a greater return than the meager 0.01% by keeping money in the bank. So now money is spent in the economy and the money supply is larger. This works in reverse too. If the Fed wants to reduce the money supply throughout the United States, the Fed can incentivize people to keep cash in the bank by raising interest rates and offering a higher risk-free rate of return.

This is important for innovation strategy because it determines how easy it is to finance innovation ventures. If everybody is investing money because the federal interest rates are low, capital financing becomes less scarce and therefore less expensive. A firm can more readily take on larger projects with less financial risk. For this reason, a low interest rate is an external factor that supports technological innovation. The same is true in reverse. When capital financing is more expensive the risks become larger and stepwise innovation becomes less attractive. Capital spending is reduced and in lieu of large technological projects, Lean Innovation is preferred for its smaller risk proposition.

Another external factor that is important to consider when shaping an innovation strategy is the volatility of the marketplace coupled with the firm's own risk tolerance. When the economy is stable it is predictable. When it's predictable it's easier to anticipate the effects of organizational activities, like opening up a new location, hiring more people, and of course innovation. So when businesses are considering ventures with high capital costs and longer lead times they can do so with more confidence that the result of the venture will ultimately be worth their while. Conversely, if the economy is up one day and down the next, it's harder to anticipate the impact of such a venture. Capital financing might become more expensive, project lead times might change, and economic consumption might diminish. Even customer behavior might change drastically like it has since the COVID pandemic. In light of everything thus far discussed, uncertainty begets risk which may exceed the risk tolerance of an organization and its stakeholders.

One of the biggest economic factors that dictate the direction of innovation, and therefore innovation strategy, has significantly grown in prominence within the last decade or so. The impact and influence that social movements and politics have on a firm has grown at an astounding rate and cannot be ignored. Because of the increased weight of public opinion, some opportunities cannot be pursued because of the social backlash. It's hard to say how many of these innovations haven't happened because of social pressures, but there are enough examples of social backlash to make an example of. Because the American social landscape is so dynamic, and many of these social pressures are also controversial, I mention only one, and do so quickly.

Fracking is an astounding innovation by any measure. It allows oil and gas companies to obtain scarce natural resources with greater efficiency than many other methods of extraction. But of course, there are social consequences to the innovation. Both in terms of the personal impact it has had on people near fracking sights as well as the environmental concerns that come with fracking. The controversy surrounding fracking clearly demonstrates the way an innovation's impact can be curtained by social factors and may even cause blow-back to damage the reputation and brand of the entire organization. This is not a value statement for or against fracking. Please don't write me letters.

All of this is to say that just like an unstable financial environment, the often polarized and volatile social environment we find ourselves in should be another external factor to be considered when drawing up an innovation strategy. If these factors are not attentively assessed, the initiatives and efforts of the organization could be undermined and may even be detrimental to the entire organization. Similar to the internal initiative mapping exercise I recommended earlier in this chapter, these factors should be analyzed to determine which innovation strategy is most amenable to the factors of the environment external to the firm and then also amenable to the aggregate of external and internal factors.

To Innovate or Not to Innovate?

There is a final option to determining an innovation strategy and that is simply to abstain from innovation for a time. Innovation does not *always* have to be part of the organization's strategy and it might be the case that given the internal goals and factors of the organization coupled with an inhospitable external environment, it's prudent to hold off on innovation for a season of time. In 2017, Pepsi released a commercial with Kendall Jenner that created an incredible amount of social backlash for the apparent insensitivity of the marketing campaign. An industry incumbent with strong market share and profitability is facing external hostility. Now is not the time to come out with a new product line. And I already mentioned the incompatibility of any sort of innovation with a "Flee" strategy.

Conclusion

Lean Innovation should be thought of like the default setting of innovation strategy. There is much less risk associated with Lean Innovation outcomes and activities and it supports longer-term strategies. Technological innovation should be thought of as more of a high-impact quick strike. Guided by the organizational goals, traditional technological innovation should always have a specific target it's tied to. It ought not be pursued in perpetuity, but should be treated more like a project with a well-defined scope, and set outcomes and objectives. An organization that is mature in formulating an innovation strategy supportive of its goals will have a good balance between these two forms, moving toward the quick strike of technological innovation when the moment is right, and then falling back toward Lean Innovation to mitigate risk and consolidate the advantages realized.

Innovation, especially technological innovation, is often portrayed as a silver bullet, a cure-all elixir that can help the health of the business by encouraging growth in new markets. But upon closer analysis, it seems to be the case that this is an over-simplification of the truth or a mistruth altogether. Innovation is just one pillar that supports an organization's strategy, not its own tour-de-force that can be pursued and realized despite of the internal and external factors facing the firm. Quite the contrary. By thoughtfully pulling back the curtain, it's clear that the effectiveness of an innovation strategy, any innovation strategy, is based on a myriad of dynamic elements some of which the firm controls, others that it does not control. Organizational goals like efficiency, revenue, and profit along with the responsibilities the firm holds to different stakeholder groups are all, more or less, controllable factors that help shape the firm's innovation strategy and emerge collectively to create the identity of who the firm wants to be. Meanwhile, the competitive marketplace and macro-economic trends can likewise shape the efficacy of an innovation strategy without paying much heed to what the firm wants. All of these elements should be considered in shaping the innovation strategy that best aligns with and supports the overall goals of the organization.

References

[1] Isidore, C. (2021). "GE Dismantles the Business That Ended Its Dominance a Decade Ago". *CNN Business*. https://www.cnn.com/2021/03/10/investing/ge-capital-close-aircraft-leasing-sale/index.html
[2] Christensen, C., Overdorf, M. (2009). "Meeting the Challenge of Disruptive Change". Harvard Business Review One Point Article. http://innovbfa.viabloga.com/files/HBR___Christensen___meeting_the_challenge_of_disruptive_change___2009.pdf
[3] Boston Consulting Group. (2021). "What is the Growth Share Matrix?" *Boston Consulting Group*. https://www.bcg.com/about/our-history/growth-share-matrix

Chapter 10

Innovation and Competitive Advantage

In the previous chapter, competitive advantage was briefly mentioned. It was stated that for strategists, regardless of industry, organizational size, or economic climate, achieving competitive advantage is the chief objective of development and deployment of business. To give a definition, competitive advantage is any circumstance that puts one firm in a more favorable position than its competitors. And for this reason, it's important to understand how organizations who tactfully employ the Lean Innovation Cycle in congruence with the internal and external dynamics discussed in the previous chapter can achieve competitive advantage.

One of the best ways to think about and discuss competitive advantage is the very popular five forces framework, illustrated in Figure 10.1. Developed in 1979 by Harvard Business School professor, Michael Porter, the five forces framework is a business analysis model that helps decision-makers discern their own competitiveness within an industry and explains why and how industries are able to sustain different levels of profitability [1]. By fully analyzing these forces, industry incumbents can determine which strategies ought to be pursued to take advantage of opportunities within the industry. And through the same calculus, prospective industry entrants can decide whether a new venture into the industry carries with it the possibility of success and profit.

The first of Porter's five forces is the "bargaining power of customers." This is the ability of industry customers to force prices downward. Industries where there are few customers or where the customers can

DOI: 10.4324/9781003206347-11

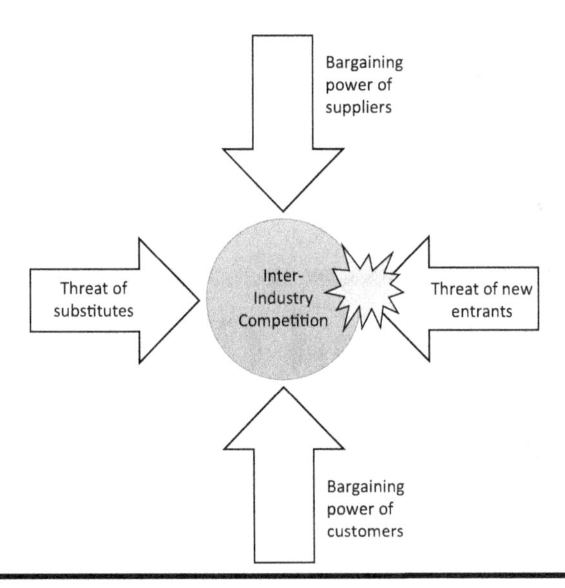

Figure 10.1 Porter's five forces.

organize to create a stronger negotiating position, experience strong bargaining power of the customers and therefore make the industry less attractive. On the opposite end of the spectrum, when customers have no bargaining power, the industry is much more lucrative to the firm. College textbooks, where the customers are college students who have no choice but to buy the textbook required for the class would be an example of an industry with low bargaining power of customers.

The second of the five forces is naturally the bargaining power of suppliers. This is essentially the same as the force of the bargaining power of the customers but just on the other side of the value chain. Firms must purchase supplies and materials to make their products or deliver services. If suppliers have the power to fix the sales prices of these materials, then it will directly influence the profitability of the firm buying these materials, and therefore, its competitiveness. Conversely, if these suppliers cannot exercise this power, then the industry will be more profitable to incumbents and more attractive to new entrants.

As an example, take the airline industry. There are a myriad of options when it comes to air travel: American Airlines, Delta, Southwest, and JetBlue. But book a flight on any of these airlines and you'll almost certainly be flying on a plane manufactured by either Airbus or Boeing. Because there are few aircraft suppliers relative to customers, the suppliers have high bargaining power and are able to fix their prices regardless of the wants of the customers. Likewise, Facebook and Google demonstrate the same paradigm in a different industry. Both are strong suppliers of online advertisements. Because of their size and web traffic on their platforms, they have become predominant platforms for online advertisement [2]. They have very high bargaining power; they can set the rates of advertisement with near impunity.

The caveat of the first two forces in the five forces framework is that they are really just a matter of perspective. How the bargaining power of customers or suppliers is characterized will change depending on where you sit within the industry value chain. The airline industry would characterize its industry as one with very high bargaining power of suppliers for the reasons mentioned above. However, aircraft manufacturers, considering the exact same firms, but from a different perspective, would characterize *their* industry as one with low bargaining power of customers.

Next on the list of forces is threat of substitutes. Threat of substitutes is the ability for a consumer to purchase a product that is not in direct competition with an industry firm but can replace the product or service of the industry firms. For this reason, threat of substitutes is closely related to the bargaining power of the consumer, in that if an industry or product can be easily replaced, it increases the negotiating position of the consumer and weakens the firm within the industry. In today's economy, this force is becoming much more important. Seemingly every new emerging, disruptive company is capitalizing on creating a substitute service for an incumbent industry. Airbnb has totally disrupted the hospitality industry which used to be dominated by incumbent hotel chains owned by companies like Marriott, Hyatt, IHG, and Hilton. Airbnb is finding success not through direct competition with the big hotel chains but specifically because they're outflanking them by creating substitutes.

The fourth of the five forces is inter-industry competition: the fierceness of competition is between industry incumbents themselves. This force is perhaps the most straightforward strategic force. Industry firms compete against one another for the same customer. The fiercer the competition between these firms the tougher it will be to be successful. Automobile manufacturers provide a wonderful example. There are so many players within the industry, and each of them is in intense competition with one another for every inch of the market in whatever segment. Ford is in competition with GM and Toyota but so are their luxury brands Lincoln, Cadillac, and Lexus. Any gain of one company comes at the expense of the other. The automobile industry also demonstrates the keyway firms within industries of fierce competition try to compete with one another, namely through differentiation. By creating a strong brand, and differentiating a product line, feature, or aesthetic within that brand, a firm hopes to woo a customer to its goods or services and eventually build loyalty between brand and customer. In fiercely competitive industries, such as commodities, there is little differentiation between products of services. In these circumstances, firms must compete entirely on price, and as such profitability severely decreases. Try to differentiate all you want, I don't care where my patch asphalt comes from. I'm taking the cheapest option.

The last, and most important of Porter's five forces, is the threat of new entrants. The threat of new entrants is synonymous with barriers to entry. These are the mechanisms that make it difficult for new firms and technologies to enter the marketplace and oust the industry incumbents from their position within the industry. If this force is kept high, it leads to direct competitive advantage for the industry incumbents and is the highest leverage and most sustainable option. Firms can achieve barriers to entry in a variety of ways, which are discussed later, but for now take for granted that one of the most easily demonstrable barriers to entry is high up-front capital investment.

One of the most well-known industries that have high, up-front capital costs is the communications industry. Think of the high capital investment needed to provide communications services to a customer, even in a very small service area – cell towers, cables thousands of miles long, a field service and repair team, a customer service center, programmers, IT professionals. And even as service offerings like premium cable and landlines go out of vogue and are usurped by substitutes, like streaming services, there is even further reliance on these industries for delivery of these services.

For any firm, no matter the industry, decreasing the threat of new entrants should be the most important strategic initiative that a firm considers. At a fundamental level, creating barriers to entry prohibits rivals from doing what another firm can do. It is the very definition of competitive advantage. No other feature of the competitive landscape has such an impact on dictating the choices and options a firm has in making strategic decisions. Only by erecting barriers to entry can a firm engage in the strategic choices dictated by the other four forces [3]. Without barriers to entry, there is no strategic landscape because there are too many competitors to keep track of. A sea of new entrants can easily enter the marketplace, drive down profitability, and oust the incumbents with little standing in their way. And without barriers to entry, this carousel of new entrants usurping industry incumbents cannot stop.

Moreover, the impacts of barriers to entry are not just limited to new industry entrants. Barriers to entry have a decisive role in restricting the expansion of competitors who are already in the industry. Take, for example, Walmart. Walmart has created substantial barriers for any prospective competitor entering the discount retail industry and for all of the current industry incumbents. Walmart's influence goes far beyond its brand recognition and its business model. Due to its massive size, Walmart is able to negotiate lower prices and operational luxuries from its suppliers that Walmart's competitors cannot replicate. In order to compete in the industry, competitors are restricted in their options in virtue of what Walmart has accomplished. They cannot engage in a price war because they're sure to lose. They cannot compete in supply chain operations, for they're already beaten. As a successful competitor, Amazon exemplifies this paradigm. Amazon must compete on a totally separate service offering – personalized delivery – to compete against Walmart.

Three Types of Competitive Advantage

The Walmart example along with Porter's five forces anticipate the much more fundamental question about how a business actually achieves competitive advantage. In essence, there are only three avenues by which an organization can achieve barriers to entry and therefore competitive advantage. First is economies of scale. Of the three types of competitive advantage, economies of scale is straightforward and the easiest to understand. As a firm increases its volume its cost per unit decreases because the fixed costs are spread out over a greater number of products [4]. This creates an advantageous circumstance for the organization that can sell the product on the market for cheaper than the competitor or sell the product for the same market price, but realizing greater profit. One thing that often gets muddled in with economies of scale is the ability to negotiate lower prices. But price negotiation and bargaining are not the same thing as economies of scale; this is a wholly different phenomenon called economies of scope [5]. Economies of scale are only realized by decreasing the per unit cost by spreading out fixed costs over greater total volume.

The issue of negotiating position that often muddies the water of economies of scale is part of the second avenue of competitive advantage, Supply. A firm can achieve competitive advantage over its competitors if it's able to procure the resources it needs to make or distribute its product/ service at significantly lower prices. The Walmart example from above is indicative of this type of advantage. Walmart can negotiate a per unit reduction in price from their suppliers because they can guarantee greater volume which may create economies of scale for the producer. It's a winning proposition for customers and suppliers. But also, this advantage can be manifested in other ways. For example, if a firm has property in Saudi Arabia, where oil is easier to extract than the tar sands of Canada, it has achieved a supply-side competitive advantage. Rather than achieving a supply-side advantage by negotiating, some firms are simply endowed with advantageous assets, like oil-rich property. And already, it might be easy to see how creating barriers to acquiring this land would improve the competitive position of the firm. But as often the case, supply-side competitive advantage is realized by new, advanced, and proprietary technology. By innovating the way a product is created, or raw materials are obtained, a firm can decrease the cost of supply and realize greater profitability in the marketplace.

Finally, an organization can realize competitive advantage through controlling demand. Demand-side competitive advantage is far more than differentiation or new products. Rivals in the marketplace can easily differentiate themselves and release new products that will erode any competitive advantage a firm thinks it has from differentiation [6]. Instead, demand-side competitive advantage is about gaining access to segments of the market that rivals cannot gain access to [7]. The most expeditious way to achieve this is by capturing the customer either through habit or switching costs. Capturing a customer by habit relies on creating a behavioral pattern in the customer. Switching costs are anything to impede a customer from looking for a substitute or replacing a firm's product/service with a rival's. Switching costs are barriers that are erected to make the customer stay put.

Together, these three avenues, economies of scale, controlling supply, and controlling demand are the only levers a firm needs to create and maintain sustainable competitive advantage within a marketplace. As briefly noted, other methods for achieving competitive advantage will quickly erode, mainly because they can be imitated and copied by new entrants or rivals relatively quickly. In each of these cases, competitive advantage is achieved not through internal efficiencies, superior products, better customer service, or anything similar. The advantages are achieved through an external focus on the competitive landscape so that only the firm can do what it does while ensuring that new entrants and competitors cannot.

Localized Advantage

Before getting to how the Lean Innovation Cycle facilitates the building of these barriers to entry, one more concept must be introduced. If the threat of new entrants is the most important force in the competitive landscape, and if barriers of entry, which decrease this threat, are achieved through economies of scale, controlling supply, and controlling demand, then how does a firm realize any of these competitive tactics? Surprisingly, the answer is the same regardless of whether a firm is looking to achieve economies of scale, supply-side dominance of a captive market; Localization.

The dominant strategy for creating barriers to entry is through creating localized dominance in a particular area. This area could be geographic but can also manifest itself in the geography of product market share. As an example, take the dichotomous competition between Microsoft and Apple. For years, Microsoft has been a company based on one thing and one thing alone – the Windows operating system. Microsoft was able to achieve undisputed market dominance by focusing on a narrow scope – the operating system – and then later on adding all kinds of applications, from graphics, to spreadsheets, to computer games. But it was all based on the core of the Windows OS. Meanwhile, Apple pursued a more comprehensive strategy. Apple created a diverse palette of applications and graphics. Their operating system was just one asset in the portfolio. And in many ways, the products offered by Apple were superior to Microsoft. So why did Apple lag behind Microsoft for years? By focusing on narrowly scoped excellence in the operating system, Microsoft was able to dominate the OS market space. With the space dominated, the costs to relearn a new operating system, applications, and communicate with others established barriers by means of switching costs. Microsoft had created a captive customer base. It wasn't until Steve Jobs cut 70% of the products in Apple's portfolio that Apple started to turn things around [8]. Subsequently, Apple only became dominant after the smartphone revolution started. The iPhone, which is an entirely new operating system, started this revolution and freed the Microsoft's captive customers. The new operating system which focused on applications and mobility made Apple a prominent competitor to Microsoft. Figure 10.2 demonstrates Apple only passed Microsoft in Market Capitalization once the smartphone phenomenon took hold in 2009 and captive customers were freed by the new Operating System [9].

Briefly, two other examples illustrate the importance of localized dominance, but in different ways. As already discussed, Walmart did not achieve

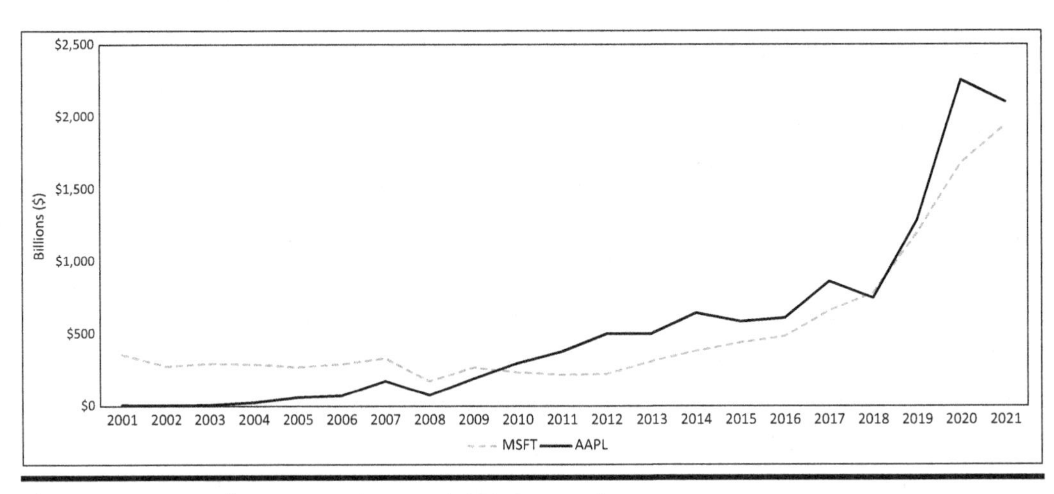

Figure 10.2 Market cap: MSFT vs. AAPL [10, 11].

dominance through proprietary technologies or innovation. Before it was a nationwide juggernaut it was a regional power in Arkansas. After creating and consolidating its regional, local position, it continued to expand at the peripheries of its footprint. It didn't do this by vertically integrating the supply chain or gobbling up adjacent marketplaces. It grew through replicating the core business in different geographic areas thereby creating multiple localized markets that it could dominate in.

And finally, before Intel was a manufacturer of microprocessors it was a manufacturer of memory chips. Eventually, when IBM decided to use the Intel 8088 microprocessor in its first PC, Intel made the conscious decision to stop producing memory chips and focus primarily on microprocessors. Even though it was part of the Intel history and legacy and was still profitable, Intel created and sustained dominance through the economies of scale afforded by focusing on a narrow market focus, microprocessors. Since Intel had captured the niche market of microprocessors, it was able to expand with the market and keep others out as the industry became larger and more attractive.

These three examples illustrate that barriers to entry are first achieved through narrow competitive advantage, either in a particular market space or in a geographical location. The first order of business for any firm is to establish a competitive advantage and consolidate it. Once the advantage is established the firm may expand the advantage in three archetypal ways. It can grow like Walmart, replicating its core business in multiple markets on the periphery and then consolidating before expanding again. It may continue its focus and dominance in a growing product space like Intel did in the microprocessor market. Or, it can gradually expand its activities to augment an existing dominant position like Microsoft did with its suite of applications around its core operating system.

Creating Barriers to Entry through Traditional Innovation

As mentioned above, the most common way traditional innovation creates barriers to entry is through decreasing supply costs. Technological inventions that reduce the cost, time, or effort in earlier stages of the value stream translate to higher profitability for the firm that develops these techniques. Mentioned cautiously in the previous chapter, hydraulic fracking is an illustrative example of how technological innovation can create supply-side competitive advantage. For the companies that possess the capabilities and technologies of hydraulic fracking, they can supply natural resources to their customer at substantially lower prices or at the same price with higher profitability. Because fracking produces a greater yield with less resources, the operating costs are greatly reduced compared to other forms of extraction. And since fracking can extract natural gas and oil in more varied geological scenarios, oil and gas companies have more flexibility on where to mine, thereby decreasing scarcity of land resources and further improving their position. Enough about fracking, please don't write me letters.

Oftentimes, the technological innovations aren't well known to the public or even the industry. These innovations have the added bonus of being a trade secret. Rather than publishing a patent to protect the intellectual property of the technological advancements, firms will choose not to disclose the supply-side changes, which decrease legal costs and makes it harder for competitors to imitate the advancement, all of which results in an improved competitive position for the firm that develops such a technology.

But what opportunities are held for controlling market demand through technological innovation? The high-powered first-mover advantage is essentially the only mechanism that traditional innovation has to suggest that any type of barriers to entry could be attained from technological innovation. And there is no guarantee that such an innovation will create a first-mover advantage or that this advantage will actually result in a captive market. TiVo had a decisive head start in the DVR industry. Started in 1997, TiVo partnered with Philips Electronics to manufacture the DVR services and began to do so in 1999, far ahead of any of its would-be rivals [12]. Through technology, TiVo created a new market that didn't exist before the invention of the DVR. Nevertheless, the DVR industry is a fragmented marketplace where all kinds of DVR suppliers and cable companies compete to offer you the same service. Yet there was a clear and decisive first-mover advantage. TiVo is synonymous with the DVR the same way Kleenex is with facial tissue or Frisbee is with...Frisbees. But despite this clear advantage, resulting from a tremendous technological innovation, TiVo was not able to sustain a competitive advantage for the reasons we've already mentioned. Figure 10.3 shows TiVo's stock value from its inception to its disintegration when it merged with Xperi in 2020. Though TiVo was able to experience a meteoric rise in popularity after the introduction of its devices in 1999, it wasn't able to sustain its market dominance. Seeing the high profitability of TiVo, competitors were incentivized to break into the market place and because there were no established barriers, they were able to enter the market unimpeded. As more entrants entered the marketplace, they found success at the expense of TiVo's market share and profitability.

TiVo could not create a supply advantage through protected intellectual property. In the electronics market, TiVo was not well positioned to achieve economies of scale in the manufacture or distribution of its product, after all, TiVo is more of service, than it is a device. And finally, TiVo did not create a captive customer base through high switching costs. As new competitors entered the marketplace, customers could abandon the incumbent TiVo by doing little more than returning the equipment, canceling the subscription, and learning how to use a competitor's remote.

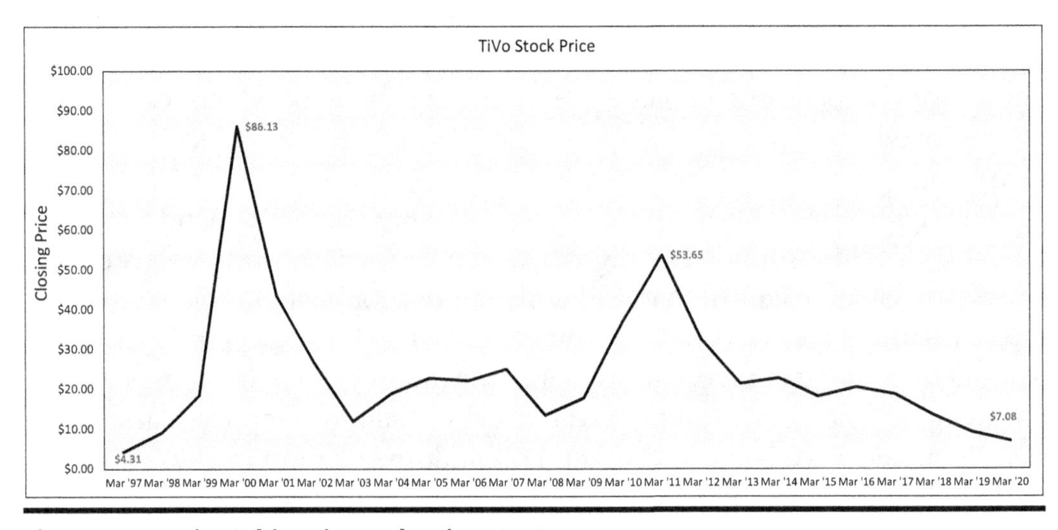

Figure 10.3 TiVo's historic stock prices [13].

The aim of this example is not to point out what TiVo did wrong or prescribe how it could have fared better if it pursued different business practices. Surely, the firm could have found ways to captivate their customers in the market that they created themselves. But more to the point, TiVo is a company that illustrates how traditional innovation alone is not enough for a firm to achieve a sustainable competitive advantage. Traditional innovation can support the strategic goal of reducing supply costs or increasing switching costs in the marketplace, but it cannot, by its own volition, create circumstances that are safe from imitation by its competitors unimpeded by barriers to entry.

Competitive Advantage and the Lean Innovation Cycle

To students of innovation and the Lean Innovation Cycle, the principles of how firms achieve competitive advantage are illuminating. Perhaps most telling is how these principles bring together concepts from the previous chapters regarding the formation of strategy and sustainability. Barriers to entry, and therefore competitive advantage, are not achieved through capturing market share, expanding into new markets, or building a reputation for being innovative or forward-thinking. Instead, barriers to entry are created through determined focus on the current value proposition to the customer, resiliency in building that value proposition and creating circumstances that preclude other rivals from achieving the current value proposition. Growth and expansion are secondary to the principal focus of delivering irreplaceable customer value. Likewise, sustainable innovation and creation of barriers to entry are both characterized by deep focus on the core value proposition with innovations that augment and run adjacent to the core product or service.

This is all very welcomed news. The business activities that make up the Lean Innovation Cycle are fully aligned with and the disciplines that support erecting barriers to entry. The Lean Innovation Cycle produces outputs that are natural extensions of the core value proposition of the firm's product/service. Whether the innovation is the first in a new product line altogether or the next iteration in a multigenerational product plan, the customer insights that were gathered, analyzed, prototyped, and finally put into the design of the innovation fuel the innovation forward and become assets for creating barriers within the industry itself.

In support of this conclusion, take again the concept of localization. Intel, Walmart, and Microsoft all demonstrated that competitive advantage is born out of localized dominance either in a real physical geography like Walmart or in a product space. Through this lens, the Lean Innovation Cycle has a direct role to play in this dominance. First, by scoping the particular market space in the Hoshin Kanri and then by systematizing customer feedback to ensure continued dominance in that space.

Moreover, the example of Microsoft in conjunction with the Lean Innovation Cycle create an actionable blueprint for expansion through innovation. Intel and Walmart did not rely on innovation to achieve their success. Intel relied on economies of scale in a growing marketplace, and Walmart replicated itself in other geographic locations. Only Microsoft relied on innovation to achieve competitive advantage. And how did Microsoft use innovation to achieve its position? Microsoft used innovation to augment the utility of its core product – the windows operating system – making it the dominant industry standard. This is prescriptive for how the Lean Innovation Cycle ought to be used. The direction of innovation created by the Lean Innovation Cycle does not have to be focused on producing a stand-alone "next best thing" but to create a system of innovations that work together, build off one another, and add superior value to the customer. In my mind, this elicits similar ideas as the customer journey and value stream map. Innovations that are directed at improving the customer experience throughout a process, and interconnecting these experiences build a web of customer experiences and opportunities that further solidify the position of a firm.

Switching Costs and Innovation

It has already been noted that of the three ways to achieve barriers to entry, technological innovation usually works on the supply-side of the equation. Proprietary technology begets cheaper procurement or manufacture which in turn bolsters profit. Only in the case of intellectual property protections can a firm that is reliant on stepwise, technological innovation hope to achieve any level of demand-side customer captivity. And even in the case of intellectual property, there is no protection against crafty imitators and substitutes. But what of Lean Innovation? How does Lean Innovation support the construction of barriers to entry?

Lean Innovation achieves these barriers mainly by affecting the demand-side of the equation, that is, customer captivity. To briefly restate, customer captivity creates circumstances that make it difficult for customers to switch to a competitor or substitute. These barriers are erected in two ways – either through habit formation or through the establishment of switching costs. Habit formation is noteworthy because it also entails a small corollary to switching costs: searching costs. As an example, think about why doctors have preferred medications that they like to prescribe. Or better yet, why do we go to the same restaurants again and again and don't venture off the beaten path? Searching costs acting as barriers explain these phenomena. It's not that there aren't other medications that work just as well, if not better, than the medications the doctor is accustomed to prescribing. But in order for the doctor to be able to prescribe it, he or she would have to research medications, learn their uses, doses, side effects, and interactions with other medications, all for small if any material gain. Likewise, trying a new restaurant involves researching restaurants, looking at the menu items and pricing, determining where you can park, or how long you'll wait for a table or if the restaurant takes reservations. All of this for a change of atmosphere with no guarantee the experience will be any better.

Throughout this book the importance of pulling insights from the end-user, experiencing the gemba, and letting the customer define value has been of tantamount importance. Here again, it is a conspicuous reason as to why the Lean Innovation Cycle can help businesses achieve their aim of competitive advantage through habit formation. The principles of habit formation have a lot to do with the user experience. If a customer is genuinely satisfied, they remain loyal. It's only when they become dissatisfied that the end-user actively pursues the searching costs associated with breaking their habit. What is the Lean Innovation Cycle if not an insurance policy against this dissatisfaction? The Lean Innovation Cycle prescribes a boots-on-the-ground approach of emersion with the customer – not just to hear what could be better about a particular product but to truly empathize with the end-user's experience. The Lean Innovation Cycle entails business activities that seek out problems to solve and then design their solutions. The focused investigation and immersion with experts and extreme users are critical to pushing the boundaries of a product's usefulness and further anticipating expectations of the more generalized, larger market.

Regarding customer captivity vis-a-vis habit formation, the benefits of the Lean Innovation Cycle come from the process itself. This is because habit formation is much more about the end-user experience than the actual product/service. Therefore, to elicit feelings of being cared for and satisfaction, the best approach is focused, diligent interaction with the end-user that produces specific actionable recommendations and improvements as a result. In contrast, the other lever or customer captivity, switching costs, has much more to do with the outputs of the Lean Innovation Cycle. In particular, to create higher switching costs, a business should look to extend and deepen the range of products and services that it provides, while still remaining adjacent to the core platform of its business.

To demonstrate this principle, take the current dominant business model of the software industry today, Software as a Service (SaaS). SaaS is a business model that entails licensing software and support to a client usually in the form of a web-based platform. This has replaced the old business model of selling a product key and downloading the software directly onto the machine (though this is still preferred for some applications – Tax Software as an example does this to mitigate privacy risks). This new model is a master class in customer captivity. By providing web-based software and support, the service provider is effectively taking over the development and administration of the product for the client. This of course has its advantages to the customer, but it also comes at the expense of the client firm's ability to develop its own internal competencies to troubleshoot, administer, and even develop its own replacement for the product later on.

Moreover, by making modular add-ons that augment the core software platform, the service provider deepens and extends its offerings and therefore its customer captivity. I worked with an HR SaaS company that executed this business model flawlessly. Starting with the core personal information of the client organization, the SaaS company built all kinds of analytics, charts, and tools. Eventually, it released new modules that brought in other parts of the HR organizational footprint – learning and development, talent acquisition, compensation, terminations and exits, and performance management. Now for the first time, all these are in one centralized place. It's a huge value to the client. But it's even better for the customer captivity.

With all of these product offerings surrounding the core platform, how could a new entrant hope to compete? At the very least they would need to develop all of the functionality of the incumbent system and would need to do it right from the start before any revenue is generated. The incumbent had the advantage of gradually adding additional functionalities and modules while still realizing some level of profitability. This is the true first-mover advantage. And how excited will the current client be to switch? They're already cared for. The system is reliable. The reports look familiar and are generated on schedule. No more integration is required. As long as the supplier keeps pace with the industry and provides an acceptable level of service, the client will be theirs for a very long time. And this begets another consideration. With all of this working like a well-oiled machine, how price sensitive is the captured customer? Would the client really become dissatisfied if the licensing cost of the SaaS is gradually increased by 5%, 10%, and 20%? Would they leave if a competitor undercut the SaaS incumbent by the same amount? Through adjacent innovation, companies like SaaS providers are creating enormous switching costs that they use to control the size of the marketplace and reap sizeable profits.

This strategy of adjacent product augmentation and modular add-ons is at the heart of the Lean Innovation Cycle. Recall the multigenerational products that were discussed in Chapter 8. These products extended the product life cycle and augmented customer satisfaction. Moreover, multigenerational products came with additional operational and financial benefits as well. Because the core of a multigenerational product plan was already designed, subsequent iterations and add-ons took less time to develop which further reduced costs. Because the client was already familiar with the product and brand, marketing and promotion costs decreased as well.

The same principles that allowed organizations to reduce operational costs and improve innovation sustainability are the same mechanisms that directly lead to decisive competitive advantage by way of erecting barriers within the consumer marketplace. Moreover, the analysis of the previous chapter showed that Lean Innovation is more or less a default setting for companies. Without a direct goal linked to growth, the tools and tactics of pursuing a technology-based innovation strategy are wholly incongruent with the needs of the organization. But this is an extraordinary conclusion. The internal and external conditions affecting an organization are almost always amendable to pursuing a strategy of Lean Innovation. This means that in most conditions using the Lean Innovation Cycle will produce competitive advantage by controlling market demand through customer captivity and erecting barriers to entry for rival firms and new industry entrants. Further, the Lean Innovation Cycle will increase operational profitability through decreased development, lead times, and burdens on marketing and promotion. And finally, the Lean Innovation Cycle is self-perpetuating and sustainable. It is a means to create an innovative culture in the organization without disruption as well as long-lasting value to the end-user.

References

[1] Porter, M. (1979). "How Competitive Forces Shape Strategy". *Harvard Business Review*. https://hbr.org/1979/03/how-competitive-forces-shape-strategy
[2] Vogelstein, F. (2012). "Network Effects and Global Domination: The Facebook Strategy". *Wired Magazine*. https://www.wired.com/2012/05/network-effects-and-global-domination-the-facebook-strategy/
[3] Greenwald, B. (2005). "Competition Demystified: A Radically simplified Approach to Business Strategy". Penguin Group, pp. 9–10. http://csinvesting.org/wp-content/uploads/2012/05/competition_demystified__a_radically_simplified_approach_to_business_strategy.pdf
[4] Reem H. (2019). "What Are Economies of Scale?" *Investopedia Website*. https://www.investopedia.com/insights/what-are-economies-of-scale/
[5] Surbhi, S. (2017). "Differences between Economies of Scale and Economies of Scope". *Keydifferences.com*. https://keydifferences.com/difference-between-economies-of-scale-and-economies-of-scope.html
[6] Greenwald, B. (2005). "Competition Demystified: A Radically simplified Approach to Business Strategy". Penguin Group, pp. 17–18. http://csinvesting.org/wp-content/uploads/2012/05/competition_demystified__a_radically_simplified_approach_to_business_strategy.pdf
[7] Greenwald, B. (2005). "Competition Demystified: A Radically simplified Approach to Business Strategy". Penguin Group. p. 11. http://csinvesting.org/wp-content/uploads/2012/05/competition_demystified__a_radically_simplified_approach_to_business_strategy.pdf
[8] Nesnidal, T. (2018). "The Apple Portfolio Strategy". *Bestsystemtrader.com*. http://bettersystemtrader.com/the-apple-portfolio-strategy/
[9] Winck, B. (2019). "Apple Surpasses Microsoft as the world's most valuable company". *Business Insider*. https://markets.businessinsider.com/news/stocks/apple-market-cap-surpasses-microsoft-becomes-worlds-most-valuable-company-2019-10-1028611689
[10] Market Capitalization of Apple (AAPL). https://companiesmarketcap.com/apple/marketcap/. Retrieved June 2021.
[11] Market Capitalization of Microsoft (MSFT). https://companiesmarketcap.com/microsoft/marketcap/. Retrieved June 2021.
[12] TiVopedia. (2021). "TiVo History". *TiVopedia*. https://www.tivopedia.com/tivo-history.php
[13] Dogs of the Dow. (2021). "TiVo Stock Price History + Charts (TIVO)". *Dogs of the Dow Website*. https://www.dogsofthedow.com/stock/tivo.htm. Retrieved June 2021.

Index

Pages in *italics* refer figures

Printed in the United States
by Baker & Taylor Publisher Services